Paul H. Glaser

Australia

A Natural History

Howard Ensign Evans
and
Mary Alice Evans

Smithsonian Institution Press
Washington, D.C.
1983

Library of Congress Cataloging in Publication Data

Evans, Howard Ensign.
Australia.

Bibliography: p.
Includes index.
1. Natural history—Australia. I. Evans, Mary Alice. II. Title.
QH197.E93 1983 508.94 83-10471
ISBN 0-87474-418-0

ISBN 0-87474-417-2 pbk.

Printed in the United States of America
Designed by Polly Sexton

The paper in this book meets the guidelines for permanence and durability of the Committee on Production Guidelines for Book Longevity of the Council on Library Resources.

Contents

PREFACE

THIS BOOK is a by-product of three trips to Australia, totaling about twenty-four months, made primarily for research purposes. These trips were supported by the National Science Foundation, the John Simon Guggenheim Memorial Foundation, the National Geographic Society, and by a fellowship to Howard in the Department of Entomology at the University of Queensland. Various technical papers resulting from this research have been published elsewhere.

Like many persons trained in biology, we quickly became enthusiasts for the Australian environment, and as early as 1969 we began to think about and gather ideas for a book on Australian natural history for Americans. There must be many persons like ourselves, we thought, who would profit by having available a broad-scale introduction to the plants, animals, and people of that continent—for who does not like to dream of distant lands, even when they are beyond his reach? When in 1979 Mary Alice received the Martha Catching Enochs Endowed Fellowship from the Educational Foundation of the American Association of University Women specifically to do such a book, we began in earnest to put together the framework of this volume.

Through much of the writing, we were fortunate to have available the excellent libraries of the University of Queensland, in Brisbane, as well as the freely given thoughts of biologists and conservationists in Brisbane, Canberra, and elsewhere. Illustrative material was generously contributed by many persons, as acknowledged in our captions, but we would especially like to thank Allan Hook and John Cancalosi, of Fort Collins, Colorado, and Raymond Besserdin, of Melbourne, Victoria. The Australian Information Service, Canberra, A.C.T., and the Department of Tourism, Hobart, Tasmania, also permitted us to use several excellent photographs.

For use of previously printed copyrighted material, we wish to make the following acknowledgments:

University of Chicago Press, for permission to quote from *Love Songs of Arnhem Land,* by R. M. Berndt.

Faber and Faber Ltd., Publishers, for permission to quote from *Australia's Last Explorer, Ernest Giles,* by Geoffrey Dutton.

Secker and Warburg and William Heinemann, Laurence Pollinger Ltd., and Viking-Penguin Inc., for permission to quote from "Kangaroo," in *The Complete Poems of D. H. Lawrence,* Copyright © 1964, 1971, by Angelo Ravagli and C. M. Weekley, Executors of the Estate of Frieda Lawrence Ravagli.

Angus and Robertson Publishers, Sydney, Australia, on behalf of the Estate of James McAuley, for permission to use an extract from "Afternoon," by James McAuley, from *World of Its Own* (published by Australian National University Press, 1978).

Also, Angus and Robertson Publishers, Sydney, Australia, for permission to quote from "The True Discovery of Australia," from James McAuley's *Collected Poems 1936–1970;* for permission to quote from "Australia," from A. D. Hope's *Collected Poems 1930–1970;* and for permission to use several poems from Judith Wright's *Collected Poems 1942–1970.*

Houghton Mifflin, Boston, for permission to use extracts of four poems from Judith Wright's *The Double Tree: Selected Poems 1942–1976.*

Kath Walker for permission to reprint her poem "Oration."

Patsy Adam Smith for permission to quote from her book, *No Tribesman.*

1

IMPRESSIONS OF AUSTRALIA

"Everything was the wrong way about"

When we were children we used to believe that if we dug a hole deep enough we would come out in China. We did not realize, of course, that if we *could* dig a hole straight through the earth from New York or New England, we would come out in Australia—or more precisely somewhere in the Indian Ocean off the southwestern tip of Australia. Nor did we realize that air travel (then in its infancy) would someday permit us to travel to the other side of the earth not once but several times—or that we would become so enamored of that unique continent, Australia.

It has been said that Australia is the only continent to have been imagined before it was discovered. In the fourth century B.C., a Greek bard named Theopompus told of a continent outside the known world "with green meadows and pastures, and with big and mighty beasts." Greek cartographers plotted that fabled continent far to the south, to "balance" those of the north. They called it the Antipodes—literally "against the feet," or more freely translated, "where creatures walk upside down." To the Romans and through the Middle Ages it was Terra Australis Incognita—the unknown land of the south. That such a land might exist was a challenge to the earliest global explorers—and they found it!

Yet in many ways Australia is still the unknown continent. Although Americans are visiting the country more and more frequently, too often they see little except Sydney or Melbourne—fine cities, but not all that different from cities everywhere. Many Australians themselves are not fully aware of the riches of their country (the only continent that is also a country). We mean not just bauxite and uranium, not just wheat fields, sugar cane, and merino sheep, but crested bellbirds, red river gums, birdwing butterflies, honey gliders, and lyrebirds. We mean red sand ridges, forests black after a bush fire, multicolor coral reefs, valleys dreamy with the odor of eucalyptus. Yes, drought, heat, bush flies, dust storms, cyclones, too—this is sometimes a difficult paradise. But there are not many places, anymore, where one can follow a track into lands that few whites have visited before; or encounter living things to be found nowhere else, not even in zoos or botanical gardens—perhaps a bandicoot, or a waratah, or a pied currawong.

To biophiles (those who are attracted to living things) the special fascination of Australia is the uniqueness of its plants and animals and the fact that so many are poorly understood. Because of its long geographic isolation from the rest of the world, Australia has evolved a fauna and flora very much its own, perhaps not the "mighty beasts" of Theopompus, but things he surely could never have imagined—a duck-billed platypus, for example.

In the capital city, Canberra, in 1970, we helped to celebrate the bicentenary of Captain Cook's landing at Botany Bay by cheering the Queen and Prince Philip. Two hundred years ago—the country is that young! For a long time transplanted Englishmen were too busy struggling with the strange and often unfriendly environment to appreciate its finer features. It is little wonder that only in the past few decades have Australians begun to chronicle their wonderful plants and animals and to become aware that unless they proceed cautiously, some of these unique forms of life may be lost forever (as some already are).

There is no way of putting a continent within the pages of a book. What we have tried to do is to capture, in separate chapters, the essence of the Australian climate and geography, its trees and wildflowers, its mammals, birds, reptiles, insects, and marine life. Finally, no natural history would be complete without a discussion of the aborigines and their relationship with the land, and of Western man as he first penetrated the wilderness and finally conquered it as only Western man can do (but can never quite do!). It is very much the personal view of two people who admit to being incurable biophiles and australophiles.

We have tried to weave together these themes: the special features of the land and its plants and animals, the problems man has encountered and the ways he has met them, and our personal responses to things Australian. Not everyone will respond in the same way. But the uniqueness of Australia lies in its natural heritage, not in its transplanted Western culture. When European man discovered Australia he was awed and puzzled by that strange continent, so unlike anything in his experience. Botanists and zoologists excitedly began to delineate its unusual flora and fauna—and after two hundred years the job is by no means complete. A place that was once forbidding is now mainly a comfortable land, dotted wtih cities and villages and crisscrossed by roads and railways (though there are still some large vacant spaces).

Western man, as everywhere, remains absorbed in his own world, and there is no doubt that some of his favorite pasttimes are specially suited to the Australian environment: boating, surfing, racing, rodeo, 4-wheel driving, and simply relaxing in the sun. But to overlook or underrate the real Australia is to miss a unique and irreplaceable part of the living world.

Visitors and settlers alike have commented on the strangeness of the land and its inhabitants ever since the Dutch discovery in 1606 of "New Holland"—by more than a century the last continent to be discovered. Their reactions have varied from shock to delight, depending upon their backgrounds, their prospects, and their points of impingement on the continent—a continent which, in any case, was not much like Holland or England or anyplace else. We have gathered here bits and pieces of impressions of some of these people and we present these quotations in roughly chronological order.

William Dampier was the first Englishman to set foot in Australia, quite by accident, for he was a pirate roaming the Spice Islands for loot when his ship was driven by a typhoon to the shores of an unknown land: the west coast of what is now called Australia. When Captain James Cook arrived on the east coast slightly less than a century later, his reactions were very different indeed. Their reflections lead off the following compendium of impressions:

The Land is of a dry sandy Soil, destitute of Water, except you make Wells; yet producing divers sorts of Trees; but the Woods are not thick, nor the Trees very big. . . .

The Inhabitants of this Country are the miserablest People in the World . . . they differ but little from Brutes. They are tall, strait-bodied, and thin, with small long Limbs. They have great Heads, round Foreheads, and great Brows. Their Eyelids are always half closed, to keep the Flies out of their Eyes. . . .

—William Dampier, in *A New Voyage Round the World* (1697)

The Coast of the Country . . . abounds with a great Number of fine Bays and Harbours, which are shelter'd from all winds . . . [and] this Eastern side is not that barren and Miserable Country that Dampier and others have discribed [sic] the western side to be. We are to Consider that we see this Country in the pure state of Nature, the Industry of Man has had nothing to do with any part of it and yet we find all such things as nature hath bestow'd upon it in a flourishing state.

From what I have said of the Natives of New-Holland they appear to some to be the most wretched people upon Earth, but in reality they are far more happier than we Europeans; being wholy unacquainted not only with the superfluous but the necessary Conveniences so much sought after in Europe, they are happy in not knowing the use of them. They live in a Tranquility which is not disturb'd by the Inequality of Condition: The Earth and sea of their own accord furnishes them with all things necessary for life, they covet not Magnificent Houses, Houshold-stuff etc., they live in a warm and fine Climate and enjoy a very wholsome Air, so that they have very little need of Clothing. . . .

—Captain James Cook, in his *Journals*, First Voyage (1770)

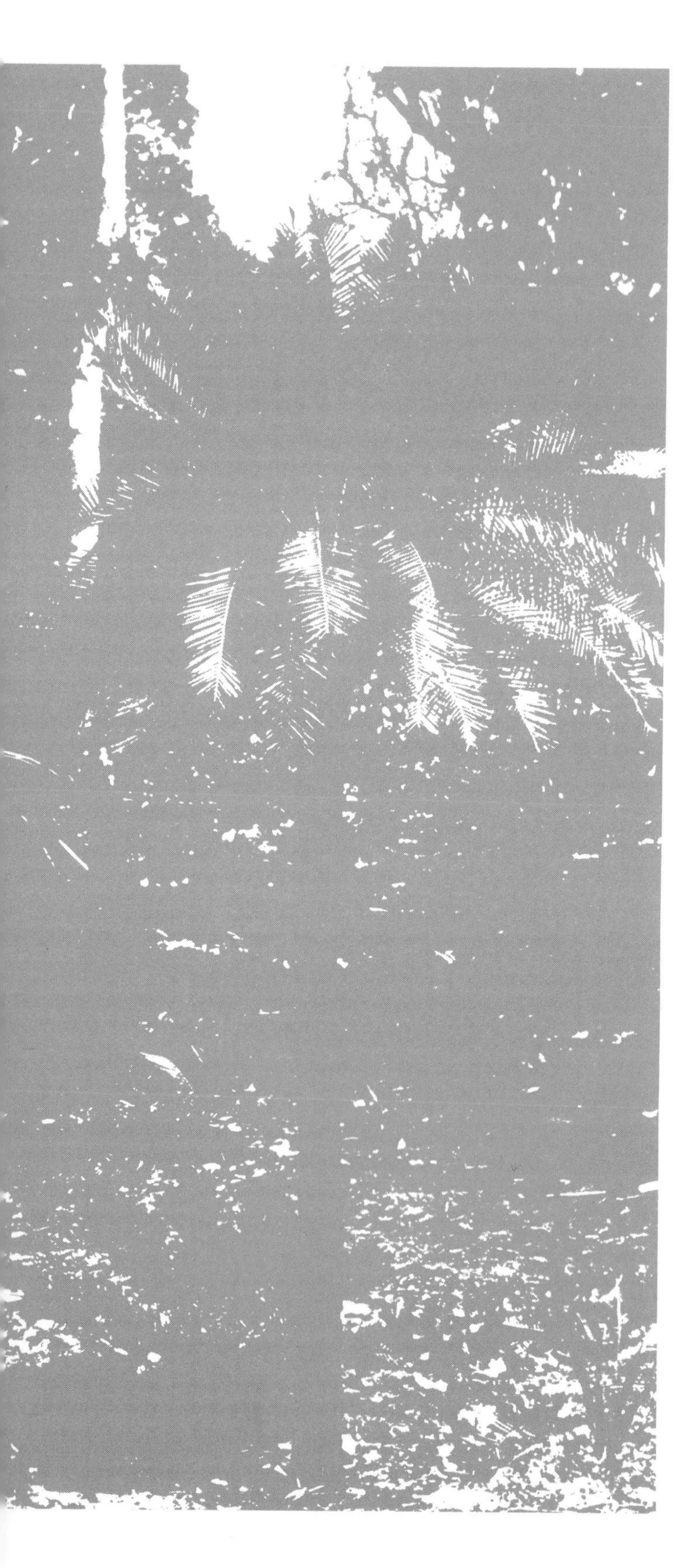

I do not scruple to pronounce that in the whole world there is not a worse country than what we have yet seen of this. All that is contiguous to us is so very barren and forbidding that it may with truth be said here that Nature is reversed; and if not so, she is nearly worn out. . . .

—MAJOR ROBERT ROSS, on arriving in Sydney in 1788

. . . supposing you to have heard something of the swiftness, meekness, and singular formation of the Kangaroo, of the Opossum, Guanoe, Lizards, etc., I may say, that not only these, but the whole appearance of nature must be striking in the extreme to the adventurer, and at first this will seem to him to be a country of enchantments. The generality of the birds and the beasts sleeping by day, and singing or catering in the night, is such an inversion in nature as is hitherto unknown.

—THOMAS WATLING, in *Letters from an Exile at Botany Bay to his Aunt in Dumfries* (1794)

When a botanist first enters on the investigation of so remote a country as New Holland, he finds himself as it were in a new world. He can scarcely meet with any fixed points from whence to draw his analogies. . . . Whole tribes of plants, which at first sight seem familiar to his acquaintance, as occupying links in Nature's chain, on which he is accustomed to depend, prove, on a nearer examination, total strangers, with other configurations, other economy, and other qualities; not only the species themselves are new, but most of the genera, and even natural orders.

—SIR JAMES EDWARD SMITH, in *A Specimen of the Botany of New Holland* (1793)

The dismayed and astonished navigator turns away his eyes, fatigued with the contemplation of these unhappy isles and hideous solitudes [the north coast of Australia] . . . and when he reflects that these inhospitable shores border those of the archipelago of Asia, on which nature has lavished blessings and treasures, he can scarcely conceive how so vast a sterility could be produced in the neighborhood of such fecundity.

—FRANÇOIS PERON, in *A Voyage of Discovery to the Southern Hemisphere* (1809)

Nature may be said to have in this country indulged in whim. She sometimes mimicks herself in giving to smaller animals, such as the native rat, the general form and characteristics of the kangaroo; she gives to a great variety of species, the false belly of that animal; in numerous instances, animals were discovered which might at first sight be considered monstrous productions, such as an aquatic quadruped, about the size of a rabbit, with the eyes, colour and skin of a mole, and the bill and web-feet of a duck. . . . The whole animal creation appears to be different from that of every other region: nor less the vegetable. . . .

—JAMES O'HARA, in his *History of New South Wales* (1817)

Australia is the land of contrarieties . . . her zoology can only be studied and unravelled on the spot, and that only by a profound philosopher.

—BARRON FIELD, in *Geographic Memoirs on New South Wales* (1825)

. . . trees retained their leaves and shed their bark instead, the more frequent the trees, the more sterile the soil, the birds did not sing, the swans were black, the eagles white, the bees were stingless, some mammals had pockets, other laid eggs . . . and to crown it all the greatest rogue may be converted into the most useful citizen: such is Terra Australis.

—JAMES MARTIN, in *The Australian Sketch Book* (1838)

I had been lying on a sunny bank, and was reflecting on the strange character of the animals of this country as compared with the rest of the world. An unbeliever in everything beyond his own reason might exclaim, "Two distinct Creators must have been at work; their object, however, has been the same, and certainly the end in each case is complete."

—CHARLES DARWIN, in *The Voyage of the Beagle* (1839)

The Flora of Australia has been justly regarded as the most remarkable that is known, owing to the number of peculiar forms of vegetation which that continent presents. So numerous indeed are the peculiarities of this Flora, that it has been considered as differing fundamentally, or in almost all its attributes, from those of other lands; and speculations have been entertained that its origin is either referable to another period of the world's history from that in which the existing plants of other continents have been produced, or to a separate creative effort from that which contemporaneously peopled the rest of the globe with its existing vegetation.

—JOSEPH HOOKER, in *On the Flora of Australia* (1859)

The fault of Australian scenery is its monotony. The eye after a while becomes fatigued with a landscape which at first charmed with its parklike aspect. One never gets out of the trees, and then it rarely happens that water lends its aid to improve the view. . . .

—ANTHONY TROLLOPE, in his *New South Wales and Queensland* (1874)

In all my wanderings over thousands of miles in Australia, I never saw a more delightful and fanciful region than this, and one indeed where a white man might live and be happy.

—ERNEST GILES, in his *Journal* while exploring central Australia (1873)

What is the dominant note of Australian scenery? That which is the dominant note of Edgar Allan Poe's poetry—weird melancholy. . . . The Australian mountain forests are funereal, secret, stern. Their solitude is desolation. They seem to stifle, in their black gorges, a story of sullen despair. . . . The savage winds shout among the rock clefts. From the melancholy gum strips of white bark hang and rustle. The very animal life of these frowning hills is either grotesque or ghostly.

But the dweller in the wilderness acknowledges the subtle charm of this fantastic land of monstrosities. He becomes familiar with the beauty of loneliness. Whispered to by the myriad tongues of the wilderness, he learns the language of the barren and the uncouth, and can read the hieroglyphics of haggard gumtrees, blown into odd shapes, distorted with fierce hot winds, or cramped with cold nights, when the Southern Cross freezes in a cloudless sky of icy blue.

—MARCUS CLARKE, in his Preface to *The Poems of Adam Lindsay Gordon* (1880)

What's Australia? A big, thirsty, hungry wilderness, with one or two cities for convenience of foreign speculators . . . populated mostly by mongrel sheep, and partly by fools.

—HENRY LAWSON, Australia's best known "bush" poet and storyteller (1896)

To my mind the exterior aspects and character of Australia are fascinating things to look at and think about, they are so strange, so weird, so new, so uncommonplace, such a startling and interesting contrast to the other sections of the planet. . . .

—MARK TWAIN, in *Following the Equator* (1897)

. . . there is no land with more beautiful aspects than Australia. . . . The grotesque English prejudice against things Australian, founded on no better reason than that they are unlike English things, still remains to vitiate the local sense of local beauty; but every year is teaching us wisdom. We are gradually learning that there are no more beautiful trees in the world than Australian gum trees—particularly if seen against the sky, when amber days or purple nights play hide-and-seek among the wayward branches. . . . And if you go up beyond the tropic line, and walk out of your tent at dawn, the air is literally weighted down with the fragrance of a hundred brilliant flowers. . . .

—A. G. STEPHENS, in the Sydney *Bulletin* (1899)

The curious sombreness of Australia, the sense of oldness, with the forms all worn down low and blunt, squat. . . . The strange, as it were, invisible *beauty of Australia, which is undeniably there, but which seems to lurk just beyond the range of our white vision. . . . And yet, when you don't have the feeling of ugliness or monotony . . . you get a sense of subtle, remote,* formless *beauty more poignant than anything ever experienced before.*

—D. H. LAWRENCE, in *Kangaroo* (1923)

. . . Australia, although officially registered as a continent, is just about exactly everything a well-regulated continent should not be. . . . In the first place, its position is so unfortunate that [it] was not actually seen by the eyes of a white man until 1642 . . . in the second place it had a very unfortunate climate . . . the fauna . . . contains a most formidable museum of animal curiosities. . . .

—HENDRIK WILLEM VAN LOON, in the chapter "Australia, the Step-Child of Nature," in *The Home of Mankind* (1933)

Everything about Australia is bizarre. . . . The three million square miles, one third of them desert, are all ancient . . . there are no great mountains and, except for the Fertile Crescent of the south-eastern coasts, few rivers, or rivers that rise fitfully, then disappear. . . .

It would seem that I have been describing an alarming, uninviting country; I have, Australia is; and yet no one who has been there can fail to be obsessed by the spirit, the atmosphere, of the continent—by its haunting, unpredictable oddity. Australia is, in the most literal sense, unforgettable.

—COLIN MACINNES, in *Sidney Nolan* (1961)

Everything was the wrong way about. Midwinter fell in July, and in January summer was at its height; in the bush there were giant birds that never flew, and queer, antediluvian animals that hopped instead of walked or sat munching mutely in the trees. Even the constellations in the sky were upside down. . . .

—ALAN MOOREHEAD, describing the reactions of the early settlers in Australia, in *Cooper's Creek* (1963)

The visitor . . . must be warned that Australia is not a country that reveals itself very easily or dramatically, and it is certainly not picturesque. The distances are vast and you have to sweat it out over many dusty, thirsty miles to get to the interesting places. You must wait and listen quietly and accommodate your eyes to apparent nothingness, and then, little by little, an awareness of another world which is antediluvian, shy, infinitely subtle and sometimes a little sad, begins to penetrate the mind.

—ALAN MOOREHEAD, describing the impressions of a modern traveler in Australia, in the Foreword to Allen Keast's *Australia and the Pacific Islands: A Natural History* (1966)

Billabongs and coolibahs. Barramundis and wallaroos. Bandicoots and bimbils. Here is a continent where all life, and the land itself, have evolved their own individual patterns.

—JOHN GUNTHER, in the chapter "The Continent that Nature Left Unfinished," in *Inside Australia* (1972)

2

The Land and Its History

"Everything a well-regulated continent should not be"

As diverse as opinions may be, they betray a common theme: Australia is different. The uniqueness of the continent is in a good part a reflection of its isolation and of its geological history, as well as of its current climate and landforms. So, for the moment we must look at the land itself; otherwise we shall never understand, or at least know only in some small measure, the plants and animals that enliven it.

Australia is located in the southwestern part of the Pacific Ocean about midway between southeastern Asia and Antarctica. It straddles the Tropic of Capricorn, with approximately 40 percent on the northern tropical side, and the rest in the temperate zone. A quick glance at the atlas will show that this same mythical line runs across the southern end of Africa and through the center of South America. And while Rio de Janeiro is technically tropical, Australia's northernmost city, Darwin, is a tropical city without doubt—as we found out on a visit in early spring (September) when the temperature reached into the nineties every day. If Australia could somehow be placed in the northern hemisphere, Darwin would be on a latitude with Vietnam's Saigon or the Nicaraguan capital, Managua; Melbourne, on the southern coast of mainland Australia, would match Washington, D.C., or Sacramento, California.

Tasmania is politically and geographically part of Australia, being separated from the continent only by rather shallow Bass Strait, which was above water only a few thousand years ago; its capital city, Hobart, is at a latitude equivalent to Portland, Maine, or Eugene, Oregon. New Guinea, too, is separated from Australia only by a shallow, island-filled water gap, Torres Strait, but it is politically separate and ecologically very different from Australia, so we shall mention it only in passing.

New Zealand is often linked with Australia in the minds of Americans, but though both were settled by Englishmen and have some similarities in their natural history, New Zealand is 1,200 miles away to the southeast, and on the whole its story is quite different (and in any case we have spent only one hour there—at the Auckland airport).

The land area of Australia is approximately equal to that of the United States (without Alaska). A flight from Sydney on the east to Perth on the west is about equal to a trip from Miami to Phoenix; one from Hobart to Darwin would be equivalent to flying from Miami well into Canada. But crossing the two continents is a vastly different experience. Starting from the east coast, one might note a remote resemblance in the wooded, heavily eroded mountains of the Appalachians of North America to the Great Dividing Range of Australia. Beyond the mountains, one would find that the verdure of the Australian landscape fades much more rapidly, to be replaced by sparse vegetation on stony or sandy soil, streaked with parallel dunes and spotted with white salt pans: a mostly empty country, with far more sheep and kangaroos than people.

Still farther west, there would be nothing equivalent to the Rockies, the Sierras, or the coastal ranges, only an extensive low plateau broken here and there by arid hills—for Australia is at once the flattest and the driest of the continents. Its highest mountain, named for the Polish patriot Kosciusko, is a mere 7,316 feet, and the top is an easy drive by car. Only a few other mountains exceed 5,000 feet, and the mean elevation of the continent, about 1,000 feet, is by far the lowest of any continent. Snow falls in winter only in the higher mountains of the Southeast and in Tasmania. (It sometimes falls in the summer in Tasmania, as we discovered when hiking in Cradle Mountain–Lake St. Clair National Park in February, the equivalent of August in the northern hemisphere.)

Not only are there few mountains to stimulate the production of rain clouds or to provide large amounts of runoff for irrigation, but the continent lies in the "horse latitudes," between the zone of tropical trade winds and that of temperate westerlies. Again, if we can imagine Australia being swung northward into the northern hemisphere (using the equator as a hinge), it would lie at the same latitude as the northern part of Africa. Superimposed on Africa, the south coast of Australia would lie along the Mediterranean, and the dry center would overlie the Sahara Desert. And indeed the climates are very similar, with pleasant coastal temperatures and humidities, and the inland hot and dry for want of clouds blowing in off the sea and for want of mountains to cause rain clouds to form.

That there are few parts of Australia as empty of vegetation as the Sahara reflects the fact that parts of the African desert receive an average of less than four inches of rain a year, while there are very few places in Australia that receive so little. However, nearly half of the Australian continent does receive less than ten inches a year, and nearly two-thirds of it less than twenty inches, while less than one-tenth receives over forty inches annually. The deserts of Chile and South Africa, as well as those of Arabia, North Africa, and our own Southwest and northern Mexico, all lie at latitudes roughly equivalent to central Australia and have much the

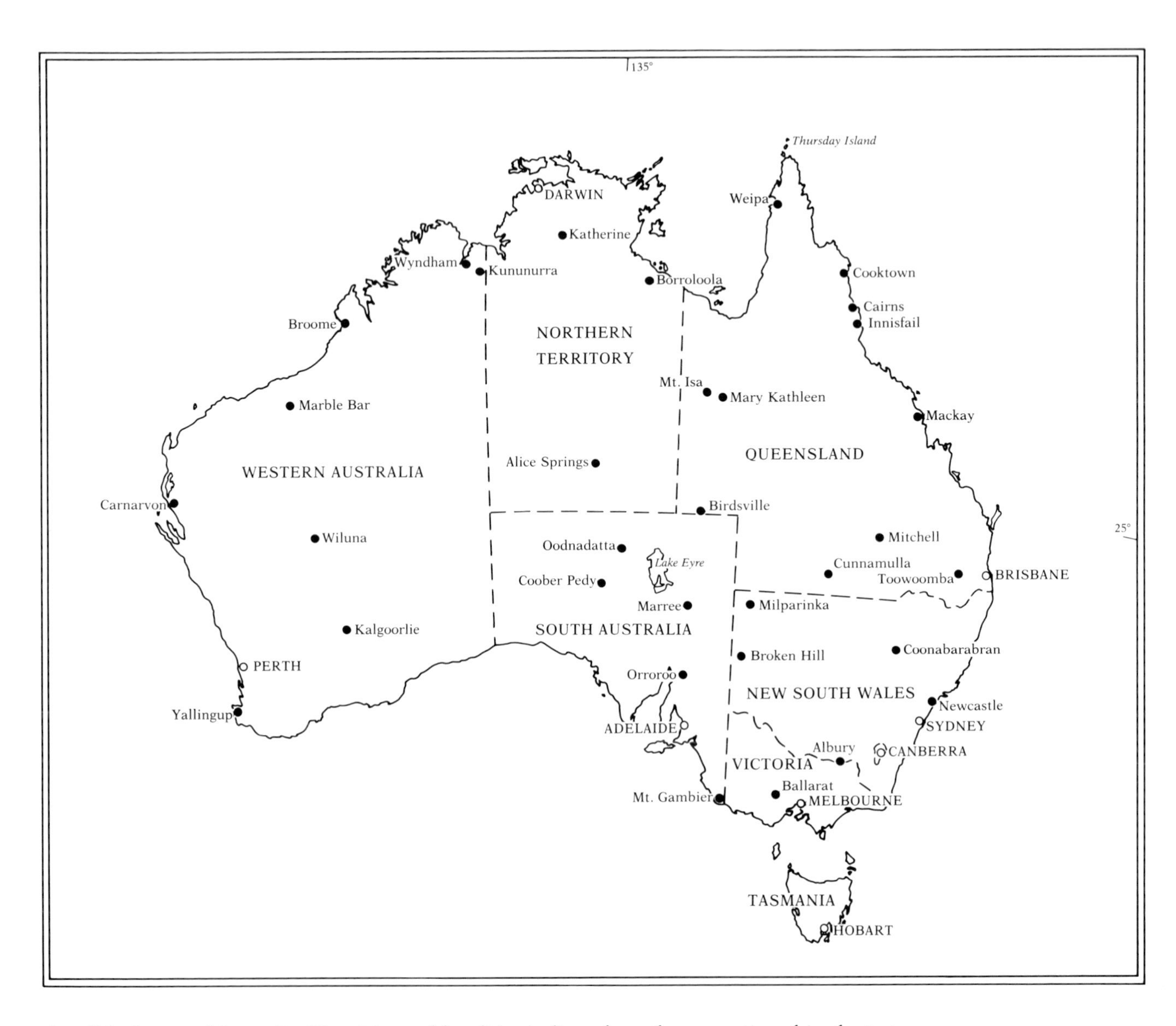

A political map of Australia. The cities and localities indicated are those mentioned in the text.

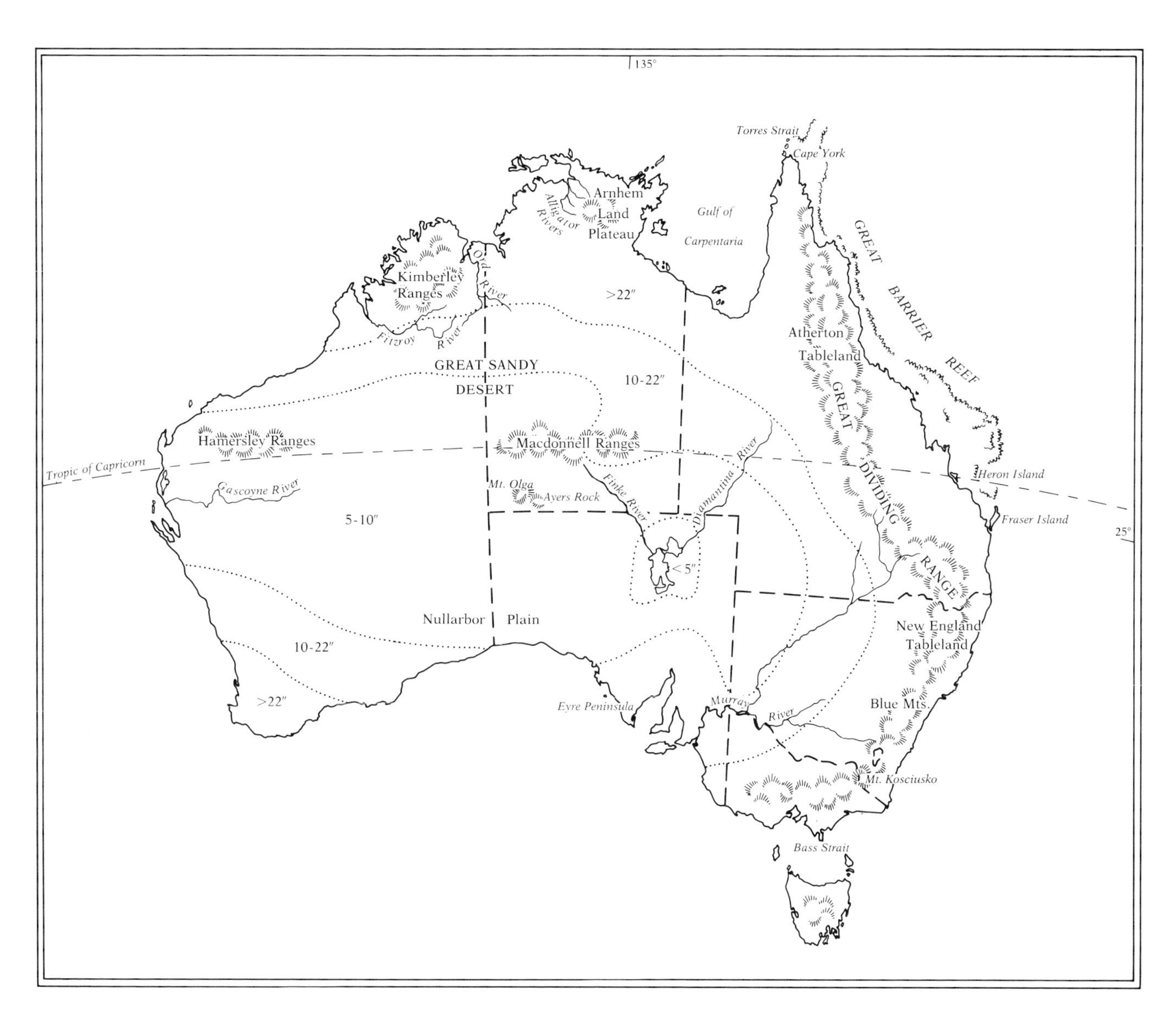

Some of the major climatic and geographic features of Australia. The dotted lines embrace regions of increasing mean annual rainfall, expressed in inches.

same origins.

When meteorologists plot mean annual rainfall on a map of Australia, they produce a series of concentric rings. The continent's center is driest, with rainfall gradually increasing toward the coasts (except in the west where the arid zone extends broadly to the Indian Ocean). But such generalities do not tell the whole story. Rains along the north coast come in the summer, the "cyclone season," when equatorial low-pressure systems bring periodic deluges and at times winds of destructive force. On the average, about five cyclones a year strike with varying and often unpredictable tracks, some considerably inland. The most destructive cyclone in recent times was one that hit Darwin on Christmas eve in 1974. The city was almost completely flattened, but when we visited it some six years later it had been rebuilt, and we saw little evidence of the devastation except for a few tattered pieces of former buildings mostly covered by vegetation.

At the same time that the cyclones are hitting the north, the southern part of the continent receives from the west a series of high-pressure systems, largely devoid of heavy clouds. Sometimes their progression is slow, and the winds turn northerly and produce very high temperatures. To illustrate, the average January temperature of Melbourne is sixty-seven degrees Fahrenheit, with an average maximum of seventy-nine degrees, but during the heat wave of January 1939 a temperature of 114 degrees was reached. However, summers along the south coast tend to be pleasant and equable. And fortunately for the Center, Australia seems to be free of tornadoes of the type that sometimes devastate parts of the American Midwest, although "dust devils," or "willy willies" as they are called in Australia , are a common sight during hot weather in the interior.

During the winter, very different conditions prevail. The greatest heat is generated north of the equator, and the cyclones (or hurricanes, as we call them) move to the northern hemisphere. The progressive high-pressure systems shift northward, providing a long, dry season in the northern part of the continent. Southern Australia is at this time influenced by low-pressure systems arising over the Southern Ocean, which bring cold winds and rainy periods—a time when Melbournites migrate to Queensland, if they can.

Meanwhile, the Center may be receiving little or no benefit from either the summer rains of the North or the winter rains of the South. The east coast, on the other hand, is influenced by easterly winds at all seasons, and these often result in showers on the coast or on the mountain ranges that parallel the coast. The highest mean annual rainfall, about 140 inches, occurs at Innisfail along the northeast coast, while the lowest occurs in the country around Lake Eyre. Marree, South Australia, for example, receives a yearly average of 5.6 inches. The major population centers lie between these two extremes, with Darwin having the highest mean annual rainfall (fifty-nine inches) and Adelaide the lowest (twenty-one inches).

These averages, however, conceal a great variability in rainfall that occurs throughout the continent. Sydney, a coastal city, has an average annual rainfall of forty-five inches; yet some years it has received as little as twenty-three inches, in other years as much as eighty-six inches. Brisbane, another coastal city, which (in our opinion) enjoys one of the best climates in the world, has twice experienced devastating floods, the last in 1974. It is, however, in the Center where the greatest variability occurs. At a place appropriately named Whim Creek, in Western Australia, only 0.16 of an inch fell in 1924, but on another occasion thirty inches fell in one day! There are places in the Center where years may pass with only an infinitesimal amount of rain, but once in a while they are transformed into quagmires, to be followed by meadows of flowers. This variability deceived many of the early explorers and settlers, whose initial impressions, gathered in a favorable season, were blasted by endless months of drought.

Since Australia is an island continent, the moderating effect of the ocean is felt all around the periphery, but like other travelers, we found ourselves surprised to see palm trees growing in Melbourne so far to the south. Winter frosts, of course, are rare there, as in most coastal localities, but they frequently occur farther inland or at higher altitudes south of the Tropic of Capricorn. Temperatures below zero Fahrenheit are very rare indeed, and have been recorded only at a few places in the southeastern highlands.

In the summer when the sun is directly overhead and the days are long, high temperatures are common, especially in the Center. In the northwest-central part of the continent, average daily maxima may exceed ninety-five degrees Fahrenheit for several months. Marble Bar, a mining town in Western Australia, is reputedly the hottest place on the continent, often registering temperatures in excess of a hundred degrees for weeks on end.

One of the local tales is of a man who died and went to hell, but immediately called for an overcoat. True or not, travelers in the Center do well to avoid the summer months and to carry plenty of water at all seasons. Nevertheless, there is much to be said (we think) for the Australian climate, which may be the driest and one of the hottest of any of the continents, but is also the sunniest. And because of that moderating effect of the ocean, the temperatures in most cities vary much less than they do in many cities in the United States. For example, the average monthly temperature in Melbourne varies from fifty in midwinter to sixty-seven in midsummer, in Brisbane from fifty-nine to seventy-seven, in Darwin from seventy-seven to eighty-six (spans of eleven to eighteen degrees); in Chicago temperatures at comparable seasons vary from twenty-one to seventy-nine, a span of fifty-eight degrees.

A sunny climate may be well and good, but in a country like Australia it can play havoc with the water supply. Water has to be stored for drinking and for irrigation, and in a hot, dry land, the evaporation loss is tremendous. The fact that Australia has by far the lowest average rainfall of any continent and one of the highest rates of evaporation means that the runoff is much lower than that of any other continent. The annual continental precipitation is 16.5 inches, but only a little over 1.75 inches remain as runoff—less than a fourth that of North America and less than one-eighth that of South America.

There are fifteen rivers in the world that carry more water to the sea each year than the total of *all* of Australia's rivers. The Murray River, Australia's largest, discharges in one year what the Mississippi carries to the sea in nine days. Although the Murray and its tributaries drain an area of 414,000 square miles, much of this is flat and semiarid, and some of the tributaries, such as the beautiful Murrumbidgee, rise in the southeastern highlands, and although at first they are steep, they later flow into relatively flat country, too. Thus most of the system has a very low gradient, dropping by only three to nine inches per mile. Someone calculated that water leaving Albury, not far from the so-called "Australian Alps," takes two to three months to reach the sea just south of Adelaide.

Paddlewheelers and other larger craft were once common on the Murray and its larger tributaries as they moved wool to market, but today most of the water is used for irrigation, and little passes through the narrow mouth to the sea. We were pleased to learn, however, when we visited the area, that there are now two or three new "old riverboats" paddling tourists over the old romantic routes of "the mighty Murray."

As mentioned earlier, the major system of mountains in Australia more or less parallels the eastern coast. It is called the "Great Dividing Range" because it sheds its water on the east into the Pacific and on the west into the Murray system or into systems of internal drainage. Whether it should be called "great" and parts of it compared to the Swiss Alps—well, all things are relative. Certainly, Australia's most scenic country occurs in the eastern highlands, where in places splendid forests, alpine meadows, and rugged cliffs and canyons are to be found. The mountains of Tasmania form a disjointed part of the Great Dividing Range, and have jagged peaks, cirques, and wild rivers that rival anything North America can offer—but they occupy a limited area that is continually being invaded for hydroelectric power.

The only natural lakes in Australia are small ones formed by the filling of old volcanic craters or by past glacial actions, and all are in or near the eastern highlands. Maps of Australia can be

Rugged Cradle Mountain, in Tasmania, bears a fresh coating of snow in February—equivalent to August in the Northern Hemisphere.

deceptive, as they show many inland lakes, including giant Lake Eyre, which is forty feet below sea level and 3,700 square miles in extent—the seventeenth largest lake in the world. In fact, most of the time these lakes are merely glaring white sheets of salt crust. Lake Eyre is said to fill about twice a century, the last time in 1975, when the water in places was over fifteen feet deep.

Australia's natural lakes make up in personality what they lack in numbers. Lake Barrine, not far from Cairns, is a jewel set in rich tropical rain forests in northern Queensland; Lake Dove is a cool mirror for ragged Cradle Mountain in northwestern Tasmania. Blue Lake, occupying an old volcanic crater of Mount Gambier in South Australia, is brilliant blue in summer but turns a somber gray in winter. Apparently, temperature changes cause minerals to go in and out of solution, changing the reflectivity of the water. Of course, there are now many man-made lakes and reservoirs, and these are often inhabited by waterfowl, as are many of the salt lakes when they fill. One of our favorite places was Fogg Dam, or rather the lake and marshes behind the dam. This area east of Darwin had originally been planned as a site for growing rice. It grew, and so did the bird population, which harvested the rice well ahead of the planters. Abandoned now by the farmers, the area is an ornithological paradise, abounding in white cockatoos, cormorants, jabiru storks, herons, geese, and many kinds of ducks.

Since the Great Dividing Range parallels the

east coast fairly closely and is in a relatively well-watered part of the continent, its east-flowing streams tend to have steep gradients, and the entire chain is strung with waterfalls. We have visited several of these and would be hard put to pick a favorite. Perhaps it would be Russell Falls, which descends in spreading tiers through lush tree ferns in Mount Field National Park, not too far west of Hobart in Tasmania; or Moran's Falls, which we came on suddenly as it roared through the mists of Lamington National Park, a half-day's drive south of Brisbane, Queensland. The highest falls is said to be Wollomombi, which plunges 1,580 feet from the New England tableland of northern New South Wales, with a single drop of 1,100 feet—fifth highest in the world. Many of these falls are inaccessible by road and provide a challenge to bush walkers.

The north coast has a number of rivers that drain somewhat limited areas but carry great volumes of water during "the wet" of summer. The Alligator Rivers of the Northern Territory (which should have been called "Crocodile Rivers," since there are no alligators in Australia) drain the Arnhem Land plateau, one branch plunging 650 feet over Jim Jim Falls, in Kakadu National Park. The Ord River, in the northern part of Western Australia, has been harnessed for agriculture. There, Lake Argyle, Australia's largest man-made lake, supplies water for a vast area of mixed crops, which unfortunately have been plagued by a variety of insect pests and are too far from markets to be grown at any great profit. We enjoyed swimming on hot, September afternoons in the Ord River behind the diversion dam, but a night of camping on the Fitzroy River in the far Northwest was sleepless because the black cockatoos resented our invasion of their domain.

Rivers of the west coast tend to be unspectacular, although the Swan provides a beautiful setting for Perth, and the Gascoyne farther north provides water for market gardens and banana plantations. When we visited the Gascoyne it had been dry for many months, but water was being pumped from beneath the sandy bottom. In June 1980 the Gascoyne was in flood, its major town partly evacuated, and the surrounding crops in large part destroyed.

Lake Violet, in central Western Australia, is typical of many of the continent's "lakes," which are dry and encrusted with salt except when filled now and then by heavy rains.

Such is the variability of Australian rainfall.

The central part of the south coast has no streams at all, for this is limestone country, and rain (such as it is) drains directly into the ground, forming caves and underground streams that run to the sea. A vast plain of some 75,000 square miles is covered with limestone rubble and saltbush, with scarcely any trees at all. The surveyor Alfred Delisser, who in 1865 made the first careful study of the area, appropriately called it the Nullarbor Plain (from the Latin *nullus arbor*, no tree). Where the plain meets the sea there are many miles of sheer cliffs, some three hundred feet high, where no landfall is possible. Little wonder that the Nullarbor long proved a formidable barrier between settlements in Western Australia and those in the east.

Bordered on the north as it is by harsh deserts, the plain is still a barrier to the distribution of many plants and animals. Now it is crossed by a highway, which in one stretch goes for ninety miles without a curve, and by a railway, which has no curves or bridges for three hundred miles! We have crossed the Nullarbor by car, by train, and by air, and each time felt that the unearthly landscape more than made up for the lack of "scenery." At many points near the coast deep blowholes penetrate the limestone, producing strange moaning sounds and air currents that sometimes suck objects into (or out of) the holes. To the aborigines, this was the breathing of Jeedara, a great serpent that lived beneath the plain. The many caves—one three miles long—provide a challenge to speleologists and spelunkers. Some are inhabited by great clouds of bats.

All of Australia's river systems together drain less than half the area of the continent. The Lake Eyre basin of the east-center is one of the largest areas of internal drainage in the world, some 480,000 square miles. Much of the western part of the continent is so flat that water merely collects in local pockets, where it evaporates to form the many salt pans. Lake Eyre receives input from the Macdonnell and other ranges of the Center as well as from inland Queensland, but water from these areas only rarely reaches the lake. The Finke River, the major "river" of the Center, is for most of the time a ribbon of sand flanked by drought-resistant trees, with waterholes here and there. The Diamantina in Queensland flows through such flat country that when it is full (about once in seven years), the water flows through hundreds of separate channels, so that the whole river is many miles wide and unfordable. But most if not all of this water disappears into the ground or evaporates before it reaches Lake Eyre.

In fact, much of the drainage from the western slopes of the Great Dividing Range, and other highlands in Queensland and adjacent parts of neighboring states, disappears into the ground, where it flows toward the west in sloping, porous layers of sandstone that are between thick layers of impervious rocks. This is the "Great Artesian Basin," where bores often 2,000 feet deep (but sometimes as much as 7,000 feet) produce a steady flow of water. This is an enormous area, some twelve hundred miles long and nine hundred miles wide, and it is surely surprising that the driest continent in the world should have the largest artesian system known. But there is a catch. Much of this artesian water is hot and mineralized, drinkable only after it has cooled, and then best for livestock.

We spent a good deal of time in areas served by artesian wells, and managed pretty well by filling our water jugs in the evening and allowing them to sit overnight, but we did tire a bit of smelling like rotten eggs after taking a shower, and drinking water with a taste of sulfur. It is little wonder that the number of pubs per capita is high in that part of Australia!

We don't mean to imply that all of Australia is flat west of the Dividing Range. The rugged Kimberley Ranges of the Northwest have scarcely been fully explored, and peaks of the mineral-rich Hamersleys, farther south, reach an elevation of 4,000 feet. The Macdonnell Ranges of the Center, in which Alice Springs is situated, are not high but are impressive, rising as they do in a long, linear series running east-west when all the stream beds run north to south, cutting the ranges with steep-sided gorges, many of which are readily accessible to tourists. The Musgrave and Everard Ranges, some two hundred miles farther south, are less readily accessible, but there was one campsite in a canyon in the Everards that we shall not readily forget: a full moon was shining on the great, red, granite domes, and a boobook owl was calling. Pictographs on the canyon walls suggested that the aborigines, too, had cherished the site.

Between the Macdonnell and Musgrave Ranges, the country is mainly a flat desert of reddish sand, but from it rise three great masses of rock: Mount Conner, a sandstone mesa rising some thousand feet; Ayers Rock, which is about eight miles west of Mount Conner; and the Olgas, still another twenty-five miles farther west. All three are remnants of an extensive plateau, most of which eroded long ago; oddly, the three are very different in form, depending upon the tilt and composition of the rock at that particular point.

Ayers Rock [colorplate 1] and the Olgas have become meccas for tourists, as well they should be. Ayers Rock is a single great chunk of sandstone 1,100 feet high above the desert floor and about six miles in circumference. By day it is reddish-brown, but at dawn and sunset it may glow an intense red. We have seen it in good weather and bad—but "bad" weather is good at "The Rock," for rain is always welcome, and a heavy rain produces dozens of waterfalls from the rock (as well as the excitement of becoming hopelessly bogged, as the nearest paved road is, or was, many miles away). To the aborigines, who called it *Uluru*, the rock was sacred, and many of the caves around the base are adorned with their paintings. The Olgas consist of a number of huge domes of darker, conglomerate rock. To the natives, this was *Katajuta*, "mountain of many heads."

Australia's "red heart," as the Center is often called, has a beauty that is both subtle and unique. "Its beauty made one catch one's breath," wrote George Farwell in 1951 in his book, *The Outside Track*. "Red sea: red sand? It was not red at all. Nothing approaching red. Yet how describe it? Crimson, carmine, red ochre, pink chrome—it had something of them all. Yet it was none of them. It had its own indigenous hue. The landscape was beyond the power of words. . . ."

What is even more astonishing than the beauty of this country is the abundance of its life: golden-yellow clumps of spinifex (porcupine grass); a variety of small trees; at times and places, patches of wildflowers; now and then a colorful parrot or a majestic eagle; at night, the howl of dingoes. But after a series of bad years, the landscape may become forbidding indeed. The trees and bushes lose their leaves, if not their lives, and wildlife seems to disappear—a silent world baking under a merciless sun. Now it is properly the "dead heart." Yet the seeds of recovery are there, for plants and animals have developed ways of surviving these

Although within sight of Ayers Rock, the equally spectacular Olgas are formed of very different rock.

A common scene in one of Australia's sandy deserts, in this case near Lake Mungo, New South Wales. (Raymond H. Besserdin)

A gibber plain in South Australia. Such plains are largely devoid of vegetation and of animal life.

extremes. Indeed, the deserts of Australia are full of remarkably adapted living things—provided one has the patience and endurance to search them out.

Australian deserts are by no means all alike. The country around Ayers Rock and the Olgas is sand plain, mostly flat and sufficiently stable to support a sparse growth of bushes and small trees. Elsewhere there are extensive areas of parallel sand ridges, some of them many miles long, generally twenty to forty feet high and separated by vales of loamier soil up to a mile wide. On tops of the ridges the sand tends to be bare and somewhat mobile, but the sides are often stabilized by bushes and grasses, and the vales between often have small trees.

There are three major areas of sand-ridge deserts, all of them largely uninhabited by man. These are the Simpson Desert, north of Lake Eyre; the Great Victoria Desert, north of the Nullarbor Plain; and the Great Sandy Desert of the inland Northwest. Both plain and ridge deserts tend to be interrupted here and there by evaporative basins (salt pans), since there are generally no stream beds to channel the waters to the sea. The reddish color of the sand results from its mineral content, chiefly iron. Altogether there are about three-quarters of a million square miles of sandy desert—about one-fifth of the continent.

By far the most dreary and forbidding parts of Australia are the so-called stony deserts or "gibber plains," gibbers being dark, rounded or jagged stones of various sizes that lie on a flat surface like an irregular pavement. Gibber plains sometimes extend for many square miles, uninterrupted by trees or hills or much of anything. These stony deserts are said to occupy some 6 percent of the continent. Elsewhere, in the dry interior, one finds extensive areas of dark, less stony soil, which is more or less covered with grasses, saltbush, or other vegetation. Much of this country is now used for grazing sheep and cattle.

The extensive areas of sand, gibbers, and poor-quality soil have resulted from weathering over a long period of time of some of the oldest rocks in the world. Recently, bits of zircon from Mt. Narryer, Western Australia, have been dated 4.1 to 4.2 billion years old, not long after the earth was formed from debris circling the sun. Rocks more than two billion years old cover a large part of the continent, in places exposed and in places covered by younger rocks or by soils. Fossil bacterialike organisms recently found in sedimentary rocks of the Warrawoona formation in northwestern Australia have been found (by radiometric dating of associated igneous rocks) to be three and a half billion years old. Thus they represent the oldest evidence of life that has yet been found on earth.

Remains of the oldest multicellular animals known to science also occur in Australia, in this case in the Flinders Ranges of South Australia. In fine-grained sedimentary rocks can be found the impressions of soft-bodied animals such as segmented worms, jellyfish, and others. These date from 670 to 550 million years ago, before any animals had acquired hard shells or skeletons. This period in the geological record has been called the "Ediacarian period," after the Ediacara Hills of South Australia. Fossils of this period are of great interest to students of animal evolution, as it is evident that much of the diversification into major groups (phyla and classes) occurred during this time.

While the rocks of the eastern third of the continent are more varied and generally less ancient, soils there have also been subject to leaching over long periods, and indeed throughout Australia soils tend to be deficient in nutrients such as nitrogen, phosphorus, and trace elements such as manganese, zinc, copper, and molybdenum. While native plants and animals are adapted to these soils, this is not necessarily true of imports. For example, lack of boron in Tasmanian soils produces a corky disease of apples, and lack of cobalt in parts of South Australia has been incriminated as causing a disease of sheep.

Appreciation of these deficiencies has made agriculture possible in many places where at first it was not. Superphosphate fertilizers are now used for pasture improvement at a rate of several million tons a year, and trace elements are supplied wherever they are needed. Thanks to intensive research on Australian soils, some of the finest fruits and vegetables in the world are now grown there.

The Australian continent is not only composed largely of very ancient rocks, but over many millions of years these have undergone relatively little change, other than erosion and degradation, over vast areas of the West. The modest mountain ranges of the East have undergone uplifting in more recent geological time, only a few tens of thousands of years ago. But on the whole, few of the geological forces that produced the scenery and variety of Europe and North America have operated to any great degree. As would be expected of a continent that straddles the Tropic of Capricorn, there were no "ice ages" at the time these occurred in the Northern Hemisphere, merely a few localized glaciers in the mountains of the Southeast.

Earthquakes are almost unheard of, and there are no active volcanoes or thermal areas. A few old craters and volcanic cores attest to the fact that this was not always so. These do afford some interesting scenery in parts of eastern Australia, as for example the series of old volcanic spires known as the Glasshouse Mountains, north of Brisbane, named by Captain Cook for a supposed resemblance to the glass furnaces of his native Yorkshire.

We hiked, one day in the rain, to Hypipamee Crater, a sheer-sided hole 200 feet wide and nearly 500 feet deep in the rain forests of the Atherton Tableland of north Queensland. The crater is said to be the result of a single volcanic explosion many thousands of years ago. Of some of the crater lakes, Barrine and Blue Lake, we have already written. Soils of volcanic origin occur in many parts of the Great Dividing Range and adjacent country and are some of the richest in Australia. When precipitation was sufficient, they often supported rain forests. Now, much of this land has been cleared for settlement and pastureland, resulting in serious erosion and invasion by weed plants such as lantana.

All the evidence suggests that the landscape had been stable for a very long time before the coming of man. Australia has often been called the most ancient of the continents, and in an important sense this is true. As we have said, large areas are underlain by some of the oldest rocks in the world. Weathering and erosion have acted upon these rocks for so many eons that they are broken into ragged hills and canyons, and over vast areas reduced to flat plains of sand or gravel. As Australian geographer C. D. Ollier has pointed out, persons in the

Northern Hemisphere are used to living in landscapes dominated by events of the Ice Age, or at most by events of a few million years ago—landscapes still influenced to an extent by earthquakes, volcanoes, the effects of ice and snow. But Australian landscapes are affected by events of the past 250 million years. "It is necessary," Ollier says, "to make a conscious effort to appreciate the vast timescale appropriate to Australia." A. D. Hope, one of Australia's leading poets, put it somewhat differently:

> They call her a young country, but they lie:
> She is the last of lands, the emptiest,
> A woman beyond her change of life, a breast
> Still tender but within the womb is dry.

The ice ages, however, did have important effects on Australia. The melting of the continental glaciers of Eurasia and America caused a rise in sea level that flooded many coastal areas, converting the lower river valleys into bays and inlets of the sea (as our Chesapeake Bay was formed). At the same time, hills along the coast became islands and peninsulas: the coast of Maine is replete with examples. In Australia the results include Sydney Harbor and, just to its north, Broken Bay, Wilsons Promontory in Victoria, and the many offshore "holiday" islands of Queensland. The separation of Tasmania and New Guinea from the continent occurred at about the same time—by the flooding of Bass and Torres Straits, still island-flecked.

At many points along the coast, highlands abut the sea, forming cliffs and headlands that are battered by the waves. Between these headlands the sediments are drawn into magnificent beaches, often backed by sand dunes. On Moreton Island, Queensland, these dunes reach a height of nearly a thousand feet. As for the beaches, surely Australia has more per capita than any other continent, and (away from the population centers) it is often possible to share a beach only with the sea birds.

The ice ages of the Northern Hemisphere also resulted in some overall cooling of the Australian continent and a considerable increase in rainfall. In the several interglacial periods, warmer and drier conditions prevailed. These changes presented challenges to the plants and animals, as we shall see.

Aside from the submergence of coastal areas, the general outline of Australia is believed to have been pretty much the same for several thousand years. However, fossils of marine animals that have been found in parts of the interior show that at one time a shallow sea covered much of the Center, all the way from the Gulf of Carpentaria to the south coast, and divided the continent into three separate land masses. (Some of the early explorers were seeking an inland sea; unfortunately they were 130 million years too late!) These seas withdrew, but a later incursion of the sea over the central south coast produced the limestone base of the Nullarbor Plain.

Fossils also show that the climate of Australia was often very different from what it is today. There are, for example, major deposits of coal, oil, and natural gas, resulting from fossilization and transformation of ancient plants, probably during a time when the climate was much wetter than it is now. Thanks to modern methods of dating rocks associated with fossils, it is now possible to time, approximately, past alternations in climate, warm to cool and dry to wet. Some of these changes occurred at the same time on other continents, perhaps as a result of changes in the amount of radiation from the sun.

Research within the past two decades has also confirmed a long-held suspicion that the world's continents have, over long periods of time, been moving in relation to one another. Actually, England's Joseph Hooker suggested, in 1853, that the continents of the Southern Hemisphere must once have been linked. But this was against all common sense—nothing seems more stable than the earth we stand on. Now a great deal of evidence has accumulated to support the "continental drift" theory, and we know that the continents are still moving—at a rate of about four inches a year, we are told. The concept of continental drift, as it applies to Australia, has done a great deal to help us understand past changes in climate, and especially to shed light on the origins of the remarkable flora and fauna.

Along the leading edges of each continental block—the west coast of North and South America, the east coast of Asia, and so forth—earthquakes and volcanoes are the expression of this movement. Fortunately for Australians, the block including that continent has its outer edge through New Guinea, the Solomons, the New Hebrides, and New Zealand, and it is these that bear the brunt of the earth's stresses—including the well-known thermal areas of New Zealand.

It is believed that more than two hundred million years ago all the continents were united in a single supercontinent. This became split in two by the incursion of a sea, one of the fragments comprising what is now North America and Eurasia (minus India), the other the remaining landmasses. The latter, called by the romantic name Gondwanaland, contained what is now Australia, India, Africa, and South America, all huddled together against Antarctica, which was by no means always the frigid and sterile place it is now.

All of this has something of the flavor of science fiction, but in fact several lines of evidence support it. Not only do the continents appear to fit together like pieces of a jigsaw puzzle, but similar rocks of the same age occur in adjacent parts of all of them. Furthermore, when basaltic rocks are formed by the cooling of magmas, they preserve a record of the direction of magnetism—in this case the south magnetic pole. But only when the continents are shifted to their original positions as part of Gondwanaland do the rocks point to the pole (which is known to have shifted by several hundred miles in the past two hundred million years). A final line of evidence is supplied by fossil and living plants and animals that could scarcely have crossed broad water gaps. For example, remains of long extinct seed ferns called *Glossopteris* occur on all the southern continents as well as India, suggesting that these areas were not only in contact but had a similar climate.

There are also groups of living plants (such as the Proteaceae, which we'll discuss in the next chapter) that occur today on the continents that made up Gondwanaland, though absent even as fossils elsewhere. Antarctic beeches, *Nothofagus*,

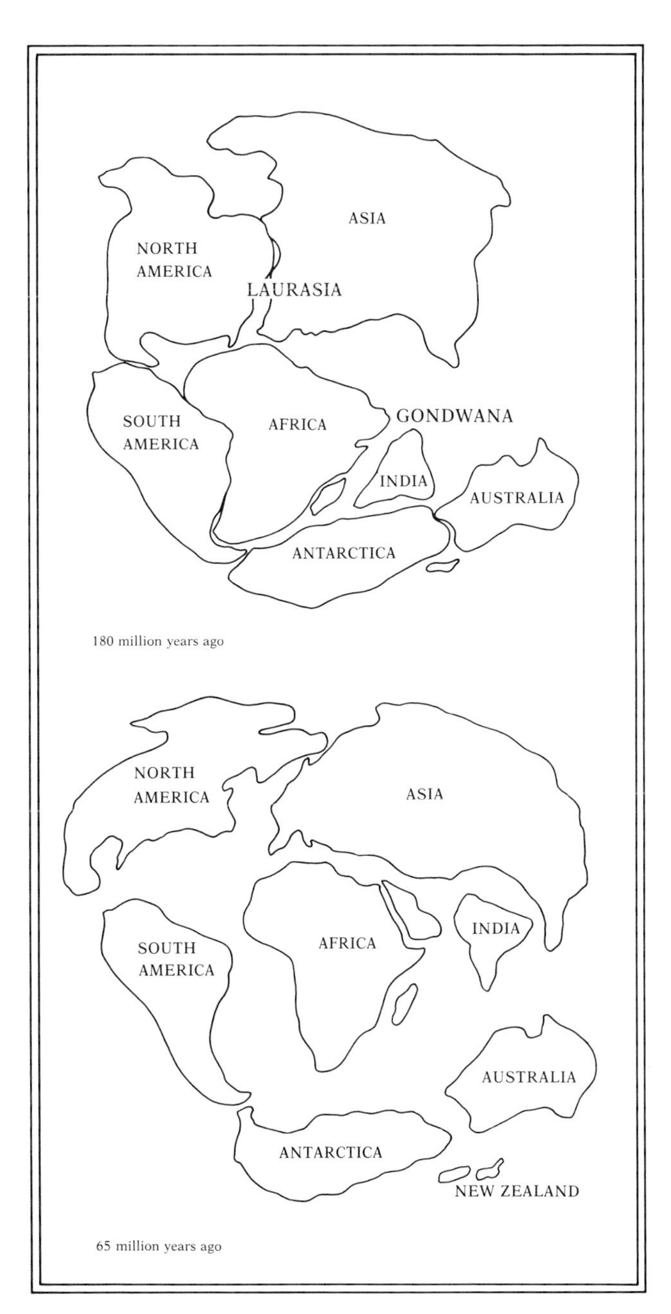

At top: *the positions of the continents at the end of the Triassic geologic period, about 180 million years ago. By the end of the Cretaceous period, about 65 million years ago, the breakup of Gondwana was partially complete* **(below).**

now occur in Australia, New Zealand, and southern South America, and are known from Antarctica by fossilized pollen deposits. These beeches do not occur in Africa and India, indicating that the group must have evolved after these landmasses had begun to break away from Gondwanaland.

Much of Gondwanaland apparently enjoyed a moist, cool to subtropical climate for a long time. This was the age of dinosaurs and primitive, nonflowering plants such as cycads (still a prominent feature of the Australian flora). As Africa and India drifted away, some seventy million years ago, Australia and Antarctica remained more or less stationary, with New Zealand apparently a separate island, but not far away. For a time South America remained connected to Antarctica, and through it to Australia. By this time the dinosaurs had become extinct, and marsupial mammals, Antarctic beeches, and other still-living plant and animal groups were becoming established in the remaining parts of Gondwanaland. South America broke away from Antarctica perhaps forty-five million years ago, but the separation is still a matter of only a few hundred miles, Cape Horn and the Graham Land Peninsula of Antarctica remaining strung out toward one another today as if the continents had just been pulled apart.

For many years biologists had thought, but could not prove, that marsupials must have been on Antarctica when it was warmer and still served as a bridge between Australia and South America. Certainly, possumlike marsupials occur widely in South America (one even ranges into North America), though because they have to compete with many higher mammals they have not become the dominant animals they are in Australia. Then in early 1982 a team of American scientists turned up fossil jawbones of a rat-sized marsupial in Antarctica, and these bones are believed to be about forty million years old. Thus it seems probable that marsupials ranged across Gondwanaland after Africa and India had drifted away, and after New Zealand had split off, too, for it also has no native marsupials.

Obviously (and fortunately) Australia eventually moved north from Antarctica, but that forbidding continent remains its closest neighbor (1,500 miles away). The separation from Antarctica began some fifty-five million years ago, and by ten million was nearly what it is now. Interestingly, New Zealand became widely separated from Australia well before that, although New Guinea and Tasmania remained part of the Australian continent, as they very nearly still are.

As the Australian block drifted north, it gradually came closer to Asia. Today, these two continents are 1,750 miles apart, and it is probable that, some tens of millions of years from now, Australia will have joined Asia, just as India and Africa have done. But at this point in time Australia remains the only continent (other than frozen Antarctica) without a land connection to another continent, in fact separated from all continents by deep oceans. That this has been true for many millions of years provides the explanation of many of the unique features of Australian natural history.

Of course, there are many islands between Australia and southeast Asia. As the continents came to lie closer together, these islands sometimes served as "steppingstones" for plants with seeds that were airborne or resistant to salt water, and for animals that could fly or drift on air currents—or build ships. That is, organisms could become established by chance on one island, then at a later time populate a more distant island, and finally, after many years and adaptive changes, reach another continent.

When sea levels were lower, as they were when much water was tied up in the continental glaciers that melted back some ten thousand years ago, New Guinea was connected to Australia, and Sumatra, Java, and Borneo were connected with Asia, leaving a much narrower water gap than there is today. But there are deep ocean troughs of long standing between the islands of the Asiatic continental shelf and those of the Australian shelf, some of these troughs as much as 1,800 feet deep. The islands between, such as the Celebes, have been geologically unstable and have provided limited habitats available for occupation. So the passage of plants and animals across these steppingstones has been limited.

On the whole, Asiatic stocks have been much more successful in crossing to the south than have Australian stocks in crossing northward. Doubtless this is at least partly because the Asiatic landmass is so much larger and more varied, and so closely associated with other continents, that diverse and competitively vigorous groups evolved. On the other hand, Australia's flora and fauna developed on a smaller land mass, with less diversity of habitat and little interchange with other continents, at least since the breakup of Gondwanaland. Perhaps, too, prevailing winds and ocean currents had something to do with it, as did the movements of early man as well. We know that the Australian aborigines arrived, presumably via island steppingstones from Asia, some thirty to forty thousand years ago, and Asiatic and Melanesian fishermen often touched on the north coast of Australia long before Europeans settled there.

In any case, we know that many of the "less unusual" components of Australia's flora and fauna have an Asiatic origin, mainly in fairly recent geologic time. Stocks of bats, rodents, birds, and insects invaded from the north from time to time and adapted to the rather different environments.

Many Asiatic plants reached New Guinea, where the tropical climate was not very different from that of Malaysia and Borneo, and some of these trickled into Australia. But none of Australia's distinctive creatures—kangaroos, possums, echidnas, and so forth—got beyond New Guinea. Only one species of *Eucalyptus*, Australia's most distinctive contribution to the trees of the world, got as far as the Philippines, and one species of *Casuarina* managed to extend its range all the way to Africa. Throughout much of Australia, these two major types of trees are joined by another—*Acacia*. However, *Acacias* did not originate in Australia at all, but probably first arrived there via floating seeds, which are resistant to salt water. *Acacia* pollen has been found in Western Australian sediments dating from ten million years ago; now there are several hundred species in habitats as diverse as stark deserts and humid coastal forests.

At first glance it seems odd that some groups of plants and animals have as many species as they do on a continent as relatively flat and unvaried as Australia. How does one account for the presence of more than five hundred species of *Eucalyptus* and at least as many species of *Acacia*; of large, distinctively Australian groups of birds such as the honeyeaters; of groups of insects having dozens or even hundreds of species which evidently evolved within Australia?

Generally speaking, species evolve when populations of an ancestral stock are separated over a long period of time, so that genetic changes accumulate and produce, through natural selection, new populations that are closely adapted to slightly different environments. In North America, there are not only plenty of existing barriers, such as the Rocky Mountains, but we know that in past times continental glaciers several times pushed into the northern United States, greatly altering climates and distribution patterns. This produced fragmentation of many populations, which were released from their refugia only after several thousand years of separate evolution.

Even though glaciation in Australia was confined to mountains of the Southeast, the overall effect on the climate may have been considerable. During glacial periods the climate is believed to have been cool to warm, with ample rainfall in most parts of the continent. But each of the several interglacial periods was very dry, so that many moisture-adapted plants and animals survived only in isolated pockets along the coast (not unlike those we see today). Others doubtless adapted gradually to the increasing aridity, while some surely simply failed to survive the change.

There is evidence of three interglacial periods as well as another dry period about five thousand years ago, so there was plenty of opportunity for populations to be divided, adapted, redivided, re-adapted, and so forth. Today, in another dry cycle, it is easy to appreciate this, as the Nullarbor Plain, the various deserts of the interior, the lowlands separating patches of rain forest—all of these provide obvious barriers to distribution. One finds related species in the Southeast and Southwest, for example, or in rain forests of Queensland and Tasmania.

Fragmentation of populations undoubtedly long preceded the ice ages, going back to the time of the inland seas and the splitting up of Gondwanaland. Even so, it takes a bit of mind-stretching to envisage the production of so many diverse species of *Eucalyptus*, for example, from the stringybarks of the monsoon forests of the north to the ghost gums of the interior deserts and the snow gums of Mount Kosciusko. Nowadays, of course, eucalypts occur in many warmer parts of the world, and in California and Mexico they almost seem like natives. But it was man who carried them to those alien lands. Left to themselves, the Australian fauna and flora—developed while the land was part of Gondwanaland and later during long periods of isolation—had little impact upon continents of the Northern Hemisphere.

On the other hand, plants and animals derived from Asiatic stocks came to make up an important part of the Australian scene. Since the advent of Western man, there has been, obviously, a veritable flood from other parts of the world, not only deliberate imports such as pine trees and merino sheep, but rampant pests such as rabbits and lantana—the list of each could be prolonged to fill a page. The Australian scene may have changed more in the past 200 years than it did in the previous 200 million. The indigenous plants and animals are closely adapted to environments that have often been grossly modified. Some have learned to live with man, and even flourished, while others—particularly those associated with the diminishing forests—are having a hard time of it or have disappeared forever. Fortunately, Australians (at least a few of them, and belatedly—as everywhere) are developing an ecological conscience.

Australia's isolation in the far southern oceans—as well as the great empty spaces within the continent—have had a profound effect not only on its natural history but upon its human history and culture, a story well told by Geoffrey Blainey in his book *The Tyranny of Distance*. Modern methods of travel have changed all that, rendering Australia much more visible in the eyes of the world than it was for many years after its settlement by Western man. It is not only easily reached by air, but there are few parts of the continent that cannot be visited, at least by persons willing to "rough it." Some of the finest national parks are readily accessible from the major cities. But, as everywhere, the landscape and its inhabitants can be fully appreciated only by those whose eyes are backed by some measure of understanding. A kangaroo, or a baobab tree, is not just an oddity; it is the product of a particular environment and a particular history—it is odd because that environment and that history are unique.

From scenarios never duplicated and never to be repeated have arisen the most remarkable assemblage of plants and animals to be found anywhere. They deserve to be saluted, to be understood and enjoyed, to be preserved as unusually exciting inhabitants of the earth, our home. That is why we wrote this book.

3

Gum Trees and Other Flora

"There are no more beautiful trees in the world"

Since childhood most of us have known that the "kookaburra sits on the old gum tree-ee," but other than singing about an Australian bird that laughed while sitting on a gum tree ("eating gum drops"—who wouldn't be happy!), we were rather ignorant of the "bush" of which the kookaburra was king. And it must be admitted that it is not easy to become familiar with a world of trees, shrubs, and flowering plants in which every species and many major types are completely new to one's experience. This was a matter that distressed the early settlers, who responded not only by importing familiar trees from England and elsewhere, but also by giving names such as "ash" and "oak" to Australian trees, which were totally unrelated and did not even much resemble English oaks and ashes.

We found it much easier, at least at first, to recognize the many exotics found not only in gardens but as escapes along roadsides and in meadows and forests. The dandelion is a case in point, and we almost welcomed its familiar yellow head, for it was a flower we knew well. The kookaburra we discuss elsewhere, but perhaps we should define "bush" before we talk about the flora. Any wild area, usually a forest, but even a desert or swamp, as long as no cultivation is in progress, is called "bush," a convenient and all-encompassing word (incidentally, "going bush" is a good Australian phrase, and can be flattering or derogatory, depending on how it is said). And the most important trees in the Australian bush are the gums, or eucalypts. In the words of Sir Otto Frankel, a government botanist, the eucalypts "are the epitome of the Australian landscape, expressing, in the one genus, its essence and distinctiveness."

When the nineteenth-century naturalist Charles Darwin visited Australia, he was young (only twenty-eight years of age) and not yet an international figure. The same might be said of Australia, and so Darwin's impressions of this country are interesting, if not completely flattering. In January 1837, he hired a carriage and traveled inland from Sydney for about 120 miles. In his *Journal* he wrote:

> The extreme uniformity of the vegetation is the most remarkable feature in the landscape of the greater part of New South Wales. Everywhere we have an open woodland, the ground being partially covered with a very thin pasture, with little appearance of verdure. The trees nearly all belong to one family, and mostly have their leaves placed in a vertical, instead of, as in Europe, in a nearly horizontal position: the foliage is scanty, and of a peculiar pale green tint, without any gloss. Hence the woods appear light and shadowless: this, although a loss of comfort to the traveller under the scorching rays of summer, is of importance to the farmer, as it allows grass to grow where it otherwise would not. The leaves are not shed periodically. . . . The greater number of the trees, with the exception of some of the Bluegums, do not attain a large size; but they grow tall and tolerably straight, and stand well apart. The bark of some of the Eucalypti falls annually, or hangs dead in long shreds, which swing about with the wind, and give to the woods a desolate and untidy appearance.

On our first visit to Australia we also proceeded west from Sydney, but instead of riding in a horse-drawn carriage we flew in a propeller-driven airplane to the new capital city, Canberra. While the jets that now serve on that run do not even allow time for a cup of tea and some cookies (or biscuits, as they are called in Australia), we then had time both for a leisurely "cuppa" and for observing the bluish-green of the eucalypt woodlands as we circled low over the hills.

Canberra itself is full of exotics, but once outside the confines of the city, the native hues take over. A eucalypt woodland is distinctive for smell as well as color, for the leaves give off tiny droplets that not only impart the distinctive ordor, but render distant objects bluish, as a result of the scattering of light rays. As we became better acquainted with the eucalypt groves on our walks around the outskirts of Canberra (and many other places later), we found Darwin's observations, though brief, were astute.

Eucalypts are peculiarly Australian, and although some can be found in southern California and areas of similar climate throughout the world, there they have been introduced. Of approximately five hundred species,* only seven extend into New Guinea and its surrounding islands, one of them

*We should perhaps explain that *species* are kinds of living things that remain distinct because they don't interbreed with one another to produce hybrids—but unfortunately in some cases they do, posing problems in identification. A group of related species believed to share a common ancestry constitutes a *genus* (plural, genera). Scientific names of species (which we'll avoid when possible) consist of the genus plus the species name, the two placed in italics. For example, *Eucalyptus regnans* is the "moun-

continuing north into the Philippines. The rest are restricted to the Australian continent and to Tasmania. Classification is, however, a difficult matter, as members of the genus *Eucalyptus* hybridize frequently. So, to us, new "mates" to the bush, recognizing a tree as a gum was enough of a challenge, and we seldom attempted to be more specific. As if hybridization wasn't confusing enough, an additional problem is presented by the fact that a number of plants of other genera resemble eucalypts superficially. That is, they have thick, pendant, rather slender leaves (sclerophyll, in technical parlance, meaning "hard leaves")—an illustration of adaptation of diverse plants to a similar dry, sunny environment.

The flowers and fruits are the "secret" to identification, and we could almost always find one or the other on or under an individual plant. The term *Eucalyptus* comes from the Greek words *eu*, meaning "well," and *kalyptos*, meaning "covered," and refers to the protective lids covering the buds, which are thrown off when the trees, quite literally, burst into bloom. The blossoms are usually white [colorplate 2], though they range through light yellow in some species to brilliant reds in others. They are soft and feathery because they consist mainly of a mass of stamens—a bit like an uncombed wig of a tiny doll—emerging from the cuplike base. The woody, capsular fruits, or gum nuts (not gum drops), look remotely like acorns, but offer more variety in shape and sculpture. The leaves of most eucalypts tend to be long, slender, and pointed, letting through a good deal of light, as Darwin noticed. But curiously, some species have "juvenile foliage": the leaves are different in shape and broader. We have never seen an expla-

This is a river red gum, a Eucalyptus *that often reaches an impressive size in the Outback, chiefly along the intermittent and permanent watercourses.*

tain ash" of Victoria and Tasmania, the tallest of all the eucalypts. In this case the common name is misleading, for the tree is not an ash at all.

A distinctive major group of plants or animals, consisting of one or more genera, constitutes a *family*. Families are grouped into *orders*, orders into *classes*. Since from time to time we want to discuss relationships among the plants and animals of Australia and elsewhere, we'll have to use these terms occasionally.

nation as to the value of such foliage, but suspect it may be that young trees, growing in the shade of larger trees, cannot afford to let the light pass through them but must capture as much as they can.

Like virtually all Australian trees, eucalypts are evergreen in the sense that the leaves are shed individually over time and not all at once. It is the bark that is shed seasonally in many species. Actually, some shed their bark more conspicuously than others, the most striking being stringybarks and woollybutts. Other shedders are the "true" gums, whose names often reflect the color or texture left after the bark peels off—red gums, spotted gums, blue gums, ghost gums. The ghost gums are especially impressive trees, as they occur in the dry interior, and there in the bright sunlight their white trunks are in striking contrast to the red sand and rocks, as aboriginal artists, beginning with Albert Namatjira, have so vividly portrayed in their watercolors [colorplate 3].

The eucalypts with persistent or nonshedding bark can be distinguished primarily by the color and texture of that bark, but also by the characteristics of their woods. Some of these are bloodwoods (with timber suggestive of our cedars and redwoods), mahoganies (not the true mahogany of commerce), boxes, ironwoods, and others—many of them good timber trees. Eucalypts of little value as lumber are the mallees, small trees that have several trunks arising from a common base and which survive in dry areas by having long, lateral roots just under the soil surface. These horizontal roots are greatly prized by desert travelers because

A newcomer to Australia is invariably impressed by the fact that eucalypts (some kinds, at least) retain their leaves but shed their bark periodically.

they contain unusual amounts of water. To obtain it, roots are cut into sections and stood on end in a container to let the liquid run out. It is reported that over a quart of water can be obtained from twenty-five feet or so of roots, but we confess that we have never tried it and so have no idea how long such a process takes. Mallees cover vast areas in semiarid southern parts of the continent.

Another eucalypt of importance in the dry country is the "coolabah," made famous in Banjo Paterson's "Waltzing Matilda"—a song some Australians feel should be the national anthem. The coolabah needs considerable water for growth and is found along stream beds and billabongs (oxbows), but if it is seen growing away from surface water, its presence is a sign of underground water not far below the surface. We rarely sat under a coolabah like the swagmen of old to watch and wait 'til our billy boiled (translated: until our tea water boiled in a blackened and much-used tin can), but we did relax in a karri forest watching little birds with big feet, rufous tree creepers, walk up and down the vertical backs of our benches.

Karris occur in a small area only in southwestern Australia and are eucalypts, too. They are tall, straight, and highly valued for their lumber; fortunately, a few of the best stands are protected. These majestic trees, growing up to 276 feet in height, were mixed in one small area with another huge eucalypt, the tingle. Tingles are confined to a few square miles and are totally protected.

The giant eucalypts—the tingles, karris, and so-called mountain ashes of Victoria and Tasmania—all occur in the cooler and more well-watered parts of Australia. The most cold-adapted species of all is the snow gum, which occurs in the high mountains of the Southeast at altitudes of more than four thousand feet, where the winters are long and often windy and bitter. These picturesque trees are often stunted and twisted, with bark that is streaked with various shades of red, brown, and white. And yet other species of eucalypts are adapted to the steaming tropics of northern Australia and New Guinea!

So individualistic are many of the gums, with their irregular shapes and patchy, shaggy bark, that it is easy to develop an affection for them almost as one might for an animal—a kangaroo, for example. This is especially true in the Outback, where a few river red gums may be the only major trees in the landscape, and their shade most wel-

The genus Angophora, *which is related to* Eucalyptus, *includes species with curiously mottled bark (near Sydney, New South Wales).*

come. And for the landscape painters they provide untiring subjects. But one must be cautious about camping beneath old, mature gum trees, for their branches are remarkably brittle and may come crashing down unexpectedly.

Another striking species, which we came to know well in the hills around Canberra, is the scribbly gum. The dark hieroglyphics on the pale bark of these trees are caused by the larva of a small moth that bores between layers of bark and never seems content to bore in anything like a straight line. Perhaps it is telling us something; or perhaps it just likes to doodle.

One cannot conclude a discussion of eucalypts without mentioning their distinctive odor. It is aromatic (some say pungent), and probably strongest in those trees called "peppermints." Over the years there have been several attempts to build up a eucalypt oil business by gathering and boiling or pressing the leaves, but so far none have been particularly successful commercially. The legendary Australian soprano Nellie Melba was reported to have enjoyed eucalyptus chewing gum between the acts of operas. Apparently she had the habit of leaving a wad of gum on a special shelf while she was performing, and the story is told that Enrico Caruso once bribed a stage hand to substitute a wad of well-chewed tobacco. This caused considerable uproar, as can be imagined, for Melba had a temper as well as a rich vocabulary of the Australian vernacular.

One of the early experiments in the use of eucalyptus oil had to do with malaria control. It was thought in the middle of the nineteenth century that oil from the Tasmanian blue gum would counteract malarial "miasma," and with that in mind the seeds of a number of such trees were sent to Italy and to California, to be planted in known malarial areas (that was long before anything was known about the cause and transmission of malaria).

One botanist who promoted this was Ferdinand Mueller, a transplanted German working in Melbourne. Mueller became more and more eccentric over the years and was verbose and careless in personal matters, but he was dedicated to botany and almost single-handedly brought the study of the Australian flora to international attention. He sponsored a number of exploring expeditions (mainly in hopes of obtaining more plants, of course), and was himself a member of a long trip into northern Australia. He was the official botanist of the Victorian government and during his lifetime received more than a hundred honors from all over the world, including a knighthood from the British and a heritable title of Baron from the Germans. The use of eucalyptus oil in combating malaria was one of his less-inspired ideas.

Anyone who has had experience with eucalyptus trees outside of Australia—in California, for instance—cannot imagine how diverse they are in their native home, and how many creatures live among them. Insects bore in them and eat their leaves; bees and beetles swarm at the blossoms; birds crowd about the flowers and fruits; parrots and kookaburras nest in holes in the trunks; possums and gliders climb and leap in the branches; and koalas spend their days munching on the leaves. And eucalypts have many surprises, not only because they are evergreen and have (in many cases) deciduous bark, but many of them bloom in the winter time, when there are few insects about, and presumably must rely on birds for pollination.

The second dominant genus of trees in Australia is the *Acacia*, and surprisingly there are even more kinds of acacia than there are eucalypts. Although acacias grow in many other parts of the world and are relatively recent arrivals in Australia (as mentioned in the preceding chapter), the Australian species are nevertheless distinctive in their own way.

Most of us think of acacias as being covered with spines, as they are in Africa and in our own Southwest; in fact, the name comes from the Greek "*aka*," a word meaning "point," with reference to the spines. But in Australia most species have soft foliage and no spines at all. This is believed to reflect the fact that there are no native animals that browse on bushes and trees, so that protective spines would serve no useful purpose. Kangaroos and other native mammals are grazers, and it is interesting to note that it is the grasses that have evolved spines—the spinifex or porpupine grass so characteristic of the dry parts of the continent.

Australian acacias also usually do not have the rather modest blossoms they have elsewhere; rather, they tend to become covered with great sprays of yellow blossoms—sometimes, like the gums, in winter [colorplate 4]. Australians usually call them not acacias but wattles, a name with an interesting history. Because of the toughness and pliability of the saplings, early settlers in Sydney Cove (and probably other places) used them to build wattle-and-daub huts. The branches were woven together to form a wooden frame, which was then covered with mud—an adaptation of a basic structure used by many of the poor of the world. Today, the fluffy and often fragrant golden flowers of the wattles are Australian favorites, and appear on the official Commonwealth emblem as well as on many of its postage stamps.

While the genus *Eucalyptus* belongs to the myrtle family, the *Acacia* is closely related to the mimosa, and like other plants related to the legumes, produces its seeds in pods. Wattles are strictly woody, ranging from small, scrubby bushes up to fairly large trees, whose woods can be used as timber. They are widely distributed throughout the continent, often mixed with eucalypts, which they replace completely in some arid areas. Like eucalypts, many wattles have slender, pendant leaves, thus presenting less surface to the direct rays of the sun. In the deserts, some species do not have true leaves at all, but instead bear needlelike phyllodes (modified leaf stems) to help reduce water loss.

Two of the many species of acacia are so widespread that they deserve special mention. In Queensland, away from the coast, but where the rainfall averages twenty inches or more a year, much of the countryside was once covered with brigalow, a handsome small acacia that tended to form dense thickets. The brigalow belt—more than ten million acres in extent—was the home of great numbers of birds and of wallabies, echidnas, and a host of other animals. Other interesting trees grew among the brigalow: cypress pines, sandalwood, and others. Now most of the brigalow has yielded to bulldozers and to defoliants applied from airplanes. This is prime agricultural land and doubtless needed to be cleared to feed a growing world population; but it would have been nice if a little more of the brigalow belt had been left for posterity.

The same fate may not befall the mulga, for this is a tree of the Center, where rainfall generally does not exceed ten inches a year and little ground water is available for agriculture. Mulgas are small trees with slender, gray-green leaves (actually phyllodes), providing only limited shade. But over vast areas they are the dominant trees, often the only trees away from watercourses with their fringe of coolabahs and river gums. Mulga, spinifex, and red sand—the traveler in the Center sees too much of these. But when the setting sun turns the sand vermillion, the spinifex gold, and the mulgas a rather dreamy noncolor—well, things churn around inside and one is hooked on the great Australian "emptiness."

Next to the nearly ubiquitous acacias and eucalypts, the trees and shrubs most likely to attract attention belong to a diverse group called the Proteaceae—appropriately named for the Homeric god Proteus, who could change his shape at will. Visitors from the Northern Hemisphere find Proteaceae strange and striking plants, for with their typical Gondwanaland distribution, they are rarely seen outside of their native habitats. Early in its history, New South Wales chose as its official emblem one of these, the waratah—a bush whose large red flower heads grace a limited area along the coast of that state.

Much more widely distributed are the many species (over two hundred) of grevillias, sometimes called "spider flowers," evidently because the long, curved pistils protruding from the masses of flowers suggested to someone the legs of spiders. These flowers, although not usually large, are always brightly colored and have unusual shapes and scents—making them much prized as ornamentals. Those which attain tree-size are generally known as "silky oaks."

Without much doubt the most striking proteaceous plants belong to the genus *Banksia*. They grow mainly in coastal, sandy areas and have huge clusters of flowers, rather like erect brushes, often brightly colored and eagerly sought for nectar by honey eaters and other birds. The flower heads are succeeded by thick, woody cones, which release their seeds chiefly after bush fires. Aborigines were known to prepare a sweet drink by soaking the flower heads in water, and a common name given to banksias (and some other proteaceous plants) was "honeysuckle." These remarkable plants were appropriately named for Joseph Banks, the wealthy and influential naturalist who accompanied Captain Cook on his first voyage and collected the first specimens at Botany Bay (we'll have more to say about Banks in a later chapter).

One proteaceous plant that has become familiar to Americans is the macadamia tree. This is a native of Queensland that has been cultivated widely in Hawaii, where its nuts have become a local delicacy of considerable economic value. The Hawaiians have developed a thin-shelled variety that is easily harvested; native Queensland macadamia nuts have remarkably tough shells. At both of the places where we lived in Brisbane we had macadamia trees growing in the yard, and we soon found that we needed a hammer and a good solid stone beneath the nuts to crack them. But they went very well indeed with the local beer.

Sir Joseph Banks's contributions to botany have been recognized in the name of one of Australia's most striking and characteristic trees, Banksia, *of which this is the flower.*

Grevillias, banksias, and macadamias are quickly noticed as being unusual, but members of another group, belonging to the genus *Casuarina* in its own distinct family, look so much like some of our pines that we at first believed they were (when grown in Florida and elsewhere they are called "Australian pines"). On close inspection the "needles" prove to be divided into sections, rather like the stems of horsetails (*Equisetum*). Thus the needles are really twigs, and each of the sections terminates in a whorl of minute, scalelike leaves. Technically, casuarinas are flowering plants, not conifers at all, although the fruits do look rather like small cones.

As mentioned in the preceding chapter, casuarinas are one of the distinctively Australian groups that have to some extent successfully invaded other continents. With the help of man, these trees now occur in many subtropical parts of the globe. Australians call them "she-oaks," for reasons not clear to us. There are numerous species, some growing as understory in eucalypt woodlands, others in sandy, coastal areas or riverbanks. In the Center, groves of stately "desert oaks" here and there provide a welcome change from the vast expanses of mulga. At one time, we were told, casuarina wood was used to make very durable shingles.

Australia does have its quota of true coniferous trees, though they do not form the continuous forests that one finds in Canada or in the Rockies or Sierras. There are no native pines, though imported pines (chiefly Monterey pines from California) are now grown in extensive plantations as a source of soft wood. Native "cypress pines," related to our cypresses and junipers, grow in various parts of Australia, generally in sandy soils where there is moderate rainfall. These are handsome trees, usually rather small, but some attain a height of over a hundred feet.

The most impressive conifers, however, are the *Araucarias*: tall, straight trees with spreading branches that bear most of their foliage toward the end of the branches. These trees are restricted to the southern continents, with fossil pollen having been found in Antarctica. A Chilean species has a particularly striking type of branching and is often called "monkey puzzle tree." Like other *Araucarias*, it is grown as an ornamental in other warm parts of the world. "Norfolk pine," which is sold in nurseries in the United States as an indoor plant, is an *Araucaria* hailing from Norfolk Island, a tiny island that is politically part of Australia although closer to New Zealand.

In eastern Australia, the most common *Araucaria* is called "hoop pine," a tree sometimes reaching 150 feet in height and growing not in pure stands but scattered among other trees in well-watered areas. A giant hoop pine grew near our home in Indooroopilly, with the Brisbane River as a backdrop, and it was a joy each morning to look out and watch the birds among its open branches: sometimes kookaburras, at other times butcher birds or blackfaced cuckoo-shrikes. A related tree, the bunya pine, has a more limited distribution, but was formerly much valued by the aborigines for its large seed-bearing cones. The seeds are said to taste rather like roasted chestnuts.

Some of the conifers don't look much like the conifers we are used to. *Podocarpus*, variously called she-pine or brown pine, has leaves rather like willows. The related huon pine of Tasmania is greatly esteemed for its canary-colored, very durable timber resembling teak. These trees grow only in remote, roadless areas of western Tasmania, but so valuable is their timber that they are "hunted down" by loggers who camp in the forest and float the logs down the rivers to the coast to be milled or shipped elsewhere for milling. Huon pines are slow-growing trees, and many of those being harvested are several hundred years old. Most of the harvestable trees have been taken, but now that parts of western Tasmania have been made into a national park, perhaps there is hope for the few remaining. Patsy Adam Smith (Australian journalist and storyteller) describes the lives of some of the last of the "piners" in her book *Tiger Country* (1968). (To Americans, all of this will have the familiar ring of "Save the Redwoods!")

This completes the roster of conifers (omitting a few kinds of local distribution), and a strange and fascinating lot they are. Even stranger are the primitive seed plants called cycads, which have foliage rather like palms but bear huge cones, the male and female cones being on separate plants. Further, their roots support nitrogen-fixing organisms. When we camped in Queensland's Carnarvon Gorge, we were amazed at the size of the cycads, some with trunks five or six feet high and two feet or more in diameter, their fronds waving freely over our heads. As cycads are very slow growers, these may have been several hundred years old.

Australia is supposed to have the greatest diversity of cycads in the world, including some growing as much as sixty feet tall, and others (or maybe the same ones) being ten to fifteen thousand years old. The remains of cycads have been found in rocks 150 million years old, and probably they flourished in the age of dinosaurs. At Carnarvon, the presence of a giant sand goanna (monitor lizard) near our campsite made it easy to imagine that that age had not really passed at all. We cannot resist quoting Judith Wright, because we think that no one has characterized the cycads so beautifully as has this Australian poet:

> Only the antique cycads sullenly
> keep the old bargain life has long since broken;
> and, cursed by age, through each chill century
> they watch the shrunken moon, but never die,
>
> for time forgets the promise he once made,
> and change forgets that they are left alone.
> Among the complicated birds and flowers
> they seem a generation carved in stone.

Altogether there are reported to be somewhere between twelve and fifteen thousand species of

Cycads near Darwin grow tall and resemble small palm trees.

plants in Australia, and no one but a professional botanist can hope to learn more than a few of the more conspicuous and common ones. One endemic genus of woody plants that is especially likely to attract attention is the tea tree, *Leptospermum*. Captain Cook and his crew were reported to have made tea from the leaves of members of this group, as did the early settlers. Like the eucalypts, the tea trees belong to the myrtle family, but there the resemblance ends. Most tea trees are shrubs and have five-petaled flowers, usually white but sometimes pink or red. Horticulturists like these shrubs because they are so hardy, enduring poor soil, periodic dryness, and even strong winds. We liked them because they blossom early in the spring, long before most plants except the wattles, and the blossoms attract a variety of interesting, often colorful insects.

As we flew along the northern coastline to Darwin, we were impressed by the vast expanses of mangrove swamps. Mangroves are found along many tropical, subtropical, and even some temperate coasts and river estuaries of the world, and Australian mangroves, like all, do not belong to one family but represent members of several families that have become modified for this special kind of environment. Thus they look more like each other than like members of their various and respective families. For reasons not yet fully understood, these diverse mangroves occur in different combinations in different areas, each species having its own tolerance of salinity and submergence. In northern Australia there are over twenty genera of more than fifteen families. The one mangrove endemic to Australia, we noted with interest, also belongs to the myrtle family.

One scene we especially appreciated, perhaps because it reminded us of our own Rocky Mountains, was the midsummer alpine display in the Snowy Mountains south of Canberra, especially on Australia's highest peak, Mount Kosciusko. Below the tree line were snow gums, above it fields of wildflowers, most of them composites: yellow billy buttons, white snow daisies, varicolored everlastings. One unusual high-country flower (which has relatives in the deserts) is the dainty pink trigger flower, which has a unique manner of achieving pollination. The blossom has a sensitive column or "trigger" which, when an insect touches it, springs up and either deposits pollen or collects it from the invader.

The wildflowers of Western Australia are perhaps the most famous of all, and a tour of that state in the spring should be on the itinerary of every visitor. Probably the most unusual flowers are the various kangaroo paws. It is hard to describe them, for they are neither beautiful nor like any other flower, but their odd colorings and pawlike shapes make them unforgettable [colorplate 6]. A red and green one is Western Australia's floral emblem: a further demonstration that in Australia "nature is reversed," for it is the stem that is red and the flowers that are green! Many flowers of the pea family also form part of the display, as indeed they do in many parts of Australia. The best known, though most unusual one, is called Sturt's desert pea, after the explorer Charles Sturt, and it is the floral emblem of South Australia. The flowers of this plant are about two inches long and of a brilliant, glossy red with a buttonlike black center.

Members of the portulaca family are well represented in Australia, where they are often called purslane, as some of them are in the United States. The most conspicuous one, found on the Nullarbor Plain and in other barren areas, is known as parakeelya. It has bright pink flowers and thick juicy leaves, and provides both food and water for animals feeding in these areas. Cattlemen have claimed that in times of drought their animals have not only survived but fattened on this plant. Further, some claimed, such cattle were hard to move to market because they had never learned to drink water directly.

Australia has many orchids, some of them springing from the ground and others growing on trees as epiphytes. Perhaps the best known is Queensland's Cooktown orchid, once commonly found in rain forests around that northern city, but becoming increasingly rare with the clearing of those forests and the exploiting of the lovely pink sprays by nurserymen and orchid fanciers.

Some of the finest displays of wildflowers occur in Australia's extensive coastal heathlands. These include not only true heaths, but many Proteaceae and members of the pea family, as well as tea trees, orchids, and many others. Most of these are bushy plants, seldom over two or three feet tall, often so gnarled and dense and covered with harsh and prickly leaves and fruit that one can hardly walk through them. Yet the flowers are often delicate

Parakeelya, a plant that grows in sandy areas of the Interior, provides both food and "drink" for grazing animals.

One of Australia's many orchids, this was growing not far from Sydney.

and fragrant. The heathlands occupy sandy soils of low fertility and occur in places that are often windswept and subject to fires. The soils are especially deficient in phosphorus, and they evidently survive by recycling the nutrients in the dead and fallen leaves and branches.

Heathlands were once easy to find around the major cities, but this is no longer so. Both heathlands and mangrove swamps are prime targets for developers. One of the finest heathlands in Australia, just south of Brisbane, is now covered by streets and high-rise buildings—Australia's equivalent of Miami Beach and called "The Gold Coast." The real gold has vanished. There are other places, however, and we found one on the southwestern coast. Even though summer was over when we were there, and most of the flowers had gone, the thick foliage remained, and in the low clouds and mist it presented as lonely and haunting a scene as any English moorland.

Along parts of the east coast, behind the mangroves and heathlands, and often on the east-facing slopes of the Dividing Range, occur some of Australia's most fascinating assemblages of plants: the rain forests. Kenneth Clark, the spokesman for the English world of art, once wrote that he did not consider the jungle (*i.e.*, rain forest) "authentically Australian." True, the tropical rain forests do contain a majority of trees common to the forests of New Guinea and to the East Indies and southeast Asia. But surely they are as authentic as eucalypt woodlands and red deserts—and particularly precious as they are so limited in extent and so different from other aspects of Australia.

Although the forests are not continuous, but occur in patches, this adds to their fascination, for no two patches are quite alike—the tree species differ and so do the associated ferns, insects, birds, and mammals. Australia is one of the very few places in the world where one finds tropical rain forest grading into subtropical and eventually into temperate or subantarctic rain forests of totally different composition. A rain forest-hopping trip from Cape York in the north to Tasmania in the south can provide more botanical excitement than perhaps anywhere else on earth.

As one enters a tropical rain forest [colorplate 7] from eucalypt woodland, the contrast is striking. Instead of gray-green foliage letting in a good deal of light, the foliage is deep green and closes over the canopy so that one's eyes must adjust to the semidarkness; lianas fill the spaces between the trees, and epiphytes adorn the trunks, often at a height of fifty feet or more.

Our first acquaintance with a tropical rain forest was at Eungella National Park near Mackay in Queensland. Once we had entered the gloom of the forest via one of the trails, we saw that many of the trees had enormous buttresses at their bases, measuring sometimes six to eight feet out from the trunk proper. The function of the buttresses (root outgrowths) is still being debated, but some suggestions that have been made include mechanical support, increased absorption of light or moisture, or devices to keep other trees from growing too close.

In the luxurious tropical rain forest, it is seldom possible to find any dominant species, but rather many species tend to occur within a short distance. As the nineteenth-century naturalist A. R. Wallace put it, "if a traveler notices a particular species and wishes to find more like it, he may often turn his eyes in vain in every direction. Trees of varied forms, dimensions and colour are around him, but he rarely sees any one of them repeated." To illustrate, between Townsville and Cooktown there are more than six hundred species of trees in the rain forests, and on a quarter-acre plot 164 different species were counted.

To persons brought up in the gentle woodlands of North America, the rain forest is both bewildering and awe-inspiring. Fortunately for us, many of the trees at Eungella were labeled, although the names did not really mean a great deal to us: white cedar, red cedar (not even remotely like the cedars we knew), swamp mahogany, bonewood, satinash, camphor, Mueller's walnut, and so on. The epiphytes, too, ranged from delicate orchids to huge staghorn ferns that must have weighed many pounds. The lianas, which occasionally hung across the trail, almost tempted us to try our luck at swinging through the jungle instead of sedately walking down the track. Below the tops of the giant trees, the fronds of palms formed a second tier of greenery, picking up and scattering the few sunbeams that penetrated the overhead canopy. The forest seemed almost eerie in the diffuse light (nice on a hot day!) and quite a tangle, which it was not, because the brush turkeys chased each other easily through the undergrowth. The one sunny stretch through the gloom, the Broken River, bubbled along, and its cool pools offered shelter to the platypi.

There were tree ferns at the sides of the pools of the Broken River, though not in the rain forest itself. One giant, which stood beside a swimming pool we shared with a platypus or two, must have been sixty feet tall. In Mount Field National Park in Tasmania they seemed more plentiful (and we appreciated a nonskid trail made of tree fern stems as we made our way through the rain and mist), but not as tall. Tree ferns, which are reminiscent of the carboniferous ages, are a common denominator in most of Australia's rain forests.

Most rain forests also contain strangler figs. Each tree begins as an epiphyte on another tree, then sends down roots to the ground, and eventually enmeshes or "strangles" the host tree. With time the fig itself may grow into a giant tree, betraying little evidence that it began as a parasite. Stages in the process can be seen in almost any rain forest. On the Atherton Tableland in tropical Queensland there is a "curtain fig" that is something of a tourist attraction: the host tree grew in an oblique position, and the many hundreds of roots of the fig hang from it like a great curtain. We visited this attraction, and as so often happens in the low light of the rain forest, found it difficult to photograph.

As one proceeds down into southern Queensland and northern New South Wales, there is, one notes, less variety among the rain forest trees, and certain kinds tend to repeat themselves more frequently (for example, brush box, *Tristania*). Epiphytes and lianas, too, are smaller and less abundant, though still in evidence, and fewer trees have buttresses. Still, these are lush and exciting forests (usually termed subtropical), and in some of them one may hike up to higher (and colder) altitudes and enter patches of temperate rain forest, festooned with mosses and lichens and dominated by just a few species of trees. Chief among these is antarctic beech, *Nothofagus,* a relative of beeches of the Northern Hemisphere, but evergreen and with much smaller leaves. We found them to be great, shaggy trees, and as we walked among them we could almost imagine ourselves back in ancient Gondwanaland, the ancestral home of these trees.

Pollen of antarctic beech has been found in sediments in southern Australia dating from eighty million years ago—well before the final breakup of Gondwanaland. This, and pollen from deposits in Antarctica as well as lush forests of *Nothofagus* in Chile, provide evidence for continental drift as neat as Thoreau's trout in the milk.

The presence of so many Asiatic trees in the forests of northeastern Australia led some botanists to believe that these forests were relatively recent incursions from Asia—having arrived by "island hopping," much as had many birds and insects. Some recent studies have suggested that this is not so. Rain forests can move only as a community of closely interdependent species. It is hard to imagine this occurring by way of seeds borne on the wind or carried on the feet of birds—and there has evidently always been deep sea between Asia and Australia. Yet rain forests in parts of India are very much like those in northwest Australia; as many as forty-seven plant genera are the same in both areas. Perhaps, according to some researchers, these rain forests evolved in the northern, more tropical parts of Gondwanaland—after all, India was once part of that landmass. Further, Australian rain forests contain a higher percentage of more primitive types of plants than those of any other part of the world. Perhaps, then, its rain forests evolved *in situ,* as part of a great forest that eventually, after many changes, provided the basic substance of rain forests everywhere.

At present these are only theories, but it seems certain that many components of Australia's rain forests were present long before that continent drifted toward Asia. Dr. Helene Martin, of the University of New South Wales, has discovered fossil pollen at a depth of a thousand feet in semiarid country in the Murray River basin. This pollen includes a species of holly related to one now occurring only in the Far North (Australia's only living species of holly).

These and other samples of fossil pollen indicate that there were rain forest trees in many parts of Australia well before the breakup of Gondwanaland. The increasing aridity of the continent through many millions of years has squeezed the remaining forests to pockets along the east coast where they are subjected to enough rain, mists, and clouds from the sea to retain some semblance of their former condition. And doubtless some species have indeed arrived from southeast Asia in more recent geological time.

The forests of Australia (defined as any woodland with a relatively closed canopy) occupy only 2 percent of the area of the continent, as compared, for example, to 38 percent in Canada. But true rain forests occupy only 0.25 percent—and doubtless less than that, as they fall to the axe and bulldozer daily. To the settlers this was the "Big Scrub," an enemy to be cleared for agriculture and a source of timber for building and for export. Rain forest trees are generally soft woods, and over the years some, such as the cedars, have been logged to use as cabinet woods. Australia's greatest monument to culture, the Sydney Opera House, has had much of its interior done in brush box *(Tristania)* and carabeen *(Sloanea)*, and the effect is beautiful. But we wondered which rain forests had come down to provide these woods in such abundance.

Much of the destruction of rain forests in recent years has been at the hands of pastoralists, with the thought that soil that would produce such luxuriant growth would be ideal for pasture for dairy herds. But removal of the forests has resulted in rampant erosion as well as invasion by lantana and other noxious plants. And now that England has joined the Europe Economic Community, there is not nearly the market for Australian butter that had been anticipated! Rain forests do not grow back readily, and it is virtually impossible to undertake reforestation when there are hundreds of mixed species involved.

Fortunately, many of the remaining areas of rain forests are in national parks, and visitors who have read of the "monotony" of the Australian landscape should make it a point to visit one or (better) more of these. Not only is the vegetation rich, so is the diversity of animal life, Mammals thump in the underbrush and a variety of strange bird calls emanate from the trees—some fifty species of birds are restricted to rain forests and another fifty occur most abundantly there. Many of the smaller denizens of the forest have hardly been studied; a recent survey of the snails and slugs of Queensland rain forests found that nearly half the species were new to science.

Incidentally, visitors should stay on well-marked trails unless they are hardened and experienced bushwalkers, for untamed rain forests are not friendly places. It is easy to become entangled in vines, and some of these, such as the lawyer vine, are armed with formidable, hooklike spines. Then there are the infamous stinging trees, whose broad leaves are covered with irritating hairs said to produce an effect much like nettle but much more prolonged. Elspeth Huxley put it well in her book *Their Shining Eldorado:* "Give me the savage animal any day, rather than the savage plant."

The rain forests have no monopoly on odd trees, however. In the far Northwest, in the Kimberley Region, are grotesque trees called baobabs, which occur nowhere else save in parts of Africa. These trees have great, swollen trunks that give rise to short, misshapen branches. In the dry season the branches are bare, as if the trees had died in agony: for these are among Australia's few deciduous trees. The trunks may be fifty or sixty feet in circumference and are often hollow; they have sometimes been used for storage, and one or two are reputed to have been used as temporary jails, holding up to twelve prisoners.

"A veritable pachyderm," John Bechervaise calls the baobab, and Ernestine Hill, in her tome *The Great Australian Loneliness*, describes it as a "Caliban of a tree . . . friendly ogre of the great North-west." It is indeed a friendly tree, for during the wet season it collects water in cavities at the base of the branches, and this can be tapped for drinking during "the dry." The trees also exude a gum "rather like macaroni" that can be fermented to produce an intoxicating beverage. When in bloom, baobabs are covered with fragrant blossoms, and the fruits are juicy and edible. Truly a multipurpose tree!

Another tree that struck us as unusual was the pisonia, which grows on various islands of the Great Barrier Reef. These trees are remarkable for their soft, spongy wood and for the very sticky stems that bear the fruit. These stems adhere to the feet of sea birds, which have been responsible for spreading the tree to various islands. On Heron Island, we sometimes saw noddy terns so covered with sticky pisonia seed-stems that they could not fly at all, and presumably perished.

Perhaps the most peculiar tree of any is the "grass tree" or "black boy." It is a common sight in hilly, sparsely wooded country in many parts of Australia, and it is not a tree at all, but a lily. Grass trees live for hundreds of years and may reach heights up to eight to ten feet. From the top of the trunk a "grass skirt" of narrow leaves hangs down, while at times a narrow flowering stalk may shoot up two or three feet more. As the black trunk suggests, these plants survive numerous bush fires and in fact seem to survive best when there are occasional fires. Grass trees growing at various heights and in various attitudes provide a surrealistic atmosphere to many Australian landscapes.

Australian woody plants, in general, seem to bear an unusual abundance of flowers. This is especially true of dominant trees such as eucalyptus and acacia, but it is also true of shrubs of the heathlands and of banksia, grevillea, and even "grass trees." It comes as a surprise to North Americans to learn that many of these plants are pollinated by birds and mammals rather than (or in addition to) bees and other insects. Australia has more vertebrate-pollinated plants than any other continent.

Among the birds, certain species of parrots and most members of the large family of honeyeaters are nectar-feeders, and it is common to see these birds emersed in a cluster of eucalypt or banksia blossoms. These two groups of birds, and several others, have independently evolved brushlike tongues which serve in extracting nectar from blossoms.

The baobab tree of northwestern Australia has its closest relatives in Africa.

Among the mammals, the honey possum and the sugar glider are especially well adapted for taking nectar, pollen, and insects from flowers. Some rodents and bats, too, visit flowers for nectar and so serve as pollinators. Mammal-pollinated flowers tend to produce large quantities of nectar at night and many of them have musky odors. Bird-pollinated flowers, on the other hand, tend to have sweet odors and to produce most of their nectar by day.

As we traveled around Australia, we could not help but notice two exotic plants, lantana and blackberry, which, without natural enemies, seem to be usurping a considerable part of the countryside. Lantana, a member of the verbena family, has attractive pink and yellow flowers, and was originally introduced as a garden plant, in spite of the fact that it has a pungent, rather unpleasant odor. It escaped, and now, in tropical and subtropical eastern Australia, it grows wherever it can gain a foothold, especially in cleared or neglected areas. The dense, prickly thickets smother other vegetation and attract only honeybees and a few butterflies.

Blackberries, which are rampant in the more temperate Southeast, produce big and delicious fruit, but in areas such as those we saw along the Cotter River near Canberra, the brambles make impenetrable barriers around the streams. As yet there is no way to fight off the blackberries short of a large machete, but small beetles have been introduced to eat the lantana. Let us hope that these and other weeds can be brought under control successfully, as was the once dreaded prickly pear cactus. And this leads us to mention one of the most surprising features of the Australian deserts (to Americans): there are no native cacti!

Bush fires are a way of life in Australia, and one can do little traveling in the more wooded parts of the continent, by road or air, without seeing columns of smoke rising from the hills. The

A bush fire sweeps through an open forest in the Northern Territory, a very common scene in Australia.

aborigines set fires to drive the wildlife to within range of their spears; and of course there have always been fires set by lightning. White man used fires to clear forests for settlement and for pastures, and today he still uses fire to clear undergrowth and stimulate the growth of new grass. Grass trees, eucalypts, certain palms, cycads, bracken fern, and heathlands are relatively resistant to fire and in fact do well in a natural regime of occasional fires.

It is commonly believed that if a woodland is burned once a year, little undergrowth will develop and little damage will be done to the trees; conversely, if it is burned too infrequently, bushes and fallen trees will accumulate and a raging, uncontrollable blaze will result. Fires prevent the building up of humus in which the small organisms live that are important in recycling nutrients. On the other hand, fires release phosphorus from the ground cover and stimulate the growth of nitrogen-fixing plants. It seems to be a question of "damned if you do and damned if you don't." One thing is certain: to persons interested in plant and animal life, a recently burned forest has little to offer.

In the past few years, a disease of eucalypts noncommittally called "die-back" has made its appearance. In 1980, when we visited the University of New England in Armidale, New South Wales, we found the rolling hills there to be a scene of desolation. Die-back seemed to have started in small stands of trees around pastures and along roadsides, and then spread in all directions. Those trees still alive were infested with small leaf-feeding scarab beetles, but the educated guess was that they were opportunists and not the basic cause of the almost total destruction.

In Western Australia, jarrahs, which are tall eucalypts valuable for lumber, were also dying, and their problems were attributed to a common fungus in the soil, though why it suddenly became so virulent no one could say. One explanation involves fire, because it is known to reduce the numbers and balance of soil micro-organisms. Thus it could enable the die-back fungus (a survivor) with fewer natural enemies to become an increasing menace to the eucalypts. Further, when fire removes top soil nutrients, the trees are less able to resist attack. Whatever the cause, or causes, it is obvious that the fungus reproduces rapidly in disturbed soil, and so large areas of jarrah reserves have been declared off-limits to vehicles and hikers.

Perhaps Australians have been taking their eucalypts too much for granted; perhaps they have been subjecting them to too much uncontrolled burning and clearing, to too many cattle and sheep trampling the ground around their roots. However, the calamity of die-back has brought about a massing of state and federal funds for research, so perhaps there is hope that "the old gum tree" will make a comeback and be more fully respected and apreciated. After all, eucalypts *are* Australia!

4

THE MAMMALS

"A most formidable museum of animal curiosities"

Nothing astonished the first European arrivals in Australia more than the furred animals, the mammals. Francis Pelsaert, wrecked off the coast of Western Australia in 1629, spied several "cats" of "miraculous form . . . under the belly the females have a pouch into which one can put a hand" [these were tammar wallabies]. To Captain Cook, nearly a century and a half later, the kangaroo was rather like a "wild dog" that "jumped like a hare." As for the platypus: there was nothing to compare it to, even in the medieval bestiaries. The beak and webbed feet of a duck attached to the body of a beaver, with skeletal parts and reproductive organs rather like those of a reptile! Surely this was a hoax, perpetrated by some nature-faker for whatever profit he could glean from human gullibility.

But that was not all. Dissection revealed that this creature, though furry and having a four-chambered heart, like a mammal, had no teats and had a common opening for the anus, urinary, and genital organs, like birds and reptiles. Perhaps, said the French naturalist Geoffrey Saint-Hilaire, it might even be found to lay eggs! This was a point of much debate among biologists until, in 1884, a young Englishman, W.H. Caldwell, shot a female carrying a large, yolk-filled, rather leathery egg. Quickly he cabled the British Association for the Advancement of Science: the platypus is indeed an egglayer. We now know that the female does suckle her young after it emerges from the egg, but the milk oozes from pores rather like the sweat glands of other mammals, where it is licked from the fur by the growing offspring.

This was all rather a shock to zoologists, who like to put animals in neat little pigeonholes containing creatures of supposed common ancestry. Where did the platypus fit? The only solution was to create a new pigeonhole and call it the "Prototheria" (literally meaning "ancient beasts"). For the weight of evidence suggests that the platypus is a surviving relic of a time when mammals still retained many features of their reptilian ancestors. Mammals they are—furry, equipped with milk glands, and able to maintain a constant warm temperature (more or less)—but of a type called monotremes, a word meaning "single opening," with reference to the common orifice for the anus, urinary system, and reproductive organs. Zoologist G.G. Simpson calls them "mammals by definition rather than by ancestry"; in fact, he regards them as highly modified survivors of an ancient stock of reptiles, and not "real" mammals at all.

But one does not need scientific jargon to appreciate the platypus. Although we had first seen one in a tank in the Taronga Zoo in Sydney (and seen it swimming and feeding underwater), our first sighting of the animals in the wild was, as mentioned in the previous chapter, in the Broken River, where they cavorted in the pools below our campsite on the edge of the rain forest in Eungella National Park. They hid when tourists were wading in the river, but not long after each party had gone, the little animals reappeared, chasing each other in circles or floating quietly for a few minutes. Now and then they dived for worms or insect larvae, then resurfaced for air; but mostly they just swam placidly back and forth, quite unmindful of the honored place they fill in the annals of science.

We are glad to report that platypi (which sounds rather better than platypuses) are still fairly common in some places despite damming, channeling, and polluting of many of Australia's rather limited river systems. They are quiet animals, active mainly at dawn and dusk, but there to be seen and enjoyed if one is also quiet, and out at dawn or dusk in the right places.

A duck-billed platypus, one of the world's few egg-laying mammals.
(Australian Information Service)

Platypi spend much of their time in a burrow in the streambank, above the water line, and it is said that the burrow is so narrow that it squeezes the water from their soft fur as they enter. After mating, the female makes an especially long burrow and lines the end of it with leaves. Then, after plugging the entry with mud, she lays one to three white eggs, less than an inch long. When the eggs hatch in a week or so, the tiny offspring feed by licking milk from their mother's fur. After a few weeks they are large enough to venture forth into the stream. Oddly, the young have baby teeth that are later shed, even though the adults have no teeth at all. When a platypus dives, the eyes and nostrils are closed; it is able to stay under water no more than about three minutes, probing for food with its broad, sensitive bill.

While it is true that there is nothing quite like a platypus, there is in fact another monotreme, with much the same mixture of mammalian and reptilian features, though at first glance one would hardly suspect any sort of a relationship with the platypus. This is the echidna, or spiny anteater, a thorough landlubber and voracious predator on ants—or much more commonly on termites. It was Captain William Bligh (of *Bounty* fame) who first recorded its existence during a voyage to Tasmania. "An animal," he said, "of very odd form. . . . It has no mouth like any other animal, but a kind of duck bill two inches long, which opens up at the extremity. . . . [There are] quills about an inch long, as strong as those of a porcupine."

This echidna, or spiny anteater, has extended its tongue to feed on termites.
(Australian Information Service)

Many years later it was learned that the echidna, too, is an egg layer. The female lays only one egg at a time and holds it in a fold of her skin until it hatches in about ten days. The tiny offspring is little more than an embryo, but it remains in the skin fold and feeds on milk that oozes from pores in the mother's skin. After about twenty days, the mother places the baby in a hole in the ground, where she feeds it periodically until it is able to fend for itself. Echidnas have powerful front claws, which they use for digging into termite nests; they lap up their prey with a sticky tongue, which may be over a foot long when fully extended in an adult animal. Captive echidnas have been known to live up to fifty years, but they rarely breed in captivity.

Echidnas occur widely in Australia, and despite their secretive habits are fairly frequently seen by bushwalkers. When disturbed, they bury their head quickly in the soil, using their powerful front claws, exposing only their back and rear end with their formidable spines. Once in Tasmania (actually not far from Launceston, a fair-sized city), we heard some rustling in a ditch beside an old road. There, coming along was an echidna that apparently was not aware of us until we leaned over him to take a picture. Then he rapidly moved under a bush on the bank, dug in, and no amount of prodding by us could get him loose and out into the sun to be photographed.

In New Guinea there is a larger species of echidna with a long, curved beak. Otherwise, the echidna, like the platypus, is unique. It is interesting that "anteater" types of animals have evolved on other continents, but the South American ant-bear, the pangolin of Asia, and the aardvark of Africa are wholly unrelated to the echidna and not very closely related to each other.

There are no monotremes, fossil or living, in any other part of the world. Did they once occur more widely, or have they always been confined to Australia and New Guinea? A good guess might be that they were once widespread, as a link between reptiles and mammals, but today only the very specialized platypus and echidna survive, and only in Australia, where, because of the continent's isolation, they have been shielded from competitors and major predators. Fortunately, Australians are well aware of how precious they are. The platypus is even engraved on the Australian twenty-cent piece, the echidna on the five-cent piece!

Although the echidna and the platypus are the strangest of Australia's motley array, they make up only a minor element in a fauna made up mostly of marsupials. Marsupials, unlike monotremes but like most mammals we are familiar with, give birth to living young, have quite a normal mouth opening, a separate anus and urogenital opening, and so forth. The female has teats, but oddly enough the young have no ability to suck; the milk is discharged through muscular action of the teat itself. The teats occur in a pouch, where the young are carried for a period. Hence the name marsupial, which is based on the Latin word for "pouch."

In the early days there was much puzzlement as to how young got into the pouch. Since the penis of many marsupials is double, it was thought by some that the male inserted his penis through the nostrils of the female, and she later moved the embryos to the pouch. Others thought that the male placed his sperm directly into the pouch and the young grew directly from the nipples. It was not until 1830 that an officer of the HMS *Success* saw a minute baby kangaroo emerge from the mother's vagina and crawl to the pouch.

Marsupials are not confined to Australia. The common North American opossum and a number of related animals in South America are marsupials, and fossils of this group have been found in many parts of the world. But it is in Australia that the group has flourished, again probably because of that continent's isolation from the many kinds of predators and competitors that evolved elsewhere but never made it to Australia.

Because of their need to retain the young in a pouch for a period of time, marsupials necessarily reproduce rather slowly as compared to such mammals as rats and rabbits. Yet there are advantages in the marsupial mode of reproduction. Pregnancy is short—only about a month in the largest living marsupial, the red kangaroo. The young are very tiny and undeveloped when born (less than an inch long in the kangaroo) and crawl laboriously into the pouch, where they grow slowly for several months. Even after they are old enough to leave the pouch and graze for themselves, they often return to the mother's pouch, and it is not unusual to see a female carrying a fairly good-sized "joey" with parts of his anatomy (often the large legs and feet) protruding from her pouch. But as soon as the baby is born and enters the pouch, the female usually mates again and begins another pregnancy. However, as long as there is a joey in the pouch, this embryo will remain in a state of suspended development. This means that if conditions are bad, for example if drought severely restricts the available forage, the young in the pouch can be sacrificed, to be replaced promptly by another that may stand a better chance of surviving if conditions improve. Thus this mode of reproduction serves animals well when they live in an unpredictable environment such as the interior of Australia.

As in higher mammals, including ourselves, reproductive cycles in marsupials are controlled by hormones. In fact, marsupial hormones are much the same as those of other mammals. As long as joeys are sucking inside the pouch, prolactin is secreted by the mother's pituitary gland, and this suppresses development of the embryonic second young. Biologists of the Australian Division of Wildlife Research have found that if the joey is removed prematurely and prolactin injected, the second young will still not develop. But if a substance that suppresses prolactin is administered to a female carrying a joey, she will soon be found to be carrying two developing young of different ages.

Marsupials have rather small brain cases, and are often assumed to be rather "stupid" animals. Dr. Robert Kirkby, of the Lincoln Institute, in Carlton, Victoria, one of the leading authorities on marsupial behavior, feels however that recent studies of learning and problem-solving suggest that marsupials are by no means "primitive" in their behavior. They often do well in competition with so-called "higher" mammals. The North American opossum is certainly a successful beast, and kangaroos thrive in cattle and sheep paddocks in many parts of Australia despite the relentless efforts of many graziers to get rid of them. The scarcity and

The thylacine is sometimes called the Tasmanian tiger, with reference to its stripes—at other times, the Tasmanian wolf, with reference to its body form. (Tasmanian Department of Tourism)

even extinction of a number of kinds of marsupials in recent years is indeed the result of stupidity—but not on the part of the marsupials.

Altogether there are about 125 species of marsupials in Australia. These range in size from the tiny planigales (pigmy marsupial mice), less than two inches long, to the red kangaroo, males of which may weigh 200 pounds and measure seven feet in height. Formerly there were giant kangaroos, much larger than this, and even a hippopotamuslike marsupial called Diprotodon, but these became extinct a few thousand years ago, perhaps partly because of hunting by the aborigines.

A most remarkable characteristic of marsupials, taken as a whole, is their superficial resemblance to many other major types of mammals occurring elsewhere on the globe. The wombat is rather like a marmot or woodchuck, and like a marmot lives in a burrow and feeds on grasses and herbs. The Tasmanian devil is suggestive of a wolverine, and like that animal is an aggressive predator. The gliders leap from trees and glide on expanded folds of skin between their limbs, like flying squirrels, while the hare wallabies are so-called from their resemblance to true hares.

The "native cats" are rather more like the civets of Asia and Africa than they are like true cats; while "marsupial mice" are in fact analogous to our shrews, since they feed mainly on insects and other small invertebrates. The marsupial mole is remarkably like true moles in other parts of the world, having a cylindrical body covered with fine silky hair, scarcely any eyes, and powerful claws for digging through the soil. Yet it is a true marsupial, with a pouch that opens backward—a pouch that opens forward would hardly be practicable when pushing through the soil. Unfortunately, marsupial moles are quite rare, and few people have seen one alive.

Even rarer—in fact possibly extinct—is the most unusual example of all of convergence in form and behavior to a totally unrelated mammal occurring elsewhere. We refer to the thylacine, or Tasmanian wolf (also called the Tasmanian tiger because of its stripes, though otherwise it is much more wolflike). Thylacines were at one time widely distributed in Australia and New Guinea, as indicated by skeletons found in caves. Carbon dating of these skeletons suggests that extinction on the mainland occurred about 3,000 years ago, probably soon after the time that dingoes became widespread. Sheep farmers in Tasmania did not appreciate thylacines, and a bounty was placed on them—one pound for an adult and ten shillings for a pup. Some of the skins were tanned and sent to London, where they were made into waistcoats for gentlemen. In 1930 the last thylacine was shot in the wild, and in 1934 the last one died in the Hobart zoo. In 1938 the Tasmanian government declared it a protected species—but there were none left!

Yet there are those who believe the beast still roams in the wilds of southwestern Tasmania. World Wildlife Fund Australia recently voted $55,000 for a fresh search for the thylacine. Eric Guiler, Dean of the Faculty of Zoology at the University of Tasmania, has devoted years to the search, and is fully convinced it survives. "If there were not a sporting chance," he is quoted in *The Bulletin* of Sydney, "I wouldn't be wasting my bloody time charging around the bush like this." Using cameras equipped for night photography, he has (according to *The Bulletin*) obtained some excellent shots of "cows' backsides," possums, and wallabies, but no thylacines. One can only admire a person who clings so tenaciously to the dream that this special animal may have eluded man's destructive powers.

Adult thylacines were up to six feet long (including the tail) and stood two feet high. The head was decidedly wolflike, and the jaws could be spread widely; the head seemed disproportionately large for the body. The hind quarters were somewhat kangaroolike, the joint in the hind leg being well below where it is in a wolf or dog, while the body tapered gradually behind the hind legs to a rather stiff tail. An animal well deserving the expression "as if put together by a committee"! As Michael Sharland put it in "Tasmanian Wild Life":

> A true wolf put beside it would seem to be a better-proportioned and more alert animal in every way. For one thing a wolf, or a dog, would be able to express its feelings not only by the play of its countenance but also by the movement of its tail—a snarl, a smile, a wag of the tail would each convey the prevailing emotion. But the tiger, as far as can be determined, has no such means of revealing just how it feels at any given time, either by facial expression, tail-wagging, or voice. Some say it cannot even growl. . . .

Fortunately, the related but smaller Tasmanian devil is still fairly common, although we have seen it only at the Tasmanian Devil Park, a private establishment near Hobart. Like the thylacine, it was once widespread on the mainland but is now confined to Tasmania. We were just as happy not to meet any in the wild, as devils are heavily built, short-legged animals, with a wicked set of teeth, a whining growl, and a generally fierce demeanor. They feed mainly on carrion, although they also eat fish, reptiles, and small wallabies—as well as an occasional lamb. The Tasmanian devils' unpleasant disposition evidently extends even to other members of their species, as they seem to spend a good deal of time snarling and gaping at one another or actually attacking one another with open jaws

The Tasmanian devil is a predator and scavenger with an unpleasant disposition. It is still reasonably common in Tasmania.

(Tasmanian Department of Tourism)

or having tugs-of-war over food. Local groups apparently establish dominance hierarchies (or "peck orders") that result in the more aggressive individuals getting the best parts of the available food. Much of the pioneering research on the Tasmanian devil was done by T. T. Flynn, a professor of biology in Tasmania—a man who became better known as the father of actor Errol Flynn.

Also in the Tasmanian Devil Park were some of the so-called "native cats" that belong to the same group as the devil. These are beautiful, spotted animals, able to climb readily and possessing a voracious appetite for insects, mice, and birds. The largest of these, called the tiger cat, reaches a length of four feet from nose to tip of the long tail. Captain Arthur Phillip, the first governor of New South Wales, aptly dubbed these animals "spotted martens" because of their resemblance to martens of the Northern Hemisphere; rather a better name than "cat," at any rate. Unfortunately, these animals sometimes get into poultry yards and kill far more than they can possibly eat. So they are not very popular, and have largely disappeared from settled areas. They are nocturnal, like most marsupials, and so are rarely seen in the wild, although it is said that they make good pets if taken while young.

This completes the roster of what might be called "major predators" among the marsupials. There are, however, many lesser predators, smaller animals that feed mainly on insects, worms, and the like. These include a number of species of "marsupial mice," which, as we mentioned earlier, are really much more like shrews. They also include a group of slightly larger but still smallish creatures called bandicoots, which have sharp noses and ratlike tails; superficially they are the most like North American opossums of any Australian marsupials. Bandicoots are nocturnal, ground-dwelling animals that devote much of their energies to digging grubs and worms from the ground. In some areas they are still quite common and although we have rarely seen them active, at times we have seen numbers of road kills. They often suffer from predation by introduced foxes, and many are killed in bush fires and in the burning of sugar cane fields, where they tend to congregate to feed on grubs in the fields. These elegant and beneficial little animals deserve a better fate.

A number of strange and rarely seen animals belong to the bandicoot clan. One of these is the rabbit-bandicoot, often called by the aboriginal name "bilby," justly regarded as one of the most beautiful of Australian mammals. Although bandicootlike in many respects, its ears are rather like those of a jackrabbit, and its tail is hairy. The fur is soft and silky and dark in color, but the tail is white on the outer half and is carried like a banner. The hind legs resemble those of a kangaroo, and bilbies hop much like kangaroos, although they are also efficient diggers and live in rather deep burrows in the semidesert country where they occur. (If a committee put this one together, it did a rather better job!) Aborigines considered bilbies a delicacy and used their tails as body ornaments, but it was white man with his guns and his introduced rabbits and foxes that caused their decline, and now they are restricted to remote areas in the Center.

At least the bilby still survives. The same cannot be said for the pig-footed bandicoot, which has not been seen in at least half a century. This odd creature was first discovered by Major Thomas Mitchell on one of his parties of exploration in 1836. Its legs were somewhat hoofed, suggesting a pig to Mitchell, though in fact the slender legs and rather long ears gave the animal more the appearance of a small deer. The pig-footed bandicoot was apparently never common, and it is now listed as one of four species of marsupials that are undoubtedly extinct (another fifteen are listed as of "obscure status").

Another bandicootlike animal of considerable interest is the numbat, or banded anteater. This is a small creature, not much over a foot long and much of that tail, weighing only about a pound. Its fur is reddish-brown, its back barred with transverse, alternating black and white stripes. With its pointed nose and long, wormlike tongue it probes for termites (only occasionally taking ants, despite its name).

The numbat has a number of characteristics that seem odd for a marsupial: it is active by day, and it has no pouch; the young are held securely by the teats, which swell in their mouths. The numbat is especially interesting to zoologists because it has fifty teeth—more than any mammal aside from dolphins. Numbats are confined to southwestern Australia, though formerly they were more widely distributed. They live in hollow logs, and if cornered are said to produce a noise rather like escaping steam. We have never seen a numbat, but well remember seeing Australia's best known naturalist, Harry Butler, extract one from a log on his popular television program "In the Wild." The numbat apparently stands a good chance of surviving permanently in faunal reserves, although most of its original habitat has been converted to agriculture.

The remaining types of marsupials are primarily herbivorous, and as might be expected they have very different teeth from the carnivores: there are only two incisors in the lower jaw, and canines are reduced or absent, so that there is a gap between the front and the hind chewing teeth, as in most herbivorous mammals. By and large the plant-feeders are much more abundant and successful than the carnivores; these are the mammals everyone has heard about, and which a visitor to Australia may hope to see, at least in zoos and faunal parks. There are three major groups: the kangaroos and wallabies, the koala and wombat (which are somewhat related), and the possums. We will discuss these in reverse order, saving those most familiar of Australian mammals, the kangaroos, until last.

Although the word possum is a corruption of the word opossum, applied to American marsupials, in fact these are very different, unrelated groups of animals. Whereas the North American opossum is an unprepossessing beast, with a full, carnivorous-type set of teeth, the Australian possums are primarily herbivorous and have handsome faces and a rich coat of fur, which often also clothes their tails. These are tree-dwelling animals, and the group includes the gliders, which we mentioned earlier as suggesting flying squirrels [colorplate 8]. Perhaps the best known of these is the sugar glider, a delightful little animal that lives in small groups in cavities in gum trees. At night they emerge and bury their faces in clusters of eucalyptus flowers, licking up the nectar and at the same time devouring any insects in the blossoms.

One of the most remarkable species is the feather glider, a tiny, mouse-sized animal in which the hairs of the tail grow only on the sides, like the vanes of a feather. It is a beautiful sight to see a glider launching itself into space and landing securely on an adjacent tree. One of the larger species, called the fluffy glider, has been recorded as gliding as much as 370 feet, descending at an angle of only thirty degrees from the horizontal.

Gliders line their nests with leaves and are said to carry sprays of leaves in a twist of their tail. They have scent glands that are used to mark their home territories, and while members of a clan seldom fight with one another, those of alien clans are sometimes attacked fiercely. All of this goes on at night, and only a few dedicated naturalists have ever looked deeply into the lives of these fascinating creatures.

On the other hand, it is fairly easy to become acquainted with the brush-tailed possum, one of Australia's commonest marsupials. Both of the houses where we lived in the Brisbane suburbs were haunted by these creatures—haunted because we only rarely saw them, but every night they clamored noisily over the iron roof to the trees outside our bedroom, where they chattered and fussed intermittently most of the night. One of them returned faithfully each morning just before dawn to a bed he had made in the rafters of the garage, where he would look down at us trustingly if we disturbed him during the day.

We were often visited by brush-tailed possums at campsites in various parts of Australia, and in the parks they would occasionally take food from our hands. In Carnarvon National Park we had a favorite female that came along just after dark each evening with a baby half her own size clinging to her back; both would take our tidbits and then go on to the next campsite.

It is possible to make a case against brush-tailed possums, since they are sometimes rather hard on young trees and bushes, but one cannot but admire an animal that adapts so well to man's

The feathertail glider, a tiny species with a flattened, featherlike tail.
(E. C. Slater, Division of Wildlife Research, CSIRO, Australia)

A brush-tailed possum focuses curious eyes on the camera.
(Raymond H. Besserdin)

presence. The fur of the brush-tail is much esteemed, and it is reported that over 200,000 skins were harvested in Victoria in a single year. The possum has also been introduced into New Zealand in the effort to develop a fur industry, but it became so plentiful and so damaging to trees that it was necessary to wage a campaign against them. At one time New Zealand had a postmark: "Kill that possum."

Not all possums are as ubiquitous as the brush-tail. A small, attractively patterned possum was discovered in southeastern Victoria in 1867 and named after the taxidermist who prepared the first specimens, a man named Leadbeater. Following the clearing of the forests in the area, it appeared that the species had become extinct, as many efforts to find it had failed. Then, in 1961, a group from the Field Naturalists Club of Victoria discovered a colony only seventy miles from Melbourne! Since that time several additional populations have been found, all in dense regrowths of mountain ash, apparently the normal habitat of the species. Thus Leadbeater's possum has been removed from the list of extinct species—giving hope that others on the list may someday follow suit.

Like the possums, the koala is arboreal, in fact leaving its tree only briefly, to move to another. Its arms are admirably adapted for clinging to trees [colorplate 9], even when it is sleeping in a crotch; the fingers are thick and supplied with large, curved claws, and there is a gap between the first two and the last three fingers, so that a vicelike grip can be maintained. Its warm fur, small, beady eyes, and tufted ears give the koala an endearing aspect, hardly appropriate to its sluggish behavior and piglike voice.

Factory-made "koala-bears" are often sold in souvenir shops as teddy bears (we succumbed on one of our early trips to Australia, when our children were young). Actually, they are usually made of kangaroo skin and stuffed with cotton. Real koalas can be seen in various faunal parks, and in some of these it is possible to have one's picture taken holding one of these "cuddly" animals.

The koala was not discovered by the earliest settlers, and it was not until 1803 that a description appeared in the *Sydney Gazette*:

> This creature is somewhat larger than a waumbat, and, although it might at first appearance be thought to resemble it, nevertheless differs from that animal. . . . The graveness of the visage . . . would seem to indicate a more than ordinary portion of animal sagacity, and the teeth resemble those of a rabbit . . . its food consists solely of gum leaves, in the choice of which it is excessively nice.

Although attributing more "sagacity" to the koala than it deserves, this account is perceptive regarding the relationship to the wombat and regarding its fastidious diet. Not all early references to the koala were complimentary, as the following paragraph in a natural history book of 1811 shows:

> Whether we consider the uncouth and remarkable form of its body, which is particularly awkward and ungainly, or its strange physiognomy and manner of living, we are at a loss to imagine for what particular scale of usefulness

or happiness such an animal could by the great Author of Nature possibly be destined. . . ."

But of course we now know that the koala was destined to amuse the tourists and to advertise Qantas Airlines! On a more serious note, we may feel fortunate that this curious animal has been saved from extinction. As mentioned, it is a fastidious feeder, consuming nothing but eucalyptus leaves of about twelve kinds, all smooth-barked species having a high oil content. As an aid in the digestion of these tough, aromatic leaves, the koala has a special intestinal sac some six to eight feet long, somewhat like a huge appendix. Adults eat about two and a half pounds of leaves a day. They reach quite a large size, males weighing up to twenty-five pounds, and they live twelve years or more. The koala is a slow reproducer, with usually only one offspring each year.

As can be imagined, clearing of the forests had a devastating effect on this specialized feeder. Also, its sluggish behavior made it an easy target for hunters. Actually, the koala's flesh is relatively unpalatable, and the fur much inferior to that of the brush-tailed possum. Nevertheless, for a century it was slaughtered ruthlessly, a story angrily recounted by the late A. J. Marshall in his book *The Great Extermination*. In 1908 New South Wales harvested over 50,000 skins, and in 1924 two million skins were exported. In 1920 South Australia harvested over 100,000 skins, resulting in the extinction of the koala in that state. It remained abundant in Queensland, but in 1927 the acting premier of that state, angling for the rural vote, declared an open season. It is said that nearly 600,000 koalas were slaughtered in a few months—although the skins were worth per dozen only fifty-six shillings nine pence (about five dollars). "The most sordid episode in the history of Queensland," according to Marshall.

Fortunately, the tide has turned and koalas are not as rare as they once were. In 1979 we first saw wild ones in eucalypts around what was otherwise a miserable trailer park in central Queensland. The lack of humans (understandable) was probably encouraging to the koalas, however, and so we put up with the facilities to enjoy the wildlife. A strong effort is being made to reestablish the species in many parts of its former range. Several private koala farms and sanctuaries breed koalas not only as a tourist attraction but as a source of animals for distribution. The Department of Fisheries and Wildlife of Victoria has been especially successful in assisting the comeback of the koala.

On Phillip Island, not far from Melbourne, koalas now thrive in a seminatural condition in groves of ribbon gums, many of which were planted for that purpose, we were told, by groups of Girl Guides. We have visited Phillip Island, strolled down a road through the groves, and can vouch for their abundance, as Marshall says "enveloped in a protective wave of benevolent sentimentality." From these nuclei, koalas have been reestablished in a number of areas. "Beware of koalas crossing the road" is one of the more welcome of road signs.

Although the wombat's bearlike form, lack of a tail, and buttonnose suggest its relationship to the koala, it is quite a different animal with respect to its mode of life. Wombats are large animals, weighing up to sixty pounds, and they bulldoze huge burrow systems in the soil, often many feet long and as much as six feet deep (they were "badgers" to the early settlers, but the badger is an altogether more unpleasant creature). The common wombat of southeastern Australia occurs mostly in forested or scrubby areas and is fairly common.

Wombats are reported to make excellent pets if taken young, and we believed that when we saw a young pair in the aforementioned Tasmanian Devil Park. We were greatly tempted to pick one up and cuddle it—warned off only by the park signs and the knowledge that when they grow up they can wreak havoc about the house and gardens. There are three species of hairy-nosed wombats which occur in the Interior, and these are generally less abundant, having suffered through competition with imported rabbits and through conversion of much of their habitat to agriculture.

Wombats have but one young a year, carried in a pouch that opens backward (as befits a burrowing animal). It is said that they are a good deal

The wombat, a marsupial that is in many ways reminiscent of the marmot or woodchuck in North America.
(Australian Information Service)

better eating than koalas, and wombat stew and cured wombat hams and bacon are prized in parts of the Outback. Farmers often take a dim view of them because the burrows they dig are capable of causing a broken leg if livestock come afoul of them; and wombats are forever breaching rabbit-proof and dingo-proof fences.

Surprisingly, there have been few efforts to study wombats carefully to determine what sort of territories they maintain, how they interact with other wombats, and the like. Also, wombats have received little of the publicity of koalas and kangaroos—they advertise or symbolize no airlines or insurance companies, they are figured on no coins or coats-of-arms, and even the tourist bureaus seem to ignore them. Only a twenty-cent stamp issued in the 1970s has done the wombat justice with an appealing portrait.* Yet these animals are deserving of a more careful study and more recognition as one of Australia's priceless novelties.

Finally, as far as marsupials go, we reach the kangaroos—almost the symbol of Australia: indeed the symbol of both Qantas and Trans-Australian Airlines, as well as sharing the national coat-of-arms with the emu. The word "kangaroo," like koala and wombat, is aboriginal. Kangaroos form the centerpiece of a group of nearly fifty species that make up a family called the Macropodidae (which literally means "big feet," with reference to the huge hind legs).

Kangaroos proper include only the great gray and western gray kangaroos [colorplate 10], which occur mainly in wooded country; the red kangaroo of plains of the Interior; the euro or wallaroo, a long-haired species occurring mainly in hilly and rocky country in the Interior; and a lesser known species of the far North, the antelope kangaroo. The remainder are various smaller and sometimes more specialized animals built on the kangaroo pattern: the tree-kangaroos, the rat-kangaroos, and the wallabies, the latter distinguished from kangaroos rather arbitrarily by their smaller size (in fact wallabies are more like kangaroos than the rat-kangaroos and the tree-kangaroos).

It is easy to see kangaroos in the wild if one is willing to spend some time in the back country and to be about in the early morning or late evening, or after dark with a good flashlight. And the sight of a group of 'roos bounding through the bush is one not to be forgotten.

Kangaroos differ from other marsupials in their semierect posture, resting tripod-style on their huge hind legs and their large, muscular tail. When feeding or walking slowly, the much smaller front legs are used to some extent, but when moving rapidly 'roos bound along on their hind legs, holding their tails upward as a counterbalance—giving the nickname "boomer" to some of the large males. Kangaroos are the only large animals anywhere that employ a hopping gait, and it is natural to ask what the advantage may be and why other mammals have not adopted it. Kangaroos cover from four to fourteen feet at each bound and maintain average speeds of about fifteen miles per hour (though if pushed they can hop up to thirty-five miles per hour).

A park ranger once treated us to a pursuit of

*But in 1981, Australia issued a series of stamps of endangered species, including the Queensland hairy-nosed wombat, the bilby, and Leadbeater's possum.

Ring-tailed wallabies are one of many species of smaller marsupials. This scene was photographed in a faunal preserve near Adelaide, South Australia.

kangaroos in a jeep—great fun but, we thought, rather pointless. They readily out-distanced us in the rough terrain, and it occurred to us that hopping was specially suited for this type of country, since the 'roos readily skimmed rocks and bushes that we had to circumvent. Kangaroos hop fences readily (though often reluctantly). If there were an animal equivalent of the *Guinness Book of World Records*, a certain red kangaroo would be in it: he is recorded as covering twenty-seven feet in one leap, during which he cleared a woodpile ten feet high!

Recently, Dr. Terry Dawson, of the University of New South Wales, has been studying critically the possible advantages of hopping. Some of his work was done at Harvard in collaboration with Dr. C. Richard Taylor of that university. We were at Harvard at the time and in fact had an office just down the hall from Dawson and Taylor's treadmills. More than once we looked up to see a kangaroo hopping down the hall or staring in at our door—a pleasant treat for a pair of incurable australophiles. Dawson showed that hopping rate (hops per minute) remains relatively constant over a wide range of speeds, although stride length increases considerably at higher speeds.

All marsupials have lower metabolic rates and body temperatures than other mammals, and thus their maximum energy output is relatively low.

Kangaroos, in fact, move more economically at moderate or high speeds (in terms of oxygen consumption) than do four-legged runners. They compensate for energy deficiencies by their constant hopping rate, maintained via the natural elasticity of the tendons and muscles of their hind quarters. As Dawson explains: "energy may be stored in various elastic components in much the same way that energy is stored in the spring of a pogo stick."

With their lower metabolic rate, marsupials require relatively less food than other animals of similar size. Yet, given the irregular patterns of rainfall and resulting fresh vegetation in the Interior, it is imperative that they move about freely. The hopping gait is in every way a marvelous adaptation for achieving fleetness on a low energy budget in a rough and uncertain environment.

While wild kangaroos keep their distance, those in parks and preserves are usually easy to approach and pet (and feed). In Carnarvon National Park they nuzzled us at our picnic table at almost every meal, until finally we reluctantly had to shoo them away. They are difficult to resist, especially those with joeys, and we were frequently amused when they would stand and stare, often with one ear down and the other up—seemingly bent on catching every word of our learned conversations. We particularly like D.H. Lawrence's impressions of a kangaroo:

> Her sensitive, long, pure-bred face,
> Her full antipodal eyes, so dark,
> So big and quiet and remote, having watched
> so many empty dawns in silent Australia.

Stanley and Kay Breeden have an appealing vignette of a joey that was well grown but still very dependent on his mother:

> At this age the joey, though inquisitive and spirited, is still very insecure when more than two hops from his mother. Every now and again he becomes panic stricken at his own audacity and races back and tries desperately to get into the pouch. But there is no real danger and his mother refuses him entry. She does this simply by standing upright. No matter how hard he struggles he can get no more than his head and shoulders into the pouch. But his panic soon passes. Hiding his head for a minute or so, and perhaps a quick drink, reassures him and he dashes off again. Should real danger exist, perhaps a hunting Dingo or eagle, the mother would call her joey with soft sucking noises. These are instantly obeyed and as soon as he arrives his mother leans forward and the joey climbs quickly into the pouch head first, does a tumble-turn inside and confidently pokes his head out.

Kangaroos are not usually solitary animals, but move about in "mobs," which are loosely organized family groups, usually a mother with young of various ages, often also an adult male. Sometimes a few nonrelatives join the mob for a short period. Mob size in the red kangaroo rarely exceeds ten animals, although much larger mobs have been seen. Legend has it that mature males maintain harems by boxing rival males, or if necessary slashing them with their powerful hind feet. There is no doubt that an adult male is a formidable beast if cornered (in a reserve one growled as we slowly approached, and we hurriedly backed off). Occasional fights among males have been seen in the wild, but there is no real evidence that males retain harems in the manner of deer.

Much has been said about the widespread slaughter of kangaroos, most of it true. We have seen "kangaroo graveyards," heaped with rotting carcasses, and we have seen crews in pickups plying the highways at night, shooting 'roos as they became dazed by the powerful spotlights. A. J. Marshall presents many accounts in *The Great Extermination* and concludes that "the organized savagery with which Kangaroos are being hunted today [this was in 1966] is equalled in our history only by the appalling massacre of koalas in 1927."

It is often believed that kangaroos may be sharing the fate of the North American bison and will soon exist only in a few preserves. In 1973 the United States placed kangaroos on the Register of Endangered Species, thus banning imports of meat as well as any items made of the skins (this ban has now been lifted on a trial basis).

There is another side to this story. The *Melbourne Age*, on April 1, 1980, carried banner headlines: KANGAROO EXPLOSION (and it was not an April fool's joke). Queensland's National Parks and Wildlife Service (said the *Age*) reported at least eleven million kangaroos roaming the state, and in all of Australia "the total may well be thirty million." One grazier was quoted as saying that his losses from kangaroos eating his crops and pasture and damaging his fences come to at least $30,000 a year. We had recently returned from a trip through parts of outback Queensland when this report appeared in the papers, and can vouch for the fact that kangaroos and wallabies were, indeed, plentiful. Visitors and residents in the more heavily populated areas, to be sure, rarely see a wild kangaroo, but Australia is a big country, most of it sparsely populated. The Outback is the home of the kangaroo.

The fact is that 'roos are remarkably resilient animals, able to build up their numbers rapidly when conditions are favorable. It is possible that there are more kangaroos in Australia now than there were when Europeans first arrived. Wells and dams built for livestock, as well as improved pasturelands, have proved a boon to them. Undoubtedly, they do compete with livestock for forage, and it is easy to sympathize with pastoralists, who detest them almost to a man.

Actually, research shows that 'roos and sheep have significant differences in the types of plants they prefer. Kangaroos prefer short, green plants and tend to move away, cease breeding, or die when the vegetation dries up; they respond to drought more quickly than sheep, which are able to subsist on dry grass, saltbush, and other bushy plants. Graziers often see kangaroos grazing with sheep on good pastureland. Later, when the pasture has deteriorated, they tend to blame the 'roos for conditions caused by drought, overstocking, or damage from the hoofs of livestock. It is interesting that Francis Ratcliffe, in his report to the Australian government on the deterioration of grazing land (summarized in his book *Flying Fox and Drifting Sand*) says a great deal about overgrazing and about rabbits and about drought, but nothing about kangaroos.

Be that as it may, vast areas in the Interior are used for grazing livestock, and for graziers it is a hard life and often a discouraging one. One grazier told us he expected adequate rainfall only one year in seven; during the others he often had to reduce his flocks or ship them elsewhere, at considerable expense. When thunderstorms produce a local regrowth of green vegetation, kangaroos often appear in numbers. Any reduction in the amount of food available for livestock is unwelcome.

Unfortunately, many of the kangaroos shot are simply left to rot or are used only to a limited extent. There are many trigger-happy weekenders who simply kill for the "fun" of it, caring little about the size or the sex of the animals they shoot. Ironically, bans on the export of kangaroo products tend to encourage people to let them rot. Kangaroo and wallaby flesh was cherished by the aborigines and by the early settlers; nowadays it is used mainly as pet food. The fur makes excellent coats and rugs; the skins make leather suitable for gloves and shoes. Fortunately, a number of kangaroo abattoirs are now operating. For the most part these are supplied by professional shooters who take only mature, nonbreeding animals and who work in areas where 'roos are abundant enough to justify their operations. If kangaroo shooting can be more closely regulated, and if more markets can be found for meat for human consumption—as they should be—it would seem possible to satisfy graziers, hunters, and processers, while still assuring that kangaroos and wallabies will continue to grace the Australian bush in numbers.

There are some who feel that hoofed animals such as sheep and cattle have no place in the semideserts of inland Australia. There is no doubt that their movements chop and loosen the soil, so that the germination of new plants is retarded and the wind picks up soil and blows it into drifts and dunes. Kangaroos and wallabies have broad, padded feet, they eat less food than livestock per body weight, and their pelletlike droppings do not blanket pastures like those of cattle. Why not encourage these well-adapted native mammals and harvest them systematically for their meat and hides? At the very least, some very large, stock-free areas should be set aside for kangaroos and other native animals, where water is available and food supplied during periods of prolonged drought. In time, enough restaurateurs and householders, in many parts of the world, would surely be sufficiently sold on kangaroo meat to justify the substitution of these animals for the hoofed domestic animals that do so much damage to that delicately balanced environment.

As of now, the five species of kangaroos and several of the larger wallabies, despite intermittent outbreaks and periods of scarcity, seem to be holding their own in the face of loss of habitat and periodic carnage. We especially enjoyed the visits of whiptail wallabies to our campsites in Queensland, and in Tasmania we were surprised at the abundance of Bennett's wallabies. Here we also spotted several potoroos, small creatures with pointed snouts somewhat like bandicoots, and with slender, white-tipped tails. These belong to the group known as rat-kangaroos.

We have not seen a tree-kangaroo, and few persons have, as these are confined to mountain rain forests of the far Northeast. Tree-kangaroos have much more powerful front legs than most 'roos, as befits climbers. Their long tails are not used for climbing, but serve as a counterbalance when they leap from branch to branch. On the ground they proceed much like other kangaroos.

It is surprising how little is known about the lives of most marsupials. Even kangaroos are not well enough understood for us to know how much harvesting should be allowed. Surprisingly, an entirely new species of potoroo was discovered as late as 1980, and in a part of Australia as well known as eastern Victoria. Ironically, the species was described from a road kill, along with three other specimens that had been taken in traps.

Two species of smaller wallabies and one rat-kangaroo are now believed to be extinct, and several others are of doubtful status. Like other small marsupials, these have suffered from destruction of their habitat, from predation by introduced foxes and escaped domestic cats, and from eating poison put out for rabbits and dingoes. The same may be said for a number of species of rats and mice native to Australia. These are true rats and mice (for Australia does harbor quite a few nonmarsupials, though of only two groups: rodents and bats). The approximately fifty species of rodents are believed to be derived from stocks that arrived in Australia much later than the marsupials, perhaps not more than twenty million years ago. Nevertheless, they have diversified extensively and become well adapted to the Australian environments.

There are tree rats, rock rats, water rats, hopping mice, and others. These show remote relationships to species occurring in Asia and the East Indies, suggesting that their ancestors arrived from the north via island steppingstones and drifting vegetation. Like rodents everywhere, these are gnawing animals, their feeding habits quite different from those of the so-called marsupial mice, which as we mentioned earlier are carnivores in the manner of shrews. Most of Australia's native rodents are well known only to specialists. The rats and mice seen about the cities are common house mice and black and Norway rats, which have been carried to all parts of the world by man's activities.

Australia is also the home of something like fifty species of bats. Being strong fliers, bats have populated most parts of the world, and to a nonspecialist most of Australia's bats look much like bats everywhere. In typical bat style, they are nocturnal insectivores and spend their days roosting in caves, hollow trees, or deserted buildings. The surprise, to a visitor to the continent, is the abundance of fruit bats. These are huge creatures, some with a wingspan of five feet, which unlike other bats are vegetarians, feeding on blossoms and ripening fruit. Australians often call them "flying foxes," we suppose because of their large size and coarse fur, often reddish-brown in color. We have many times enjoyed watching these great, witchlike beasts flying over just at dusk. When the mangoes were ripe in Brisbane, we often heard them "making merry" in the trees. In his book *Flying Fox and Drifting Sand* (which we have already mentioned), Francis Ratcliffe describes the mass attack on mangoes:

When its queerly shaped fruit begins to ripen,

> the nights are made bedlam by the flying foxes. Just as darkness falls, they appear in thousands. They wheel and flutter around the trees, settle and screech and squabble in the branches. They bite at the fruits as they grow; and, being clumsy pawless creatures, knock them down in dozens, so that a squashy mess of mangoes on the ground in the morning bears witness of their business during the night. At times they will carry the mangoes bodily away, and, losing grip of them in the air, will drop them with ringing thumps on the corrugated iron roofs of the houses.

During the day, fruit bats congregate in "camps" in forested areas, where they hang upside down, cloaked in their folded wings. These camps tend to be traditional, the same group of trees being occupied year after year, often to the point of denuding the trees, breaking the branches or killing them completely. Ratcliffe has found camps of nearly a quarter of a million individuals. One of the ways of controlling these bats—which needless to say are not popular with fruit growers—is to enter a camp with guns blazing and slaughter as many as possible, hoping the remainder will fly off and not return (but they usually do!).

Fruit bats were a favorite food of certain groups of aborigines, who used to knock them from their perches with hunting sticks. It is said that they made acceptable food for the early settlers when soaked in wine overnight and cooked slowly, but it is hard to believe that these stygian creatures will ever find a place on modern menus.

Before concluding this brief survey of native mammals, mention should be made of those that live in the seas around Australia: whales and dolphins, dugongs (related to the Florida manatee), and several kinds of seals and sea lions. The latter do come ashore at various places along the south coast, but by and large none of these marine mammals are distinctively Australian, and we shall pass them by.

Whether the Australian dog, or dingo, is properly regarded as a native is a matter of opinion. Dingoes undoubtedly were introduced to Australia by aborigines many years ago—but at a time after Tasmania became separated from the mainland, as they have never been found in Tasmania. Perhaps that is why the Tasmanian devil and the thylacine (Tasmanian wolf) survived there and not on the continent, for the dingo may have proved a more efficient predator.

Dingoes were the domestic dogs of the aborigines, but they have run wild for a long time, and they have evolved to the point that they differ slightly from domestic dogs, with which they interbreed to a certain extent. Large, tawny yellow dogs with erect ears and bushy tails, dingoes do not bark, but howl, and unlike other dogs they have a fixed breeding season, mating in the fall and bearing young in the winter and early spring.

Dingoes are the largest wild carnivores on the continent, feeding mainly on other mammals and on birds and reptiles, which they hunt singly or in small packs. Rats, mice, rabbits, and marsupials of many kinds are commonly eaten. Sheep and calves are added to the diet when game is scarce, and some dingoes become addicted to these easily caught domestic animals. Perhaps the service they perform in controlling rabbits and rats more or less balances their depredations on livestock, but pastoralists do not think so, and destroy them whenever possible. The use of poisoned baits dropped from airplanes sometimes works fairly well, but results in the death of many other, harmless animals. Some farmers have suggested aerial baiting in national parks and reserves, supposedly because they are breeding places for dingoes!

Trapping and shooting are the more time-honored means of controlling dingoes, and the professional or parttime dingo-hunter, or "dogger," has become almost a legendary figure in the Outback. In his book *Tales of the Big Country*, Keith Willey tells of Peter Allen, reputedly the most famous dogger of Central Australia, who reckoned he had killed at least 200,000 dingoes. Allen and his sons traveled all over the Center in their Land-rover, trapping and shooting dingoes for the government bounty of two dollars a scalp—more than enough to support their simple life, free from the demands of modern society. Many aborigines, too, have taken advantage of the bounties to fulfill their needs at the local commissaries.

One of the more unusual methods of control has been the construction of dog-proof fences across vast areas of Australia. These extend for hundreds of miles, for example along much of the western border of New South Wales and Queensland, thence across South Australia, separating sheep grazing areas to the south from dingo populations to the north. The few dingoes that cross the fences are shot or killed with poison bait. Maintenance of the fences is the responsibility of individual landowners, with the aid of government subsidies. The burden of building and repairing these fences, often in remote areas, is very considerable, and is a measure of the threat that dingoes are believed to present to the wool industry.

Recently, sections of the fences have been electrified, on an experimental basis, using energizers powered either by standard electric current or by batteries. Battery-powered energizers have in some cases been equipped with solar panels, which recharge the batteries from sunlight. This ingenious use of solar technology would seem ideal for the Outback, where there is usually plenty of sunlight but a dearth of roads rendering easy access to the fences. For economic reasons, however, electric fencing will probably remain restricted to certain trouble areas, for example where wombats are plentiful, since these bulky animals sometimes bulldoze their way through the fences.

The "dingo problem" in Australia suggests problems with the coyote in North America. Both of these canines are wily beasts likely to be around for many years to come. In both cases it would be helpful if we knew the behavior and ecological relationships of these animals more intimately. It is perhaps too much to expect that ranchers and graziers could be convinced that predators such as coyotes, dingoes, and eagles are on the whole menaces on a far smaller scale than drought, overgrazing, and mismanagement. But perhaps a rifle is a way of registering frustration at the vicissitudes of nature (including human nature).

The red fox is clearly *not* a native animal, having been introduced near Melbourne in 1845 in the hope of enjoyment of good old English-style fox hunts. The red fox is a remarkably adaptable animal; it is the same species that ranges throughout North America and Eurasia. In Australia it spread rapidly, reaching South Australia by 1880 and Western Australia by 1916. Now it occurs almost everywhere except in the far north and in Tasmania. Foxes do well in surprisingly arid places and are common even on the stark Nullarbor Plain. This success is partly the result of their varied diet, for they are able to live on carrion, insects, and lizards as well as on rats, rabbits, and an occasional sheep.

Undoubtedly, they are partly responsible for the decline of some of the native small mammals, but there seems to be little agreement on how important their role has been. Perhaps more serious are the feral cats—the descendants of escaped pets—that now range widely, even in desolate parts of the Center. These cats are highly valued as food by some of the aboriginal tribes in the country west of Alice Springs.

But none of these predators has had quite the impact of that prolific herbivore, the rabbit. Rabbits were brought from England for sport and for food soon after the arrival of the first settlers, but it is generally agreed that the stock that invaded the countryside came from an introduction near Melbourne in 1859. Rabbits were first seen in Queensland in 1888 and had reached the west coast of Australia by 1907—a rate of spread exceeding that of the fox, which had got an early start and obviously did little to deter the spread of the rabbit.

Although rabbits have never done well north of the Tropic of Capricorn, they came to occupy the southern half of the country at the same time that much of it was being newly exploited for grazing. Wildlife authority Harry Frith has termed the spread of the rabbit "the greatest single tragedy that the economy and the native animals have ever suffered."

Rabbits took readily to the sandy soil of much of the Interior, building huge warrens and devouring indiscriminately all plants they could reach, even stripping the bark of shrubs and small trees. Rabbits and unwise densities of sheep quickly turned delicately balanced, semidesert environments into fields of bare, loose soil, easily carried away by wind or water. In 1891, when the rabbit was first well established in New South Wales, some fifteen million sheep were being run in the western part of that state; in 1951 the number was down to about seven million. At the same time many of the smaller native animals were being eaten out of house and home.

There are many vivid accounts of the great hordes of rabbits that infested the country. At waterholes and troughs they congregated "like seething carpets of brown fur." At times of drought they sometimes moved off by the millions in search of water and fresh vegetation, at times piling up and dying in great numbers against the fences that were built to contain them.

When it was obvious that shooting, poisoning, and fencing were inadequate to stem the tide, new methods were explored. It was known that a virus disease, called myxomatosis, attacked South American rabbits and that this disease was fatal to the European rabbits that infested Australia. There was some opposition to investigations of this disease, however. The public was understandably worried about the deliberate spreading of any kind of disease germs, and the rabbit was a source of profit to many people—in some years as many as fifty million skins and carcasses were harvested. But by the end of World War II the situation had gotten out of hand, and the Commonwealth Scientific and Industrial Research Organization (CSIRO) began field studies with the virus in the Murray Valley. These succeeded beyond all expectations. In 1951, epidemics began to sweep the rabbit population, and in some places the air was filled with the stench of rotting carcasses. Already by 1953 wool and meat production had jumped by sixty-eight million dollars.

As so often happens, natural selection over the next decade or two produced stocks of rabbits that were able to survive the infection, and the virus evolved less lethal strains. By 1960 rabbits had become noticeably more plentiful, and they continued to increase slowly, though never reaching their former levels. Following periods of rain, they tend to reproduce rapidly as the vegetation improves. But rains also cause mosquitoes to breed—and myxomatosis is spread primarily through bites of mosquitoes. Thus the disease, even in its less virulent form, tends to dampen the great outbreaks that formerly occurred.

Still other novel approaches are now being studied. It is known that rabbits produce a chemical that they use to mark their home territories. If this chemical could be synthesized and distributed around the edges of sheep paddocks, it might be possible to shield them from the intrusions of rabbits.

It appears that the rabbit will always be a major element in the fauna—an unwelcome element resulting from man's irrational desire to carry his familiar environment with him, and in so doing destroy environments that might in the long run prove more rewarding.

The rabbit is not the only imported herbivore now well established in Australia. Wild horses (called "brumbies") are plentiful in the Northern Territory, and at times are rounded up and broken for stock use or trucked south for pet food. Wild donkeys also roam the northwestern part of the continent, chiefly in the Kimberley Ranges. These are believed to be descended from donkeys brought to the eastern states in the 1880s by gold miners from California. There may be over a million now roaming the Kimberleys. The Western Australian government has recently spent more than a million dollars trying to eradicate them, using aborigines trained to shoot them from helicopters. Even so, it is unlikely that the donkeys will be eliminated.

Wild camels, descendants of the pack camels that were once a major form of transportation in the Center, can still be seen in remote areas. Although we spent two weeks far "off the beaten track" in the Interior, the best we can report is a few camel tracks. Wild pigs we did see, in the back country of Queensland, where they often do considerable damage to the environment and occasionally destroy crops. Recently there have been efforts to harvest these pigs systematically for export as food for human consumption.

By far the most spectacular of the introduced

mammals is the Indian water buffalo. These great, lumbering animals were brought from Timor into the Darwin area between 1825 and 1850 to serve as draft animals and as a source of milk and meat. They found the swampy country along the north coast much to their liking and soon became plentiful in the wild. Water buffalo are not closely related to our American buffalo (more properly called bison), but are more like huge, brown cattle with horns sometimes measuring ten feet from tip to tip. A mature bull may weigh three quarters of a ton. These are unpredictable animals, and can be dangerous at times. We saw many on our trip from Darwin to the East Alligator River, but we felt no desire to challenge them—witness our pictures of them all taken from considerable distances.

Buffalo hide makes good leather, and for many years professional buffalo hunters slaughtered the animals ruthlessly. More recently, there has been less demand for their hides but some interest in hunting buffalo for sport and for their flesh, which has often been used for pet food but is really much tastier than that implies. Domesticated buffalo are being bred and marketed for food, and these animals are surely much better adapted to the swamps of the far north than are cattle. However, they do a great deal of damage to the environment, as they trample the undergrowth, chop up the soil with their hoofs, and cut paths through the coastal swamps which allow salt water to penetrate. As a result, the paperback trees that provide the major shade in these areas are dying.

Tourist safaris out of Darwin always include buffalo on their agenda, along with wallabies and the great flocks of magpie geese, brolgas, jabirus, and other unusual waterfowl that occur in the marshes. Unfortunately the buffalo tend to destroy habitat suitable for wallabies and for waterfowl. There is something to be said for eliminating buffalo from the wild, if this can be done, and restricting them to a semidomesticated state in ranches, where they can be bred and harvested.

The fauna of Australia is vastly different from the one that greeted the early settlers. Urbanization, agriculture, and the introduction of sheep, cattle, buffalo, rabbits, and many other alien animals, as well as many plants, all have wrought profound changes. It is hard to imagine changes in the immediate future as extensive as these, so perhaps, if reason prevails, there is hope of many native animals surviving in something like their present numbers. The greatest danger is perhaps to forest-dwelling species—gliders, native cats, tree-kangaroos, and some of the smaller possums and wallabies. The forests were never very extensive, and now they are reduced to disconnected fragments.

Many of the mammals of the drier country—the bilby, for example—also lead a precarious existence. One thinks of the increasingly hectic search for oil, coal, and minerals as the world's population grows and supplies diminish. The idealism of conservation-minded people scarcely has the clout of dollar-minded industrialists and developers. Ironically, it is an industry, tourism, that may ultimately balance the scales toward permanent preservation of at least some of the more spectacular native mammals.

5

THE BIRDS

*"The swans were black,
the eagles white"*

A North American is likely to gain the impression that Australian birds are, on the whole, rather larger, noisier, and more flamboyant than he is used to, and also, at times, a good deal tamer. At our home in Indooroopilly, not far from the Brisbane River, we were constantly surprised by the variety and abundance of bird life—all the way from tiny redbacked fairy wrens foraging in the hedges to brush turkeys scratching in the dead leaves we were too lazy to rake up. Except during periods of extreme drought in the Interior, there is not a habitat that does not have its own complex of birds. And learning the birds in suburban Brisbane didn't help us much when we visited a rain forest, or a water hole in the Center!

Needless to say, a well-informed bird lover or a professional ornithologist (and we are neither) finds Australia a continent of vast rewards. It is true that Australia has fewer species of birds than any other continent—a consequence of the fact that it is the smallest continent and the one with the least varied climate and topography. The mountainous island of New Guinea, though only a tenth the size of Australia, has about as many species of birds. There are about six hundred that breed in Australia, plus several introduced species and over a hundred casuals. The novelty of the fauna arises from the fact that well over half of the resident species occur nowhere else, and a number of major groups (families) are restricted to the Australian region.

Equally striking to Americans is the fact that several groups are completely absent. There are no woodpeckers, for example, no jays, no shrikes, no pheasants, no hummingbirds. On the other hand, some familiar groups have "gone wild" and have evolved curious birds not at all familiar. Australian cuckoos are a strange lot, and the flycatchers are so diverse that some are called "fantails" and others "robins" (no relation to either the American or European robin). And the laughing kookaburra is in fact a kingfisher that has abandoned the water and turned to a diet of snakes, lizards, and insects.

The earliest Europeans in Australia often thought of birds primarily as a source of food. Sealers learned to eat shearwaters ("mutton birds") on the southeast coast and offshore islands; settlers shot ducks and doves; and cockatoo stew often sustained explorers in the Outback. Credit for the first scientific study of birds belongs to John Gould, an Englishman who had completed a five-volume *Birds of Europe* before visiting Australia for eighteen months in 1838–40.

Gould's Australian experiences were marked by tragedy. While he was birding on the islands of Bass Strait, one of his boatmen accidentally shot himself; Johnston Drummond, son of the government botanist of Western Australia, was murdered by aborigines while collecting birds for him; and John Gilbert, his major collector, was speared by aborigines in Northern Queensland while accompanying Ludwig Leichhardt on his expedition from Brisbane to the coast of Northern Territory.* Worse still, Gould's talented wife Elizabeth died shortly after her return to England, at the age of thirty-seven, after bearing him six children and completing over six hundred paintings for his books. After her death, Gould employed a number of other artists, among whom was Edward Lear, of *Book of Nonsense* fame. (Lear was, in fact, a distinguished bird portraitist; his illustration of parrots have recently been republished—selling for $1,100 a volume.)

To support his research and publications, Gould sold his volumes by subscription and also sold mounted birds and mammals. His 1,800 Australian bird specimens were offered to the British Museum for one thousand pounds, but were refused. They were later purchased by an American, Edward Wilson, and donated to The Academy of Natural Sciences of Philadelphia.** Gould's *Birds of Australia* appeared in eight volumes, from 1840 to 1848, and contained 681 carefully prepared plates. Fittingly, his name is commemorated in the "Gould League of Bird Lovers," founded in 1909, which today works through the schools to engender an interest in birds and their preservation. One is reminded of the Audubon Society of the United States, though there were few parallels in the lives of Gould and

*The birds collected by Gilbert on this expedition did, however, reach Gould, thanks to Leichhardt. In fact, Gould's *Birds of Australia* includes pictures of a pair of tree-creepers that were actually taken by Gilbert on the morning of the day he was killed.

**In offering the specimens to Wilson "without the Eggs for £800—or with the Eggs for £1000," Gould characterized his collection as comprising "the complete Ornithology so far as discovered of one entire quarter of the Globe." Even here misfortune plagued Gould. The skins were first shipped to Paris for mounting, where the original notes explaining where and by whom they were collected were removed and replaced by simplified and often ambiguous labels. But eventually they arrived in Philadelphia, where they remain well cared for, along with material collected by Audubon, Alexander Wilson, and others who devoted their lives to making known the birds of then little known parts of the world.

One of the most common and characteristic of Australian birds is the magpie, a marvelous songster quite unrelated to the American magpie.

Audubon other than their pioneering efforts.

To the visitor, it is the uniquely Australian groups that prove most intriguing. One of the most abundant of these groups is a family called the Cracticidae, which includes a number of rather large, black-and-white birds often seen in parks and suburban areas. Chief among these are the Australian magpies, which have nothing in common with American or European magpies except that they are black and white. The song of the magpie is one of the most characteristic sounds of early morning, impossible to describe but rather like a somewhat amorphous tune played on a slightly wheezy alto recorder. Magpies are robust birds with large beaks, which they use for probing the soil for insects. They are fairly long-lived, and pairs stay together for several years, but only after they are six to eight years old do they usually nest successfully in a strongly defended territory. Even though magpies are normally rather tame birds, during the nesting season they defend their territories vigorously against other magpies and even against other birds, dogs, cats, and sometimes human intruders.

An aroused magpie produces loud warning calls, and if further provoked will swoop at the intruder and sometimes lash at it with its powerful beak. There are numerous records of humans receiving scalp wounds from them. In one spring month in Perth, thirty-two magpies were shot following attacks on people. Actually, shooting them is at best only temporarily satisfying, as prime territories are quickly filled by other magpies. A better solution is to heed the warning calls and stay away from aggressive pairs during the spring breeding season. Magpies are, on the balance, friendly and desirable birds, consuming quantities of noxious insects and brightening the dawn with their caroling.

Close relatives of the magpies, the butcher birds also have a somewhat unfortunate reputation (and an unsuitable name). They are reputed to impale their insect prey on a twig while they tear it apart with their hooked beaks. Butcher birds resemble rather slender magpies and have an even more remarkable song that often carries a great distance. In fact, the several species of butcher birds are perhaps the premier songsters of Australia (the much less commonly encountered lyrebirds excepted). On our first trip into the bush we camped by a remote salt pan in central Western Australia. Each morning we were awakened by a complex melody, infinitely melancholy, we thought, and thoroughly suitable for that desolate landscape. We learned later that it was a butcher bird and that individuals often develop quite different songs. According to one bird book, the pied butcher bird often suggests the opening bars of Beethoven's Fifth Symphony, but to us butcher birds suggested a flautist trying to find just the right combination of notes to do justice to the morning.

To this same group belong the currawongs, which are rather like large, elongated magpies that prefer forested areas. Their calls are loud and clear but less varied and musical than those of their relatives the magpies and butcher birds. In several of the national parks in which we camped, flocks of currawongs descended upon us, staring at us with their great yellow eyes and loudly demanding to be fed. We soon found out that it was best to ignore them so that they would fly to someone else's camp and relieve our harried ear drums.

Another black-and-white bird, which looks rather like a slender magpie although it is not related, is the mudlark or magpie-lark. These are prim and elegant birds, not the least bit larklike and displaying only a rather shrill "pee-wit" call. At times, male and female perch side by side and call rapidly and alternately, each raising its wings over its head as it calls. Mudlarks are fiercely protective of their nests, and are often seen pursuing crows or hawks many times their size. We found mudlarks common almost everywhere we went in Australia except in desert country. Since mud is used in constructing their nests, they do not stray far from a source of water. The mudlark family, like the cracticids, is restricted to Australia and New Guinea.

There seems to be no end of black-and-white birds in Australia. Besides mudlarks, currawongs, butcher birds, and magpies, there are white-winged choughs, pied honeyeaters, pied cormorants, pied geese, and a number of black-and-white species of flycatchers. Even the famous black swans have white patches on the wings, and white pelicans have black! Why Australian birds seem to specialize in black and white is anybody's guess.

We have mentioned the lyrebirds, which belong to a group having no close relatives in any part of the world. There are two species, both confined to forests of southeastern Australia. Lyrebirds are chicken-size, brownish, ground-dwelling birds. The males have long, silver tail plumes framed with distinctive brown and white lyre-shaped feathers.

Lyrebirds were evidently once quite common, for in her classic *Childhood at Brindabella,* Miles Franklin speaks of the gullies (not far from the present city of Canberra) as being "alive with these fey creatures." But she also tells of trappers coming out of the mountains with long poles strung with lyrebirds on the way to market, many to provide feathers for ladies' hats in other parts of the world. These remarkable birds can still be seen in a few reserves if one is sufficiently patient and is afoot at the right time and place. Most Australians are familiar with lyrebirds chiefly through their appearance on their ten-cent coins!

During courtship, the male lyrebird struts and sings from a mound of soil he has prepared, spreading his remarkable tail feathers forward so that they extend over the top of his head. The song is loud and brilliantly melodic, and woven into it are the calls of many other birds that occur in the area. Since males are competing for the resident females, it is perhaps to their advantage to achieve as much variety as possible in their songs, and they do this by "borrowing" from other species ("liarbirds," one wag has called them). Lyrebirds breed in the wintertime, so these imitations cause no particular confusion among these other species, which have not yet begun to court. Male lyrebirds are polygynous—mating with whatever females they are able to attract to the several display mounds in their territory.

We had spent nearly two full years in Australia before we were able to fulfill a dream to see and hear lyrebirds in their native habitat. On a cool winter morning we visited the Tidbinbilla Nature Reserve, near Canberra, arriving well before the influx of noisy people on holiday. Judith Wright, a native-born poet and conservationist, held lyrebirds in a very private reverence:

> Over the west side of this mountain,
> that's lyrebird country.
> I could go down there, they say, in the early
> morning,
> and I'd see them, I'd hear them.
>
> Ten years, and I have never gone.
> I'll never go.
> I'll never see the lyrebirds—
> the few, the shy, the fabulous,
> the dying poets.
>
> I should see them, if I lay there in the dew:
> first a single movement
> like a waterdrop falling, then stillness,
> then a brown head, brown eyes,
> a splendid bird, bearing
> like a crest the symbol of his art,
> the high symmetrical shape of the perfect lyre.
> I should hear that master practising his art.

No, I have never gone.
Some things ought to be left secret, alone;
some things— birds like walking fables—
ought to inhabit nowhere but the reverence of
the heart.

A mating system remotely like that of lyrebirds is practiced by members of still another group restricted to Australia (and in this case also New Guinea), the bower birds. These birds have no elegant tail feathers, but as artisans they are unsurpassed. There are some eighteen species, but by far the best known of these is the satin bower bird, so called because of the uniform satin-blue plumage of the males. Like lyrebirds, the male selects a display arena in the bush, but it is of very different form, as the male builds an "avenue" five or six inches wide and about a foot long, flanked by walls ten to fourteen inches high composed of carefully selected sticks. The floor is covered with twigs and grass, and the threshold is decorated with flowers, berries, feathers, and (since the advent of Western man) with bits of glass, paper, bottle caps, and the like. Blue objects seem to be preferred to those of any other color, and neighboring birds will often pilfer especially desirable blue objects from one another's bowers. The males paint their bowers with a mixture of saliva and plant juices, using a stick as a paintbrush. Thus they are rightly considered among the very few animals that use tools.

During the breeding season, the males display in their bowers, and females are attracted to them. Males posture, flutter their wings, and produce a variety of sounds, including fragments of songs borrowed from other birds. From time to time they pick up objects from their caches and hold them in their beaks. Following mating, the female establishes a nest elsewhere and rears the young with no help from the male.

The satin bower bird is an inhabitant of moist eastern forests, but that is by no means true of all members of this group. The spotted bower bird of the dry interior is said to be an even more remarkable mimic, often including in his repertory human-made sounds such as the sharpening of a scythe or the twanging of a fence wire (also, it is said, the barking of a dog or the crackling of a bush fire). The bower of this species is not unlike that of the satin bower bird, but it is decorated with green and white objects, including unripe berries, bits of bone, and petals of white flowers.

The bower of the great bower bird is embellished with white snail shells.

Francis Ratcliffe tells of a tame, spotted bower bird that was presented with a multicolored children's marble, which it promptly rejected. Twice more the marble was placed in the bower, and twice more removed. On the fourth occasion, the bird picked up the marble in its beak and dropped it in a nearby river. The spotted bower bird has been known to steal jewelry from windowsills and has even been reported to have taken a glass eye from a bedside! Jock Marshall and Russell Drysdale, in their book *Journey Among Men*, tell of a spotted bower bird that stole the ignition keys from a parked car. "The aggrieved owner was shrewd enough to go to the nearest bower, where he found them."

In the Northern Territory, we were lucky enough to come upon the bower of the great bower bird, its floor decorated solely with large white snail shells. But it was the dry season, and the birds were not to be seen. However, in a rain forest in northern Queensland our fortunes improved and we spotted several pairs of rifle birds, their iridescent blue-green throats and tail feathers sparkling like jewels in shafts of sunlight that penetrated the canopy. Rifle birds are not bower birds, but belong to a related group, the birds of paradise. These birds reach their fullest expression in New Guinea and adjacent islands, where the elegant plumes and curious courtship displays of the males stretch one's credulity.

In lyrebirds, bower birds, and birds of paradise, the males expend much effort in seducing the females, but little or none in caring for the offspring. By contrast, in birds such as the emus and mound-builders, much of the care of the young falls to the males. The emu is the Australian equivalent of the ostrich, and is second only to the ostrich in size, often standing six feet in height and weighing as much as 120 pounds [colorplate 11]. Like the ostrich the female emu lays huge eggs, measuring some five inches long and weighing well over a pound—yet she lays eight or ten such eggs. Presumably she is so exhausted she must take time to recuperate, leaving the male to incubate the eggs and care for the chicks.

Emus are unpopular with graziers, and they are heartily detested by wheat growers, since they are grain feeders and are able to cover a good deal of ground in their search for food. Nevertheless, they are still fairly abundant in parts of the Outback, and it is not uncommon to see an adult male followed by a brood of striped chicks.

The emu belongs to a group of ancient, flightless birds called ratites, a group that also includes the cassowary, a shy inhabitant of the forests of New Guinea and extreme northeastern Australia, as well as the ostrich of Africa, the rhea of South America, and the famous kiwi of New Zealand. The extinct moas of New Zealand and elephant birds of Madagascar were also ratites. All of these are (or were) inhabitants of the Southern Hemisphere, and it may be that they evolved on Gondwanaland, though their relationships and ancestry are not well understood. In his book *Flying Fox and Drifting Sand,* Francis Ratcliffe remarks:

> I still can hardly believe in emus. Every now and then when I look at them the scales of familiarity fall from my eyes, and I see the things as they really are—monstrous hangovers from a more exciting creation, and every bit as extraordinary as any dinosaur.

The emu played an unwilling role in the development of Australia's only unique decorative art form: carved emu eggs, often elaborately mounted in silver. In the last part of the nineteenth century, it became fashionable to carve patterns into the three layers of shell—flowers, kangaroos, and even Sydney Harbor and its ships. One retailer offered silver-mounted emu eggs in fifty different patterns at prices ranging from a few shillings to twenty pounds apiece. Many have deteriorated or been melted down for their silver, but well-preserved examples now sell for as much as three thousand dollars. Fortunately for the emu, there are no modern practitioners of this "art."

Fortunately, too, the emu is no longer esteemed as food. Not so with the aborigines and early settlers. Captain John Hunter, the second governor of New South Wales, dined on emu and thought it "delicious meat. . . . A party of five, myself included, dined on a side-bone of it most scrumptiously." When explorer Ludwig Leichhardt was deep in the bush, he roasted emus over an open fire and collected the oil dripping from them to use in lubricating his firearms. He also rubbed the oil on his body as an antirheumatic and for what he called its "slightly exciting properties."

The lot of male mound-builders is even more strenuous than that of the emus. These birds lay their eggs in huge piles of earth and detritus measuring from twelve to fifteen feet in diameter and as much as three feet high. The mallee fowl, the best known of the three species of mound-builders, lives in scrubby, semidesert areas of the Interior. Male and female cooperate building a pit during the winter months; into this pit they scrape leaf litter; then, after waiting for a rain, they cover the litter with the soil they have excavated. As the season advances, the moist litter begins to ferment and produce heat. The female then begins to lay eggs, the male standing by and opening the mound each time she is ready to lay. In all she may lay thirty or more eggs, at intervals of from five to ten days.

Each egg requires seven to twelve weeks' incubation at the proper temperature—ninety degrees Fahrenheit—and it is the male's job to see that this temperature is maintained. He does this by altering the thickness of the layer of soil over the fermenting material around the eggs. Early in the cycle, fermentation is strong, and the male must open the mound early in the morning to permit cooling, then refill it before the sun's heat becomes too great. During the summer, fermentation declines but the sun's heat is intense, necessitating a thick layer of soil for insulation during the day. In the fall, reduced heat both from fermentation and from the sun requires that the mound be opened for variable periods during midday.

How does the male measure the temperature of the mound so accurately? Harry Frith, of the Australian Division of Wildlife Research, found that the male inserts his bill into the mound periodically and withdraws it full of soil. He then performs whatever needs to be done, suggesting that he has "tasted" the temperature with his tongue. When Dr. Frith artificially heated the mounds by installing electric heating elements, the birds quickly detected the changes and began cooling activities.

Because of the intervals between egg laying, plus the long incubation period, the male is kept busy virtually half of the year, and must have difficulty getting far enough away from the mound to find adequate food for himself. A hard life! When the eggs hatch one by one, the hatchlings merely push their way out and wander off into the bush, usually without ever seeing their parents. They may, of course, encounter their father still at his labors. In his book *The Mallee Fowl, the Bird that Builds an Incubator*, Harry Frith tells of a male that encountered a newly hatched chick when he opened the mound for the female to lay: "He did not miss a stroke, and ejected the chick in a shower of sand. It fell on the mound and rolled down the edge under its mother's nose, but she gave it no more than a passing glance as it struggled away into the scrub."

The mallee fowl is now a relatively rare bird, but once it was widely distributed in drier parts of the continent, where its eggs provided a welcome addition to the diet of the aborigines and early settlers. The explorer Ernest Giles, passing through parts of Western Australia empty of water and wildlife, found several nests in a time of need, and wrote in his journal: "We thanked Providence for supplying us with such luxuries in such a wilderness . . . [for] they are larger than a goose egg, and of a more delicious flavour than any other egg in the world. Their shell is beautifully pink tinted, and so terribly fragile that, if a person is not careful in lifting them, the fingers will crunch through the tinted shell in an instant."

We had an opportunity to visit the nest of a mallee fowl in Wyperfeld National Park, in northwestern Victoria. Unfortunately, the male scurried off into the bush before we could see much of him, but it was nevertheless a treat to see such an unusual structure. Another mound-builder, the brush turkey, became much more familiar to us and on one occasion stole food from our campsite when we were only a few yards away. Brush turkeys are impressive creatures, about the size of the quite unrelated domestic turkeys, with a naked red head and neck and glossy black plumage elsewhere. The males have a bright yellow, loose collar of skin between neck and breast, and this flaps about conspicuously as they chase each other through the bush. Altogether a striking bird, the brush turkey has a domestic life not unlike that of the mallee fowl, although brush turkeys are inhabitants of eastern forests rather than the dry interior.

It is hard to know where to stop when talking about Australian birds. A traveler from North America is certain to be impressed by the parrots, noisy and often garishly colored as they are. All the way from sparrow-sized budgerigars to giant black cockatoos, they form a major element on the Australian scene. On the whole they seemed to us much more approachable than the parrots of Central and South America, which always seem buried in the canopy or flying off in the distance. Species occurring in the Interior often flock to waterholes or cattle troughs, and in coastal localities parrots are readily

The scrub (or brush) turkey is a colorful mound builder of eastern Australia.
(Australian Information Service)

attracted to feeding stations, where they form a surrealistic tumult of sound and color.

Budgerigars (the name is derived from an aboriginal word meaning "good food"), or "budgies," are sold throughout the world as household pets. Their native home is the dry interior of Australia, where they often form huge, nomadic flocks. It is said that they are able to live several months without water, but they find living conditions more suitable where there has been rain. The flocks move from place to place, avoiding areas of drought, where there are few seeds for them to feed on. At a favorable time and place they reproduce rapidly, regardless of the time of year. It is a splendid sight to visit a water hole in the Center and find one's self in the midst of many thousands of these green and gold sprites and to be reminded that this is their normal habitat and not, after all, pet stores and home cages.

One of the most beautiful parrots is also one of the most abundant: the galah [colorplate 12]. Galahs are also birds of the Interior, even more nomadic than the budgerigars, since they often seek the milder climate of coastal cities during the winter. It is probable that both galahs and budgerigars are more plentiful than they once were, since Western man has sunk bores and built watering stations through much of the Interior.

Graziers and wheat growers do not hold the galah in high esteem despite its beauty and friendly disposition, for these large cockatoos consume large quantities of grain and will fly considerable distances to assist the farmer in his grain harvest. But as visitors to Australia, we developed a special affection for these lovely birds, whose calls often woke us in the early morning and cheered us when, tired from a day in the hot sun, we made our beds up for the night. To see a flock of these birds gathering in the trees in the evening is an unforgettable experience, as each bird wheels through the last few rays of the sun, flashing now pink, now silver-gray. And then to bed.

Galahs have earned a place in Australian slang, apparently because of the noise they make when gathering in the evening. To say a person is "crazy as a galah" is to imply that he is a bit of a loose talker or a bit wild in his ways. And in the early evenings of some rural areas, the "galah hour" on the party telephone line is an "institution" of long standing, or so we were told.

As we look back on our years in Australia, they seem to be punctuated by parrots—rainbow lorikeets chattering in the trees of our back yards [colorplate 13]; crimson rosellas landing on our shoulders and cameras when we tried to photograph them; a great flock of sulphur-crested cockatoos that screeched so interminably that we finally fled a woodland in Northern Territory, almost screaming ourselves. Perhaps the biggest surprise came in the mountains of Tasmania, when we were hiking in a midsummer snow squall and watched green rosellas gamboling in the antarctic beeches. It seemed incongruous, to say the least, to see parrots in a snow storm; but there they were.

There seem to be no habitats in Australia where parrots are not at home. In New Zealand, the kea, or "sheep-killing parrot," lives in the cool high country of South Island and nests in crevices in the rocks—surely no place for a member of a group so characteristic of the tropics. In his book *Zoogeog-*

Sulphur-crested white cockatoos are still abundant in parts of Australia, despite their popularity with bird fanciers throughout the world.
(Australian Information Service)

raphy, Philip Darlington asks: "does the unique diversity of parrots in the Australian region reflect place of origin. . . .?" He thinks perhaps not, but if it is true that major tropical forests developed in the warmer parts of Gondwanaland, as some are now claiming, then perhaps the parrots evolved there, too.

Whatever the case, parrots now occur throughout tropical and subtropical parts of the world, though nowhere so diverse as in Australia. Thus we have departed a bit from our plan to discuss groups that are more or less restricted to Australia. Of these, by far the largest is the family of honey-eaters (Meliphagidae—which is Latin for exactly that). Honey-eaters also occur in New Guinea and parts of the East Indies, but nowhere else. It is probably no coincidence that this large group, with over seventy Australian species, has evolved on a continent dominated by trees having an abundance of nectar-bearing flowers, especially eucalypts. In fact, trees and birds probably evolved together, the eucalypts depending upon honey-eaters as major instruments of pollination.

As the name implies, these birds are specialists at extracting nectar from blossoms, to a certain extent filling the niche occupied by hummingbirds in America. They are, however, not a bit like hummingbirds; the smaller ones are suggestive of warblers or vireos, the larger ones perhaps reminiscent of cuckoos. To a nonspecialist, honey-eaters seem a diverse group, all the way from tiny ones no more than four inches long to others measuring twenty inches; all the way from the flashy scarlet honey-eater to the drab and even rather ugly friar-birds. Some of them have cheerful songs, but this is hardly true of the wattle-birds, ungainly creatures that sometimes haunted our campsites along the east coast. James McAuley well describes their "song" in his poem *Afternoon:*

> A wattle-bird in the untidy scrub
> From time to time uncorks itself to utter
>
> Its quite peculiar metallic retching noise,
> Made with an effort that hardly seems worth-
> while.

The honey-eater family is usually defined on the basis of the slender and somewhat down-curved beak and the brushlike tongue. Some specialists believe the group is not really a natural one, derived from a common ancestor, but rather a diverse lot of unrelated birds that have all evolved similar mechanisms for feeding on nectar. Whatever the case, honey-eaters are very much a part of the Australian scene, and we had a good deal of fun trying to identify them.

One we did learn to recognize quickly was the noisy miner—though we never did learn why it is called a miner, since it does not seem to mine in anything. Noisy miners are rather tame, robin-sized honey-eaters that abound in parks and suburbs in eastern Australia. Only recently has their remarkable social life been brought to light, largely through the efforts of Douglas Dow, of the University of Queensland.

Miners live in large colonies, often of several hundred individuals. The colony territory is vigorously defended against other bird species and even against goannas, wallabies, dogs, and sometimes even people. A number of kinds of birds are recorded as having been killed by mobs of miners. Most of the species mobbed are not predators—in the way that various birds will mob crows, which feed on their eggs—but rather aggression seems to clear the area of birds and other creatures that might compete for food with the miner colony. So much time is sometimes spent in these activities that miners are sometimes said to exhibit "aggressive neglect" of their offspring—that is to say, they are so busy squabbling that their young are left to starve.

Miner colonies, Dr. Dow found, are further divided into "coteries," each consisting of several males which collectively occupy and to some extent defend a certain part of the area in which several females build their nests. Members of a coterie often feed and sleep together, and at times indulge in a "corroboree," greeting each other boisterously while moving their wings slowly up and down. Within each group there is a dominance hierarchy or "peck order." Dominant males assert themselves by calling and by assuming a horizontal body stance and "outstaring" their rivals, their apparent eye size being increased by a bare yellow patch of skin. When we lived in Bardon, in the Brisbane suburbs, our house opened onto a group of trees occupied by a troop of noisy miners, who sometimes had so much to fuss about that we had to shout to converse.

Males of a coterie visit the nests in the area, built by the females, and the females mate with them more or less indiscriminately. By such "prostitution," each female gathers about her several males, which assist in removing fecal pellets from the nest and in feeding the young. As the fledglings grow, the number of visits by the males increases, up to as many as fifty visits an hour, involving up to twenty-two different males (though usually fewer). The males may provide as much as 80 percent of the food required by the rapidly growing young. Evidently there are many more males than females, and by becoming a "helper" a male is likely, in the long run, to be helping to rear his own offspring. Miners are long-lived, and many of the helpers are young males which, with experience, may become dominant in their coterie and likely to father a higher percentage of the offspring.

Noisy miners are by no means the only Australian birds living in social groups in which some individuals are helpers. Recent studies have shown that the widely distributed rainbow bee-eaters and the blue wrens also have social groups. Bee-eaters are relatives of the kingfishers, but look more like orange and green swallows in their graceful acrobatic flights after insects (although they are quite distinctive with the central pair of tail feathers projecting). They nest, however, not in trees but in the ground, and especially banks. There they dig tunnels up to three feet long, and at the end lay five to seven eggs. Once hatched, the young are usually fed by several adults.

More detailed studies have been done on the blue wrens, which are common inhabitants of parks and gardens in southeastern Australia. It has been observed that breeding pairs are usually assisted in caring for the young by several others, usually but not always their own offspring from earlier broods. Members of a group sleep and feed together and may even preen one another. Blue wrens are not nearly as long-lived as miners, and do not survive generally beyond five or six years. By serving as helpers for a year or two, both males and females gain in experience and are in a position to take over a familiar, prime territory when their parents pass on.

Incidentally, Australian wrens are not true wrens at all, but belong to another uniquely Australian family, the Maluridae (often called "fairy wrens" to distinguish them from true wrens). These are tiny birds with upturned tails, and one cannot blame the early settlers for dubbing them "wrens" even though they differ in many ways from wrens of the Northern Hemisphere. These are among the most elegant of birds, notable for their iridescent colors, which in dim light often seem black but in sunlight shine brilliantly. The names of the various species suggest their plumage: blue wren, turquoise wren, purple-backed wren, lilac-crowned wren, red-backed wren. In one of our study sites south of Brisbane, we became especially acquainted with the variegated wren, a delightful splashing of blue, red, black, and white that often came popping out of the bushes only a few feet from us.

From the sublime to the ridiculous—the "laughing" kookaburra, the most famous of Australian birds [colorplate 14]. But in fact it is not that much of a transition. Not only is the kookaburra a much more admirable bird than its vocalizations suggest, but it, too, lives in groups containing helpers. Curiously, it was an American, Veronica Parry, who first studied the kookaburra's social system critically. She found that many pairs were assisted by from one to five individuals, of either sex.

Each group occupies territory that is defended by "laughing" duets, trios, quartets, or whatever. One display at territorial borders is called a "trapeze display," since the birds take turns flying back and forth between two fixed points, timed so that two of them pass in midair. In the meantime, a group on a neighboring territory may be chorusing and trapezing similarly. In general, larger groups are able to maintain a larger territory because of the greater intensity of their displays. Helpers provide up to 60 percent of the food for the nestlings. Again, it may be more advantageous for a yearling to help defend a territory he or she may inherit one day than to "go it alone."

The "song" of a kookaburra must be heard to be believed. It is usually performed with one or more other individuals, one beginning with a chuckle followed by a series of "hoo-hoos." Soon others join in with hoo-hoos and ha-has in marvelous disharmony until the forest quakes with "laughter." Dawn in forested parts of Australia—even in city suburbs—is not complete without a chorus of kookaburras. According to one aboriginal legend, the dawn chorus is a signal for the sky people to light the great fire that will warm the earth by day.

Many a time we have been wakened in the bush by the too-early calls of the kookaburra; but it is hard to bear a grudge against so marvelous a bird. In some of the national parks, kookaburras have become quite tame. On more than one occasion we have had these handsome birds perch on the edge of our picnic table and follow us with their eyes while we ate, and even help themselves to a bit of sausage when our attention was diverted elsewhere.

The kookaburra did not originally occur in Tasmania or Western Australia, but it was introduced there. Although this berserk kingfisher lives on insects, lizards, and snakes and is rightfully considered beneficial, it does usurp tree holes from other species and also sometimes feeds on nestlings of other birds, so its introduction to new areas has to some extent upset the balance of nature there. Northern Australia is the home of the beautiful blue-winged kookaburra, a slightly less frenetic species that also lives in small groups containing helpers.

The question is sometimes asked why Australia has so many birds that have helpers at the nest, individuals that sacrifice reproduction (at least for a time) to assist in rearing brothers and sisters or sometimes nonrelatives. We have mentioned only a few; there are also babblers, thornbills, magpies, and still others. Undoubtedly, group feeding often enhances survival of the offspring, and group defense assures a larger and better feeding territory. This may be especially important in the variable climate of Australia, where it may be critical to take advantage of benign conditions, when the next year may bring a drought or a cyclone. Prolonged drought or extreme heat waves may cause birds to cease breeding or at the very least to lay fewer eggs. There are records of widespread death of birds under these conditions. When favorable conditions return, birds may respond by increasing their clutch size and having several generations, one after another.

Whereas most Northern Hemisphere birds enter breeding condition as a response to increasing day length, there is evidence that many Australian birds are able to become reproductive rather quickly after favorable rains have occurred. Another adaptation we have mentioned earlier: nomadism. That is, birds such as budgerigars, many other parrots, and in fact a considerable number of species move about to take advantage of areas where rain has fallen or where seasonal flowers or fruits are available. Even the flightless emu has been recorded as moving hundreds of miles to more favorable habitat.

Spring migrations, so characteristic of American birds, seem a good deal less marked in Australia, doubtless because severe winters occur only in parts of the highlands of the Southeast and Tasmania. Quite a few species do migrate seasonally, at least a short distance; a number of Tasmanian birds move to the mainland during the winter, and a few species move from the southern states to Queensland, Northern Territory, or even to New Guinea in the winter. One migrant we became familiar with is the dollar bird, so called because of the circular white patches on the wings, rather like silver dollars. Dollar birds were often seen perching in the tops of dead trees near Brisbane, now and then undertaking a series of sweeping loops and turns, as if they simply enjoyed flying. Then in March, they suddenly disappeared, evidently to the north.

According to Allen Keast, formerly curator of birds at The Australian Museum in Sydney, only about 8 percent of land-bird species can be considered north-south migrants, while 26 percent are nomadic and 66 percent pretty much sedentary. Much remains to be learned about the movements of birds in Australia. One of the problems is that the rural population of humans is so sparse that recoveries of banded birds are quite infrequent.

These remarks apply only to the land birds. So far we have said nothing about water birds, which are quite a different story. We have ignored the water birds not because they are not interesting, but because most of them belong to widespread, familiar groups: Australia has its share of gulls, terns, ducks, geese, herons, plovers, and the like. Some are common enough, even in cities. It is not unusual to see flocks of ibis in city parks, probing the ground for insects with their long, curved beaks.

For a time we had to walk across a soccer field in Brisbane to catch a bus each morning, and each morning we were "dive-bombed" by a pair of spur-winged plovers that were guarding the fledglings they had reared along the edge of the field. The Australian pelican is a large and handsome representative of its kind. Then, of course, there is the elegant black swan, the state bird of Western Australia, but often seen in many parts of the country [colorplate 15]. As Colin MacInnes says: " . . . that Australia should produce *black* swans is symptomatic of her attitude to birds: only the unusual will do."

Some sea birds are essentially nomadic, like the wandering albatross, while others have well-defined migration routes. The short-tailed shearwater, for example, breeds in burrows in the sand in Victoria and Tasmania, but during the Australian winter flies north to Japan and the Aleutians, then down through the eastern Pacific and back to Australia, even, frequently, to the very same burrow. Dominic Serventy, of the Commonwealth Scientific and Industrial Research Organization, has banded nearly 100,000 shearwaters, and even though fewer than one percent have been recovered, more is known about this species than about most sea birds.

We have not encountered the short-tailed shearwater in our travels, but on Heron Island another species, the wedge-tailed shearwater, was much in evidence. As night falls, these birds return from their fishing trips at sea, making awkward "crash landings" that sometimes seem to stun them for a moment. Then each walks to its burrow in the sand, where its partner is brooding the single egg. Each parent spends a week or two in the burrow while the other spends the days at sea; then they switch roles, until the egg hatches in about seven weeks. While the parents are together at night in the burrow, they "sing" to each other with eerie moanings and screechings, all too familiar to the tourist population of Heron Island. Just before dawn, the "off duty" parent returns to the sea. When the chick hatches, both parents feed it with regurgitated fish until it becomes very fat, when it is left to "slim down" and make its way to the sea on its own.

Both kinds of shearwaters have earned the

During mating season, mutton birds (wedge-tailed shearwaters) spend the days at sea and the nights with their mates in underground nests. This was photographed by flash on Heron Island in the Great Barrier Reef.

name "mutton birds," since the fat young birds have been exploited as food. Evidently, some of the early sealers first discovered their supposedly muttonlike flavor. Harvesting these birds has become a small-scale industry, especially on the islands off Tasmania. The exploits and hardships of the muttonbirders are vividly described by Patsy Adam Smith in her book *Moonbird People* (moonbirds because of a legend that these strange birds were left by the moon when it was lifted from the Pacific). The birds are plucked for their down, which fills many Australian sleeping bags; the oil from their innards is used in suntan lotion; while the birds themselves are sold on the market either fresh, frozen, or salted. During some years half a million mutton birds are harvested, yet the total population is so large that the species still thrives. Perhaps their main threat is not from the muttonbirders but from possible oil spills from offshore wells being built not far from their breeding grounds.

Recently the Federal Department of Aboriginal Affairs has purchased Trefoil Island, off the northwestern tip of Tasmania, as a preserve. The half-caste descendants of the original Tasmanian aborigines have formed a cooperative for harvesting muttonbirds on the island, which harbors the largest commercial rookery. They expect to harvest some 100,000 birds a year. Outside the muttonbird season, a resident ranger will protect the island, which is otherwise uninhabited.

We wish there were space to tell of some of the other birds that have intrigued us. On our trip to the East Alligator Rivers in the Northern Territory, we saw water holes teeming with countless thousands of birds, including brolgas (the Australian equivalent of the whooping crane) and an occasional jabiru, a stately black-and-white, red-legged stork. Above all, magpie geese crowded the water holes by the thousands: boldly marked black-and-white geese with a caplike knob on top of their heads. Once these geese occurred widely in Australia, but their appetite for grain crops resulted

Brolgas are cranes not unlike the North American whooping crane, and their courtship displays are equally impressive.
(John Cancalosi)

in their being banished to the Far North. Much of their present range is now included in Kakadu National Park, where presumably they will continue to thrive without further conflict with man.

On a spring hike near Brisbane we found ourselves surrounded by spotted pardalotes, tiny, almost tailless birds of friendly disposition. Deep in the Outback we puzzled over the whereabouts of crested bellbirds, remarkable ventriloquists whose Morse-code-like song seems to come from where the bird isn't. We have watched the fairy penguins waddle ashore just after dark on Phillip Island, Victoria—unmindful of the floodlights and hundreds

The jabiru is the native stork of Australia, a striking and stately bird.
(John Cancalosi)

The wedge-tailed eagle is Australia's largest raptor, bearing a strong resemblance to the golden eagle of North America. (Australian Information Service)

of tourists lured to the popular "penguin parade."

We have not even mentioned the majestic wedge-tailed eagle, a much persecuted bird that we nevertheless saw in some abundance enroute from Alice Springs to Ayers Rock in the Center. This is one of the largest of the world's eagles, colored much like our golden eagle but having a characteristically shaped tail. The white-breasted sea eagle is also a not uncommon sight along the coast—such an elegant aeronaut that it is difficult to remember that he is a predator and a scavenger (it is evidently this bird that occasioned the remark we have quoted that Australia's eagles are white). Kites, rather slender, hawklike carrion feeders, abound in many areas, taking the place filled by vultures in North America. By night, there is the boobook owl and the tawny frogmouth. . . .

But we must stop; it is easy to become carried away on the subject of birds. On our several trips to Australia we have seen only a fraction of the species occurring there—but enough to enrich our days immeasurably.

6

Reptiles and Amphibians

"This fantastic land
of monstrosities"

Visitors are often shocked to hear that the majority of Australia's snakes are poisonous and that crocodiles pose a threat in tropical waters. Crocodiles did once abound, and were huge and formidable, and snakes were often a menace to early settlers, for it is true that many species are poisonous. But the fact is that one can spend a good deal of time in the bush without encountering a poisonous snake, or in coastal waters without seeing a crocodile.

Lizards are another matter: they are everywhere, and although they are sometimes frightening in appearance, they are never poisonous. The scampering of small ones over our front doorstep was always a welcome sight as we came in and out, and the bearded dragon which rustled through the leaves in our backyard was (almost) a family pet.

Although there are more than five hundred kinds of reptiles in Australia, many occur only in limited areas and are known chiefly to specialists. There are two kinds of crocodiles, about twenty kinds of turtles (several of them wide-ranging sea turtles), something over a hundred different kinds of land snakes, and about thirty kinds of sea snakes (most of them ranging through neighboring tropical seas). The balance consists of lizards, all the way from tiny geckos to giant goannas up to eight feet long. In addition to the reptiles, there are over a hundred species of frogs. These amphibians we shall defer to a later section of this chapter.

Reptiles made up an important element in the diet of the aborigines, and to a limited extent they still do. Among the Bindibu and other tribes of the deserts west of Alice Springs, lizards were consumed in quantities, as kangaroos and other mammals were often in short supply. The natives were adept at digging lizards from their burrows, then seizing them and dashing their heads on rocks. At other times they touched their firesticks to clumps of spinifex grass and caught the lizards as they ran out—a method we also used when collecting lizards with an expedition from the South Australian Museum in 1972. An aborigine in our party relished lizards, and roasted them lightly over the coals of a fire, tore them open, and devoured the flesh within the scaly skin—as his people had been doing for centuries.

Aborigines living in wetter parts of the continent made much use of turtles and snakes as food, and in the North sea turtles and crocodiles provided an especially bountiful feast. Early Europeans also hunted crocodiles extensively, not only for food but for their skins, which were used for making shoes and handbags and were worth the equivalent of from ten to twenty-five dollars apiece. Many tales have been told of crocodile hunters, a tough lot that spent the nights stalking "crocs" by boat and the days skinning them—enduring heat, storms, mosquitoes, and the threat of the crocodiles themselves.

Douglas Lockwood, who for many years covered northern Australia for the *Melbourne Herald*, tells of a hunter named Harry Blumantels whose dog was consumed by a crocodile "mid-bark in one bite." Blumantels himself once started to retrieve a crocodile he had shot only to find it was far from dead. Having left his rifle behind, he picked up a stick and jabbed it down its throat, only to have it bitten off "like a piece of matchwood." But he escaped to tell the tale.

Crocodiles still make news. A short while before we wrote this, newspapers reported the finding of the torso of an aboriginal woman in a Northern Territory billabong. The woman—with the fascinating name of Bukurra Number One Munyarryun—had been missing on a fishing trip, and a search was on for a fifteen-foot crocodile that was believed to be the culprit.

Crocodiles formerly inhabited many of the estuaries of northern Australia, and some reached prodigious size, occasionally up to twenty-five feet in length. Nowadays they are not nearly so abundant and rarely reach anything like that size. Indeed, there may be no more than about five thousand "crocs" left, and these are widely scattered, scarcely enough to maintain a stable population. In 1972 the government placed a ban on the killing of crocodiles—not a moment too soon. The United States imposed a ban on the killing of alligators when an estimated 450,000 remained!

In an effort to learn more about this possibly vanishing species, a group from the Department of Environmental Physics of the University of Sydney has launched a program of intensive observation, trapping, and tracking by the use of radio telemetry—no mean task in the wild, mostly uninhabited areas where "crocs" still occur. Young crocodiles, they found, live mainly on crabs and shrimps, but larger ones feed on fish, turtles, snakes, wallabies, other crocodiles, and even young cattle and buffalo when they can get them. Flying foxes appear to be a favorite food, and now and then crocodiles gather in mangroves beneath colonies of these large bats. Radio tracking has been accomplished using some of the techniques developed in the space program. Solar-powered transmitters are fastened to the head

The saltwater crocodile is a formidable animal, now surviving only in remote estuaries in the North. (Australian Information Service)

just behind the eyes, and signals are detected from fixed receiving stations or from light aircraft, which can detect the signals up to 120 miles away. Traps are also equipped with transmitters that are activated when they are sprung.

Why are these ugly and dangerous creatures worth so much effort? For one thing, there is pressure to harvest them commercially and thus hope that populations can be restored at least partially for this reason. More important, perhaps, is the fact that crocodiles are among the most ancient creatures on earth. The fossil record suggests that they have changed little in more than a hundred million years and that they were once contemporaries of their relatives the dinosaurs. They may teach us something about long-term survival, for they made it and the dinosaurs did not.

We have been talking about the estuarian or saltwater crocodile. There is a second species, which inhabits freshwater ponds and rivers and is often called Johnstone's crocodile, after a police inspector who discovered it slightly over a century ago. This is a smaller species, growing "only up to eight or nine feet," as the books put it, and there are no records of this species attacking man. Although the skins of freshwater crocodiles are less valuable than those of the saltwater species, they are often shot simply in the belief that "every croc is a bad croc." Both species are now protected by law, but it is impossible to patrol the wild country where they occur, so doubtless a good many are still being killed.

As for snakes (to dispense with the more unpopular creatures first!), about two-thirds of the species belong to a group called the front-fanged snakes, which includes the Indian cobra as well as the coral snakes of North America. Most of them are, however, too small to harm anything larger than a rat, and even some of the larger ones are relatively shy and retiring. But some are truly dangerous. The tiger snake occurs in many parts of southern Australia and sometimes reaches a length of six feet. This snake is especially common on islands of Bass Strait and is often a threat to the muttonbirders of those islands. Tiger snakes are said to contain enough venom at one milking to kill 118 sheep; the venom is rated as three and a half times more potent than that of the cobra.

The so-called death adder is only slightly less poisonous. This snake has a thick body that tapers off rapidly to a spinelike, pale-colored tip of the tail. This is kept in constant motion as the snake lies among the leaves, attracting curious birds and lizards to what appears to be a worm; when they are close enough, the snake strikes, paralyzes them, and swallows them whole in the usual manner of snakes. Before the development of antivenins, the human death rate from both of these snakes was about 50 percent.

The taipan of northern Australia is one of the largest poisonous snakes, sometimes reaching a length of ten feet. The fangs of larger individuals measure half an inch in length, and the amount of venom injected is considerable. But having said all this, we should mention that we ourselves have never encountered any of these in spite of a good deal of tramping about in the bush. We have encountered brown snakes (which are regarded as poisonous but not usually fatally so), but in every case they made haste to disappear in the bushes before we could see much of them. And there are no rattlesnakes or anything closely related to them in Australia.

The largest Australian snakes are pythons, which kill their prey by constriction. The rock python of northern Queensland is said to reach a length of twenty-five feet. The carpet python is widespread in eastern Australia, a beautiful and completely harmless snake that is sometimes killed in the belief that it is poisonous. On one of our first days in Brisbane, we found a carpet python about nine feet long basking near a garbage dump, where it had doubtless had a meal of local rats. (What were we doing in a garbage dump? It's one of the best places to find wildlife in an urban area!)

Sea snakes are a fascinating group, little known to most Americans since none occur in the Atlantic or Caribbean. Australian waters are among the richest in the world for sea snakes, elegant and wonderfully adapted creatures with flattened, paddle-shaped tails as well as nostrils that can be closed upon submergence. Although land and fresh water snakes cannot survive in the sea because of its salt content, sea snakes have a gland beneath their tongue that discharges the excess brine back into the ocean. In their search for small fish, these snakes often dive deeply and may remain underwater for an hour or two. They are able to avoid the "bends" upon coming to the surface because nitrogen escapes from their blood through their skin and directly into the sea, rather than forming bubbles in the blood as it does in animals (such as ourselves) that lack this ability.

Some sea snakes are beautifully colored, especially the yellow-bellied one that often turns up on surfing beaches along the east coast. All sea snakes produce venom, which they use to paralyze their prey before it is swallowed, and bites are occasionally fatal to fishermen who find them in their nets. We once encountered several while we were snorkeling, but were unconcerned—because at that point we did not realize they were poisonous!

Australia has no turtles or tortoises that are well adapted for life on land, and only a few river and pond turtles. The most unusual are the side-necked turtles, which surprise one with their remarkably long necks, which are not withdrawn but rather wrapped around the body when they are inactive or alarmed. Side-necked turtles also occur in South America; no fossils are known outside of the Southern Hemisphere. Of all of Australia's reptiles, the fifteen or so species of side-necked turtles are the only ones believed to belong to a

Side-necked turtles cannot withdraw their long necks, but wrap them around their sides between the upper and lower carapace. *(John Cancalosi)*

group that had its origin in Gondwanaland, or to have rafted between the continents when they were much closer together than they are now. All the remaining reptiles belong to groups that probably entered Australia from the north well after the breakup of Gondwanaland, although some of these groups have diversified greatly in the unique Australian environment.

Sea turtles lay their eggs on beaches of the north coast and offshore islands, but these are much the same kinds that occur in warm seas elsewhere—green turtles, loggerheads, and hawksbills. Like sea turtles elsewhere, they often undertake long migrations. Loggerheads marked on Heron Island, off the central Queensland coast, were found over a thousand miles away. They may well go farther, though always returning to the beaches where they traditionally breed.

Australia's most unusual turtle is the pitted-shelled turtle, one that we never found because it is a rare inhabitant of rivers of northern Australia and southern New Guinea. This is a streamlined turtle with a tubular nose and with flippers similar to those of sea turtles. Unlike other turtles it has no horny scales. The only relatives of this species are known from fossils dating from many millions of years ago. Evidently it is the sole survivor of an ancient lineage.

Not surprisingly on a continent that is generally rather arid, it is the lizards that are most abundant and diverse. Most of these belong to groups well known to naturalists elsewhere: geckos and skinks, in particular. One group, the snake-lizards, is unique to Australia and New Guinea, perhaps having evolved within Australia from geckos, which are closely related. These snake-lizards are not often noticed, as they are burrowers or nocturnal foragers, and to the uninitiated they appear to be nothing more than small snakes. Like snakes, their eyes are lidless, but they have an external ear opening, which snakes do not. Their legs are so small as to be scarcely noticeable, mere flaps containing vestiges of the leg bones. It is said that they mimic snakes in their behavior, flattening their necks and striking at threatening objects, but usually striking past their foe, with their mouths closed. Like other lizards, the snake-lizards are able to shed their tails when necessary to escape from an enemy, a feat beyond the capacity of snakes.

Monitors are by far the largest lizards occurring in Australia, and three-fourths of the world's species are found there. Usually they are called "goannas," apparently a corruption of the word iguana, which properly applies to an unrelated group of tropical American lizards. The famous "Komodo dragon" of Indonesia is the world's largest lizard, reaching a length of over ten feet. An Australian species, appropriately called *Varanus giganteus*, is nearly as large, however, with specimens over eight feet in length having been recorded. But both of these are pygmies compared to a fossil monitor from fairly recent strata in Australia: a monster measuring twenty-three feet in length.

Monitors are common in many parts of Australia, usually measuring between three and five feet in length and thus large enough to frighten a person who comes upon them unexpectedly—especially since they hiss loudly and lash their tails vigorously. We were so jolted on several occasions as we were passing by with our eyes on the horizon and not on the nearby river red gum and its resident

The prominent fringe beneath the head of this lizard gives it its popular name: bearded dragon. (John Cancalosi)

goanna. These animals are not poisonous but do have sharp teeth, and since many of them feed on carrion, a bite is likely to become infected. We have often seen them in parks and picnic areas, where they frequently add garbage to their usual diet of insects and small mammals, lizards, and nestling birds. Like snakes, they usually swallow their prey whole, and like snakes they have a forked tongue that is constantly flicked in and out, tasting the air.

The sand goanna frequently attacks snakes, even poisonous species, but its hide is apparently tough enough that the snake cannot usually penetrate it. The naturalist David Fleay tells of a sand goanna that devoured a tiger snake "with enormous enthusiasm," only to disgorge the still living snake suddenly and then maul it further and reswallow it—the whole process taking several hours. Although the sand goanna lives mainly on the ground, the common lace monitor is a tree dweller, and the water goanna has taken to a life in streams and has developed a flattened tail and valved nostrils suggesting those of sea snakes.

Some smaller but even more formidable-looking reptiles belong to a group called the dragon lizards, which occur in the Old World generally, but are especially diverse in Australia. The "bearded dragon" is reasonably common (we had one living in our backyard in suburban Brisbane), and noteworthy for the spiny projections or "beard" beneath its chin. The frilled lizard of Northern Australia is a particularly spectacular beast, having as it does a broad, extensible frill behind its head, which greatly increases its apparent size.

Both of these lizards are able to put on quite

Gould's sand monitor is a giant among lizards, attaining a length of 4 or 5 feet.
(Raymond H. Besserdin)

a show if approached by a predator (or prodded with a stick). They raise their heads and open their mouths wide, exposing a brightly colored throat, at the same time extending their spines or frills fully. But all of this is bluff. Like most lizards, these are good creatures to have around, living as they do on insects, rodents, and the like. We were amused by a sign we saw along a highway in a bushfire-ridden area near Darwin: "We like our lizards frilled, not grilled." The frilled lizard is said to be able to run in a semierect posture, on its hind legs only, and to be able to outdistance a human runner

If this aggressive display of a frilled lizard proves ineffective in frightening a predator, the animal is able to scuttle away quickly by running upright on its hind legs. *(Australian Information Service)*

over a short distance. Some persons claim to have seen these lizards take to the air, gliding on their expanded frills.

The most unusual of the dragon lizards is the thorny devil, a small, desert-loving species in which the entire body is covered with thick, tapered spines, including one large one on the head that is reminiscent of the horn of a rhinoceros. One thinks immediately of the so-called "horned toads" of American deserts, which have a rather different body shape and are not closely related. Thorny devils feed only on ants and station themselves on trails of ants, eating literally thousands at one "sitting."

Naturalist C. C. Sporn kept a thorny devil as a pet for several years and found that she ate ants at a rate of twenty to thirty a minute. Florence, as he called her, obligingly laid several batches of eggs in captivity, and some of the offspring were reared successfully. But in general, unless one is able to provide a good environment and a constant supply of ants, thorny devils die within a few weeks in captivity. Unfortunately, they have been long actively sought as pets and are now rare in most places. These bizarre animals have been given the scientific name *Moloch horridus*, but they are in fact harmless and gentle creatures that should be left to live out their lives in the deserts to which they are so well adapted.

Geckos are relatively small, soft-skinned, mainly nocturnal lizards that are common in the tropics throughout the world. Most of them have expanded,

The thorny devil, Moloch horridus, *is actually a small, timid lizard, despite its frightening appearance (and name). (Australian Information Service)*

adhesive fingertips, enabling them to cling to tree trunks, walls, and even to the ceilings of buildings [colorplate 16]. They are often quite musical, producing a variety of chirps and clicks that probably play a role in courtship. Some make a sound rather like "geck-o," hence the name. On our first night in Darwin we wondered what birds had been chirping around our motel in the night. In the morning we found that the walls were covered with geckos. The songs of birds seem less remarkable when one considers that their distant relatives, the geckos, can also produce pleasing, though softer and less varied, notes.

The largest Australian gecko is also one of the most unusual. The leaf-tailed gecko sometimes reaches a length of twelve inches, and has clawed toes that enable it to cling tightly to the trunks of trees during the day. In color it is mottled brown and green, exactly like a lichen-covered tree trunk, and because of its fringed sides and broad, leaflike tail, it does not even cast a shadow. At night it roams about and feeds voraciously on beetles and other insects. This is a lizard of upland forests, and we were lucky enough to see and photograph one during a night hike in the McPherson Ranges of southern Queensland.

Finally, a word about the group that includes the majority of lizards in Australia as well as in most parts of the world, the skinks. There are well over a hundred Australian species, some of the small ones ("penny lizards") often so abundant that the forest floor seems alive with them. Most are too small to provide important food for the aborigines, but kookaburras and some of the larger reptiles would be hard pressed for food without them.

Skinks are rather "ordinary" lizards to nonspecialists, but one kind that invariably attracts attention is the shingle-back, or bobtail, also called the sleepy lizard because of its sluggish behavior. Often one sees pairs, one behind the other, crossing the highway in a most leisurely manner, tempting motorists to contribute to their extinction. These are robust lizards, about a foot in length, with a short, blunt tail and a body covered with large, shinglelike scales. When disturbed, they open wide a pink mouth and stick out a blue tongue—enough to frighten anyone not aware that they are relatively defenseless and feed mainly on fallen fruit, fungi, and carrion.

Lizards of many kinds abound in the dry interior of Australia. In fact, the richest lizard fauna in the world occurs here. Eric Pianka, an American ecologist who has studied desert faunas on many continents, recorded thirty to forty species of lizards from several restricted, sandy areas in the Australian deserts. By contrast, similar places in the Kalahari Desert in southern Africa support only eleven to thirteen species, those in North American deserts only five to ten. Part of the explanation seems to lie in the fact that many Australian lizards have quite strict habitat requirements, such that seemingly minor changes in climate and vegetation in the past have caused populations to fragment. Once different species have evolved during such fragmentation, their refined adaptations have permitted them to live together when and where barriers were absent.

How do lizards survive the extremes of temperature and the long periods of drought often experienced in the deserts? Interestingly, during hot weather the body temperature of lizards is often a good deal cooler than that of the environment (which might otherwise kill them). Some are nocturnal or come out of their holes only in the early morning and late afternoon. Some are able to change color, being darker when it is cool, thus absorbing more solar radiation, and paler when it is hot, thus reflecting more. On cool mornings, many lizards bask in the sun until their body temperature is raised to the point that they can pursue their prey effectively.

Harold Heatwole, a professor of zoology at the University of New England in Armidale, New South Wales, has made an intensive study of a lizard known as the desert dragon. In the morning, desert dragons perch on or near the ground with their backs to the sun, absorbing heat from the sun and from the ground as it is warmed by the sun. As the day becomes hotter, they climb to progressively higher perches in the bushes, away from the scorching heat of the soil. Here they remain in a vertical position, presenting as little of their body to the sun as possible. In the evening they descend again and flatten out on the ground, taking up latent heat from the soil. It is wrong to think of lizards as "cold-blooded," for although they have little if any ability to regulate their body temperature internally, they employ a variety of stratagems that enable them to survive and function at diverse temperatures.

Dehydration is less serious for reptiles than for many animals, since their scaly skin is not highly permeable to evaporation. Many desert lizards obtain enough water from their food so that they do not need to drink, and they are able to utilize water resulting from normal body processes. In many cases the skin is hygroscopic, taking up moisture from soil wet with dew or damp from a rain. The scales of the thorny devil are so arranged that water absorbed onto the body surface is canalized through the scales to the corners of the mouth, where it can be swallowed. When moisture is in short supply, many lizards survive by essentially abandoning regulation of the composition of their body fluids—withstanding concentrations of sodium in their blood that would be lethal to man. With the first rain, however, the normal sodium concentration is quickly restored. Lizards have been seen darting wildly about during a shower, leaping into the air and swallowing raindrops as if they were catching insects.

Since the eggs of lizards are particularly prone to dessication, it is not surprising that egg-laying periods often follow periods of rainfall. There is no doubt that prolonged drought does cause a marked decline in lizard populations (among other things, they find little food, since insects are also scarce). It has been found that certain dragon lizards have two types of individuals, some that grow rapidly but cannot survive extreme drought, others that grow much more slowly but are more drought-resistant. Thus a prolonged dry period may kill a large portion of the population, but there will be enough slowgrowers to lay eggs and replenish the desert quickly once the rains return.

It is not unusual that Australian lizards have diverse adaptations for desert living—lizards do in many parts of the world. It is also not surprising to learn that there are no salamanders in such a generally dry continent, since salamanders are delicate, water-loving creatures. What is surprising is that there are about 155 species of frogs, some of them living in desert or semidesert conditions. Being amphibians, like salamanders, frogs have nonscaly skin and generally depend upon water for egg-laying and for the development of the tadpole stage. Actually, the majority of Australian frogs do occur in the more humid areas, including the well known (but seldom seen) corroboree frog, an inhabitant of the higher mountains of the Southeast. This is a remarkably brilliant frog, broadly striped and marbled with black and yellow, suggesting the body paintings of aborigines preparing for a tribal dance or "corroboree." The corroboree frog was first discovered as late as 1953, and by an American, John Moore, who was on a Fulbright fellowship in Australia.

The crucifix frog of the Murray River system may even surpass the corroboree frog in color, being yellow with a cross of red and black spots on its back. While the corroboree frog breeds in alpine bogs, the crucifix frog occurs in much drier country and burrows deeply when no water is available. One of the largest native frogs, called the green tree frog, also occurs well into the Interior, where it often croaks from wells and cisterns [colorplate, 17]. We once camped in a seldom-used public campground near the little town of Mendooran, which unexpectedly was provided with flush toilets. The bowls had become the home of green tree frogs, and we wondered how they would react to flushing. In fact, they simply swam about a bit and went back up under the rim, none the worse for the experience. Green tree frogs are said to make good (if rather unresponsive) pets, and sometimes live up to sixteen years in captivity.

The giant tree frog of the northeastern rain forests is reported to be fully five inches long and to be emerald green, with a white "mustache" and crimson legs. The mating call is said to resemble the barking of an angry dog and the distress call to resemble that of a cat. The so-called "bullfrogs" of Australia occur in the Southeast and are not at all related to North American bullfrogs. In the spring they migrate in great numbers to the creeks to breed, moving rather like automatons through the bush. Michael Tyler, Australia's leading frog enthusiast, once watched hundreds of them descending a steep slope: "They hopped along, falling, performing unintentional somersaults and often rolling for several meters down precipitous sections of the rock faces. . . . Within a matter of hours they had all congregated in the creek and were calling vociferously."

The American bullfrogs, and most of our common kinds of frogs, belong to the genus *Rana*. Only one species of *Rana* occurs in Australia, and only on Cape York, where it apparently represents a recent entry (through New Guinea) from a Northern Hemisphere stock. There is some argument as to whether the remainder of the frog fauna entered from the north many years ago or whether it evolved from an ancient Gondwanaland fauna. Considering the fact that most Australian frogs seem to have their closest relatives in South America, it seems probable that their ancestors occurred on a common land mass or were able to move from one to the other freely.

Whatever the case, Australian frogs have been isolated for so long that they have had time to evolve unusual adaptations. A species called Nicholl's toadlet has been found inside the nests of bulldog ants, taking advantage of the cool, humid galleries, while another often shares burrows with scorpions. The turtle frog is apparently a specialist on termites and remains in the vicinity of termite nests, thriving in the humidity there and gorging itself periodically. This is a globular frog with a small head and short, stubby legs, resembling a small turtle without a shell.

But the most striking adaptations have to do with accommodating the young when water is scarce and predators abundant. The so-called "marsupial frog" of the mountains of the Southeast actually has pouches—two pouches, to be exact, and in the male rather than the female! These frogs spawn in the water, but the newly hatched tadpoles climb onto the back of the male and work their way into pouches on his groin, rather like "hip pockets." As the tadpoles grow, the pouches swell, until finally they become so large that the male's internal organs are too compressed for him to feed. This remarkable frog, by the way, was described by Arthur Loverage, a Harvard herpetologist, who called it *Assa darlingtoni*, after its discoverer, Philip J. Darlington, Jr., also of Harvard. The Harvard Expedition of 1931–32 visited many remote parts of Australia and added a great deal to knowledge of the fauna.*

There is said to be a frog in Queensland in which the female swallows her eggs shortly after they are fertilized. The tadpoles develop in her stomach, apparently absorbing food through their skin and somehow resisting being digested by their mother. Up to fifteen tadpoles are able to develop in one female, making her rather bloated until they finally emerge from her mouth as tiny, fully formed froglets. A curious gastric pregnancy!

Desert frogs are as readily subject to dehydration through their skins as are other frogs. In fact any frog will die of dehydration within a few hours if exposed to 60 percent relative humidity at a temperature of seventy degrees. But desert species spend much of their lives in burrows, sometimes as much as six feet deep, where they live in a quiescent state and actually absorb moisture from the soil; some can even tolerate a high concentration of salt in the soil. The so-called water-holding frog of the Center makes a cocoonlike chamber, with an impervious lining, in which it spends long periods with its bladder filled with water from the most recent rains.

These frogs used to be attractive to the aborigines for their water. The aborigines would stamp on the ground in dry lagoons (so the reports go), whereupon the frogs would croak and could be dug

*This expedition was under the direction of Dr. William Morton Wheeler, whose story we told in our book *William Morton Wheeler, Biologist* (1970). Dr. Darlington was a young man when he participated in the expedition; he became an ardent australophile and later published important articles on Australian beetles as well as a book on the distribution of animals in the Southern Hemisphere. He is a good friend and did a great deal to stimulate our interest in natural history "down under."

out and squeezed, producing water that tasted perfectly fresh and pure. It must have taken quite a number of these small frogs to satisfy a thirsty person, though, especially if he developed an even greater thirst while digging them out!

Some desert frogs survive many months, even years, living quite deep in the soil. At some point rain will fall, and when it does they quickly take advantage of it—mating with few preliminaries and laying their eggs in temporary pools. Here the eggs and tadpoles develop rapidly, even though the water may become warm and evaporation concentrate the minerals. In some cases the tadpoles are able to develop in the burrows themselves when these become filled with water. Unfortunately, few people have studied these obscure creatures, which seem to have no influence on man's economy, but perhaps, in the increasingly decimated environment we are creating, they may teach us something about survival.

The mating calls of frogs are as fascinating in Australia as elsewhere. There is a species called the moaning frog, another called the banjo frog, others the trilling frog, the humming frog, the baw-baw frog, the meeowing frog, and so forth. The crucifix frog is said to produce a series of owllike "whoo-whoos," while one called the marbled frog has a high-pitched whistle. All of this we glean from perusal of Harold Cogger's excellent book *Reptiles and Amphibians of Australia*. We often enjoyed the calls of frogs on our various trips, but confess to have had little success in identifying them.

There is only one kind of true toad in Australia, and that is not a native. It is the giant toad, or more often called the cane toad, because it was introduced from Hawaii in 1935 in an effort to control grubs in sugar-cane fields. Cane growers were at first enthusiastic about the toads, which have a tremendous appetite and sometimes reach a length of nearly ten inches. They reproduce at a phenomenal rate, breeding in ponds and ditches twice a year and laying ten to twenty thousand eggs at a time. Sometimes they are incredibly abundant, their flattened bodies speckling the highways, and as many as one per square yard on lawns and in gardens.

Soon after their introduction it became apparent that the toads preferred other habitats to the cane fields, which are often dry and without much ground cover, and which are commonly burned prior to harvest. The toad has now spread over much of eastern Queensland and south into New South Wales. It is the only species of frog or toad that will feed on nonmoving objects, and at times it will consume plant tissue or even gather at dishes where dogs or cats are being fed. While most of its diet consists of insects, it will take anything it can catch. A survey of the prey taken by 114 toads showed that their diet included 314 pests, but 287 useful scavengers and 710 beneficial predators. Toads will now and then eat honeybees, and they have developed an appetite for some of the insects that have been introduced for biological control of pests. Worse, the toads themselves are poisonous if eaten, and many dogs and cats have been made ill or even killed from eating toads. They also poison water troughs from which livestock drink.

There has been a spin-off, however, which many would consider fortunate: many of the larger snakes feed on frogs and toads, and when they swallow a cane toad they, too, are poisoned. It is perhaps partly for this reason that poisonous snakes are no longer commonly encountered along the northeastern coast of Australia. Another desirable development has been the recent attempt to use their skins for leather, in a sense replacing the hides of the vanishing crocodiles with those of a flourishing, pest species. Also, cane toads have proved useful in teaching and research in schools and universities. In fact, Australia harvests 100,000 toads a year for that purpose, some being exported to France and New Zealand. In the Queensland city of Ingham, a service club sold enough toads to partially subsidize a home for the elderly—locally sometimes called "Toad Hall" (hardly what Kenneth Grahame had in mind in *The Wind in the Willows*).

By and large, the upsetting of natural balances caused by the introduction of the toad has been unfortunate. The story has a familiar ring—rabbits, foxes, feral cats; starlings and house sparrows; lantana, blackberry, prickly pear cacti. Any tampering with the native flora or fauna, either introductions or extinctions, is likely to have unpredictable and undesirable results. Clearing of the forests, heavy grazing, and the resulting changes in soil conditions, are likely to have profound effects on the reptiles and amphibians of Australia, and in the long run extinctions are likely to be more important than the introduction of the toad. But no one will shed a tear if the water-holding frog becomes extinct. Or will they?

Colorplates

OVERLEAF:
1 / Ayers Rock at sunset. This single great chunk of sandstone rises 1,100 feet above the desert floor and is about 6 miles in circumference. Once sacred to the aborigines, "The Rock" is now a major tourist attraction.

2 / Many species of Eucalyptus *have narrow leaves and white flowers that are rich in nectar, often attracting great numbers of bees and other insects. Other eucalypts, which are peculiarly Australian, have blossoms ranging from light yellow in some species to brilliant red in others.*

3 / Two ghost gums form an elegant foreground for one of the purple hills of Australia's "red heart," as the Center is often called.

4 / Most Australian acacias, often called "wattles," lack spines and have great masses of flowers during late winter and early spring.

5 / Here are three characteristic plants of Australia. In the foreground are cycads, primitive seed plants with foliage somewhat resembling palms; the peculiar "grass trees" are directly behind them; and the nearly ubiquitous eucalypts are in the rear.

6 / Kangaroo paws are one of the many wildflowers for which Western Australia is famous.

7 / A tropical rain forest in Mossman Gorge, near Cairns, Queensland. Australia is one of the few places in the world where tropical rain forests blend into subtropical and eventually into temperate or subantarctic rain forests of completely different composition.
(Australian Information Service)

8 / Gliders are the marsupial equivalents of flying squirrels. Mainly nocturnal, they are rarely seen unless one makes special efforts.
(Australian Information Service)

9 / The koala is popularly considered to be among the most endearing and "cuddly" of animals. Sluggish in behavior, with piglike voices, koalas can be seen in various Australian faunal parks as well as in zoos.

10 / A female gray kangaroo and a yearling graze in the late afternoon sun. Almost the symbol of Australia (along with the koala and emu), the kangaroo is the only large animal anywhere that employs a hopping gait.
(Raymond H. Besserdin)

11 / Emus—the Australian equivalent of ostriches and second only to those birds in size—sometimes become quite tame in parks, where their formidable beaks make them unwelcome at picnics.
(Australian Information Service)

12 / The galah is one of the most beautiful as well as most abundant of the larger parrots of Australia. It is also one of the noisiest.
(Australian Information Service)

FACING PAGE:
13 / Rainbow lorikeets often abound in the trees of eastern Australia, even in the suburbs of the larger cities.
(Australian Information Service)

14 / The "laughing" kookaburra, a famous Australian bird, is a large kingfisher, with an appetite for worms, insects, lizards, and snakes. Its "song" begins with a chuckle followed by a series of "hoo-hoos" and "ha-has."
(Australian Information Service)

15 / "The swans were black, the eagles white"; but, in fact, black swans have white cygnets. The black swan, the state bird of Western Australia, is often seen in many parts of the continent.
(Australian Information Service)

16 / A spiny-tailed gecko poses for a portrait. Note this lizard's broadly expanded fingertips, which are supplied with adhesive disks.
(Raymond H. Besserdin)

17 / The green tree frog is one of the largest and best known of amphibians, often living in cisterns and bathrooms.
(Raymond H. Besserdin)

18 / Glowworms, the larvae of midges, lurk in crevices in rocks and lure prey to sticky threads by means of a light organ near their tail end. On a dark night, the light they produce in a "glowworm city" is considerable.
(Allan Hook)

FACING PAGE:
19 and 20 / A female mountain grasshopper rests on a sidewalk **(top).** *In the dead leaves of a forest floor, it would be beautifully camouflaged. But when this grasshopper is disturbed, an orange collar is extended and the wing covers are lifted to reveal a bold pattern of colors* **(below).**

OVERLEAF:
21 / A view of the Great Barrier Reef, as seen from a helicopter en route to Heron Island. (Allan Hook)

23 / An aboriginal artist at work in the Cave of the Rainbow Serpent at Yuendumu in central Australia. (Photograph by Douglass Baglin, from Douglass Baglin and David E. Moore, People of the Dreamtime, *Walker/Weatherhill, 1970)*

PRECEDING PAGE:
22 / The reef at Heron Island at low tide. Corals and algae of many kinds provide a variety of forms and colors.

OVERLEAF:
24 / Scenes such as this may greet visitors to Kakadu National Park in Northern Territory. These are white ibises.
(Australian Information Service)

7

Insects and Their Relatives

"Millions were to be seen in every direction"

Insects are not usually thought of as part of the "wildlife" of a continent, though at times their impact on the environment may be very great indeed. In Australia about 54,000 species have been recorded to date, and probably at least that many more remain to be discovered. As insects go that is not an unusually large number, but in Australia it is not so much the numbers as the fact that some are so noticeable—difficult for even the casual visitor to ignore. We have visited places in forests of the Northeast where the butterflies were breathtakingly abundant and beautiful. Once, when camping in the Outback, we had a winged walkingstick nine inches long, with a wingspan of nine inches, fly into our light. It turns out that there is still a larger species in Australia, suitably called *Acrophylla titan,* which is fully ten inches long and has pink-spotted wings that together span somewhat more than ten inches: a formidable beast, harmless enough but doubtless consuming a great many leaves before reaching its full size.

But by far the most visible of Australian insects are the flies. It was the flies that most impressed many of the first Europeans to reach Australia. When the Dutch ship *Batavia* was wrecked off the west coast in 1629 (we shall have more to say of this later), one of the lesser problems encountered by the crew and passengers was "such a multitude of flies, which perched on our mouths and crept into our eyes, that they could not be kept off our persons." These were undoubtedly the notorious bush flies, which look rather like small house flies and are in fact closely related to the common house fly. Bush flies do not bite, but they have an inordinate love of the human skin, and even today, in our technological age, there does not seem to be much that one can do about them. Flicking the bush flies off one's face with the hand is often called "the great Australian salute." More of bush flies later!

Despite the abundance of insects in Australia, they are, in many ways, less astonishing, or at least less unusual, than the birds, mammals, and reptiles. All of the major types that occur in North America also occur in Australia, and there are no major groups that cannot be found on other continents. That is, there are grasshoppers and caterpillars consuming foliage, beetles crawling over the ground, mosquitoes hungry for blood, cockroaches in the kitchen, and so forth. To be sure, there are many lesser groups (families and genera) unique to Australia, and the vast majority of species found there are confined to that continent—except for a few that have been introduced, mainly by accident.

Charles Darwin, after his Australian visit on the *Beagle,* commented that the birds and mammals almost seemed to have required a separate creation from those of the rest of the world, but that that was hardly true of the insects. He noted, for example, that the pits of ant lions, so ubiquitous in Australia, hardly differed at all from those in England. And indeed most of the insects he observed differed only in degree from those he had learned as a boy.

Nevertheless, to a naturalist or to a professional entomologist the insects are of great interest. Once they were very much a part of the world of the aborigines, who had names for many of them and often included them in their tribal dances and rituals. One tribal song (which we have on a record and sometimes play on our stereo) salutes the sand wasp, a conspicuous denizen of the deserts of the Interior. It becomes clear, as one listens to the song, that the natives knew that the wasps dig nests in the sand and bring in flies to feed their larvae. Insects primarily, however, served as a source of food for the aborigines.

Held in special esteem were *witjuti,* more commonly known to whites as "witchetty grubs." These large, white grubs were dug from the trunks and roots of certain kinds of trees. Having found a likely hole in a tree, the hunter would insert a hook made from a thorn and draw out the grub without damaging it. Grubs were eaten either raw or roasted, and provided an excellent source of protein.

A good source of carbohydrates was provided by the honeypot ants, which with considerable effort could be dug from nests deep in the ground. These ants store sugars in solution by using some members of the colony as barrels; these individuals are fed honey until their abdomens become essentially spherical. One merely needs to bite off the abdomen, which is rather like a gumdrop with a crusty surface. Although we have never eaten them ourselves (we never had the ambition to dig them out), we hear that they are quite tasty indeed, and must have been, to nomadic hunters and food gatherers, the ultimate delicacy. Honey could also be found in the nests of stingless bees, which are common in many parts of Australia.

For aborigines in parts of eastern Australia, an important dietary supplement during the summer months was provided by bogong moths, which resemble the cutworm moths or "millers" familiar to North Americans. The adult moths emerge in the lowlands in the spring, having fed as caterpillars on weeds and garden plants during the winter. The newly emerged moths fly toward the mountains of the Great Dividing Range, where they settle in great masses in crevices among the rocks. Here they remain dormant during the hot summer months, subsisting on fat stored in their bodies; actually about 60 percent of their dry weight is fat. The aborigines used to make annual migrations to sites where these moths clustered, smoking them out or causing them to fall into a basket by rattling a stick above them. A fire was then built and after a while cleared away. The moths were placed on the hot ground and stirred so as to singe away the wings and scales. They were then pounded into cakes, which were cooked on hot stones to make what might be called a "mothburger." It is said that these were so rich that when first eaten they caused vomiting, but after a few days the natives became used to them and thrived and fattened on them.

Unfortunately, the aborigines no longer make much use of these natural foods, but seem to prefer, or at least use, European-style foods, which they purchase with their earnings or their welfare funds. But bogong moths are still around. When we were living in Canberra in the spring of 1969 we experienced a citywide blackout. It was not an air raid, or a strike by electrical workers, but a deliberate blackout to avoid great swarms of bogong moths that flew to the city lights in such numbers that they clogged air conditioners and caused slippery streets.

To the early white settlers, insects were only a small part of a generally unfriendly environment, one that included drought, sandstorms, unfamiliar vegetation, and unpredictable natives as well as flies and mosquitoes. John William Lewin, however, was an early settler who took a great interest in insects. He came to Sydney in 1800 and soon began to sketch and paint the butterflies he found. Five years later his *Natural History of the Lepidopterous Insects of New South Wales* was published in London. Lewin was a fine artist and is rightly considered the first Australian field naturalist.

A full century elapsed before the first comprehensive treatise appeared: W. W. Froggatt's *Australian Insects.* In the meantime, a great deal of research had been done, much of it published in England or on the Continent. Froggatt, the government entomologist of New South Wales, saw the need of a well illustrated book useful to students, amateurs, and professional entomologists. His book was followed in 1929 by a more comprehensive book, R. J. Tillyard's *The Insects of Australia and New Zealand,* and in 1970 by an even larger tome of 1,029 pages, with thirty authors, *The Insects of Australia.* Australia is now the center of a great deal of entomological research, and we ourselves have been a very small part of it.

Australian biologists invariably become involved in the study of evolution, since the continent is such a museum of "living fossils." The insects are no exception. A good example is provided by peculiar roachlike scorpion flies of the family Meropeidae. We used to collect these occasionally at lanterns set up in the woods of central New York State. They are known from only one other part of the world; in fact, from only two specimens found under a log in the bush in Western Australia. The fossil record, as well as the structure of these strange insects (about which virtually nothing is known), suggests that they are indeed relics from the distant past, perhaps even before Gondwanaland became separated from the northern continental landmass.

Dragonflies are another group of special interest in evolutionary studies. While Australia has no dragonflies as large as some of the giants known from fossils dating from several hundred million years ago, it does have the largest dragonfly living in the world today, one with a wingspan of about eight inches. It belongs to a group (called the Petaluridae), which has only a few representatives scattered about the globe: in Chile, North America, Japan, Australia, and New Zealand—a discontinuous distribution suggesting that these insects must once have been widespread. Their larvae are whitish, grublike creatures, with long, spidery legs. They are said to live in burrows a foot or more deep in bogs, and come out at night to prey on small insects they find on the ground near their burrows—a very different lifestyle from most dragonfly larvae, which live freely in streams and ponds. Perhaps the petalurids survived through the ages because of this unique adaptation. Although we made a brief study of Australia's dragonflies, some of which are very beautiful, we never had the good fortune to encounter one of these giants.

A number of groups of insects have what is usually described as a circumantarctic distribution, that is, they appear to have evolved when Gondwanaland had separated from the northern continents but while the continents-to-be were still clumped around Antarctica. A few years ago we discovered and described a family of small wasps (called the Scolebythidae) which has only three representatives, one in South America, one in Madagascar, and one in Australia. Unfortunately, insects do not fossilize as readily as bony animals, and no insect fossils are known from Antarctica, so we cannot be sure the group really evolved in Gondwanaland.

A better example, perhaps, is provided by small sucking bugs of the family Peloridiidae. (We apologize for using so many scientific names, but a great many kinds of insects having no great importance to man's economy simply have never been given any other names.) Anyway, peloridiids are small, flattened insects having lacelike expansions of the body suggesting those of fossils of many millions of years ago. They feed on primitive kinds of plants (mosses and liverworts) and occur only in cool parts of Australia, New Zealand, and southern South America. That they do not occur in South Africa and India may reflect the lack of suitable cool, mossy habitats there; or it may reflect a pattern of evolution that occurred after Gondwanaland had begun to break up.

Not all of the insects with this type of distribution and probable ancestry are as obscure as these examples. A group of wasps called the thynnids has over five hundred species in Australia, and they occur almost everywhere, from city parks to arid deserts. Some of these are large and brightly colored, seemingly formidable, but in fact those seen on the wing are unable to sting—they are males, and like all male wasps they lack a sting. The females are wingless and smaller than the males, and at times are carried about by the males while hanging headdown from their tail ends. In fact, the genital organs of the two sexes lock together in a complex manner, and they remain attached for long periods, sometimes several days. During this time the male may visit flowers, permitting the female to feed as well as himself, and in some species the male actually prepares a ball of food, which he presents to the female. Eventually, she drops off and enters the ground, where she attacks beetle grubs, including a number of kinds that damage agricultural crops.

In the soil, wings would provide a serious handicap to movement, but by having developed prolonged aerial copulation, these female wasps have retained the ability to disperse to new sites even though they have sacrificed their wings. Insects such as these are not likely to be successful in crossing oceans, and their present distribution—Australia, New Guinea, some of the nearby islands, and southern South America (especially Chile)—suggests strongly that they evolved when Australia and South America were in contact via a more temperate Antarctica.

But by no means do all of the Australian insects appear to have had an origin in ancient Gondwanaland. Indeed, by far the majority seem to have arrived in more recent geologic time, in stocks that advanced progressively over the East Indian chain from Eurasia. The water gaps between the islands were not especially formidable for insects any more than they were for birds and bats, and incursions from the north apparently occurred at many different times in the past. Some of the early arrivals have become widely dispersed in Australia and well adapted to various habitats there. Others have come in more recently and are found mostly in the northern part of the continent, especially in pockets of tropical rain forest along the northeast coast, which are most like those in the East Indies. A good example is provided by the lovely birdwing butterfly.

Birdwings are best known from the East Indies and are much prized by collectors, for they are among the largest butterflies known, and the males are adorned with bold stripes of green, blue, or orange. Australia's one species *(Ornithoptera priamus)* occurs as far south as the northeast corner of New South Wales, but only in patches of rain forest. The same species occurs in New Guinea, but the Australian populations have been isolated long enough so that they differ slightly in color and size from those in New Guinea, and each area of rain forest has a population recognizably different. We were thrilled to catch a birdwing one bright day in north Queensland, but after admiring its incredible colors at close hand we released it unharmed. Birdwings are protected by law in Australia, and in any case our research had nothing to do with butterflies, so we had no reason to sacrifice it.

For the moment we shall omit mention of the most recent incursions from the north: the many insects Western man has brought in, either accidentally or deliberately. These insects are very much a part of the present fauna—as we are reminded by a German cockroach that has just popped out of a drawer as we write this on a September day in Brisbane.

As an example of a group that apparently arrived long ago from the north but has become well adapted to all parts of Australia, we can do no better than mention the insects we ourselves have been studying intensively: *Bembix* sand wasps (the subject of an aboriginal chant we mentioned near the beginning of the chapter). Wasps of this group are common in North America and in fact throughout the Northern Hemisphere; there are a few species in South America and some in Africa and the East Indies. We now know that there are at least eighty species in Australia, together ranging from humid coastal areas to the most arid parts of the continent (though there is only one species in Tasmania).

Obviously, these insects have "found a home" in Australia, though it is clear the group cannot have originated there. Close study of the eighty species suggests that something like twelve immigrations from the north may have been involved. Products of later immigrations are largely confined to more humid, coastal areas, and these remain rather similar to Asiatic species. Those resulting from earlier incursions are now widely distributed in the dry Interior, and in many cases these have developed special peculiarities. Probably recurrent isolation of populations, as discussed in chapter 2, provided the mechanism for the production of so many species.

Often several of the species occur in the same place, nesting, in fact, side-by-side in some of the sandy ridges of the Interior. How do they avoid competing with one another? Of course, there is plenty of sand in which to dig their nests; but how about food? The fact is that although *Bembix* wasps prey on flies throughout the Northern Hemisphere, in Australia many of them prey on quite different things: bees, wasps, ant lions, damselflies, rarely even dragonflies. Thus they are able to live together and share available prey. It is interesting that in other parts of the world there are other groups of wasps that prey upon bees, wasps, and occasionally upon ant lions or damselflies, but these kinds of wasps do not occur in Australia. Thus, species of *Bembix* have evolved to fill those food niches, just as marsupials have evolved to occupy various niches filled elsewhere by other kinds of mammals—wolves, shrews, marmots, flying squirrels, and so forth.

One of the reasons that the Australian insect fauna is so exciting to an entomologist is that so much remains to be discovered. When we began to study *Bembix*, only about thirty-five species were known, and next to nothing was known about where they occurred and what they preyed upon. Even some very large insects have been discovered only recently. In fact, as we write this, there is much excitement over the "Cooloola monster," a strange cricketlike creature first collected in 1976 in a pitfall trap in the rain forest of Cooloola National Park on the Queensland coast. This is an area of multicolored "rainbow sands," long known to soil scientists and to tourists; yet this striking insect had remained unknown to science. Once it had been discovered and recognized as a wholly new type of insect, two successive expeditions were launched to capture specimens, but after a great deal of digging, sifting, baiting, and trapping by a group of highly qualified entomologists, none of these new insects were unearthed. Eventually a large "Wanted" poster, with a picture of the "monster," was distributed up and down the coast; anyone who found a specimen was urged to contact the Queensland Museum. Soon a second insect was collected by a

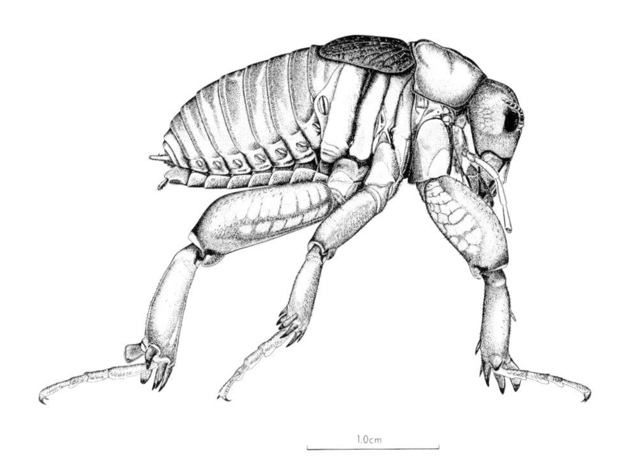

The Cooloola monster is a member of a recently discovered, wholly new group of cricketlike insects. (Queensland Museum, Brisbane)

park ranger and a third by a camper, who found it entering his tent after a rain. All of these were males, but eventually several females were also found, deep in the soil, from which they probably never emerge. Individuals of both sexes have huge, elephantine legs with fringes of large spines that evidently serve them for digging through the soil. On land they are said to move like toy tractors.

David Rentz, the government authority on this general group of insects, has now described the Cooloola monster in detail and has assigned it to a wholly new family of insects. Evidently, it has evolved independently of other cricketlike insects for a long time. Dr. Rentz believes that its closest relatives may belong to a group found in southern India.

Another recent discovery merited a lead article in *Science*, the weekly publication of the American Association for the Advancement of Science. This was the report by Robert Taylor on his finding of colonies of what is believed to be the world's most primitive living ant, called *Nothomyrmecia macrops* (literally translated, "peculiar ant with large eyes"). In fact, the existence of this big-eyed ant had been known for some years, since there were two preserved specimens in the National Museum of Victoria, which had been collected in Western Australia in 1934 by John Clark.

Time and again, collectors had searched for living colonies of this ant, the "holy grail" of ant specialists, even making trips all the way from the United States to search for it. On our earlier trips to Australia we also looked for it, feeling it would be a "coup" if nonspecialists like ourselves outdid the ant specialists. In fact it never turned up until, quite by accident, Dr. Taylor and his party found it while camping on the Eyre Peninsula in South Australia. It proved possible to establish these ants in Taylor's laboratory in Canberra and to learn a great deal about their behavior—especially important because of current efforts to understand the origin of social behavior among insects. *Nothomyrmecia* turned out to be a rather timid ant and strictly nocturnal. The nests in the soil proved to be quite simple, the colonies small (fifty to seventy workers) and with little evidence of an efficient alarm communication or territorial defense—all appropriate to a "living fossil."

Although *Nothomyrmecia* long proved elusive, members of the related genus *Myrmecia* form a conspicuous part of the Australian scene. These are the bulldog ants, famous for their large size and aggressive behavior. Bulldog ants are commonly seen roaming about hunting for small insects, which they sometimes capture by jumping upon them. The ferocity of these ants, with respect to humans, has been exaggerated. We were warned that they might actually pursue and jump at a person, but we finally had to pick one up to find if they can bite and sting as reputed. They can! On one occasion we made camp late at night in the bush and only the next morning found that we had set one of our cots directly over a bulldog ant nest. In the morning the ants were parading about, but they never bothered us. We did move the cot shortly, however.

In the northern half of Australia, one quickly becomes aware of green tree ants, as these are sometimes inadvertently brushed from foliage onto one's clothes or down the neck—and the ants can bite painfully. Green tree ants belong to a group known as the weaver ants, since they tie leaves together with silk to form nests in trees. These nests

A portrait of Nothomyrmecia macrops, *the world's most primitive ant. Its large eyes suggest those of a hunting wasp.* *(Robert W. Taylor, CSIRO)*

A scene in the nest of Nothomyrmecia. *Standing on the cocoons are two workers (right) and two short-winged queens (left).* *(Robert W. Taylor, CSIRO)*

sometimes reach the size of a basketball, and one tree may contain several of them, all part of one colony, with much communication and movement between the enclosures.

The ants themselves are most unusual in appearance, not only because they are green but because of their unusually long legs and antennae and their manner of holding their abdomen over their head and thorax. When tying leaves together, the worker ants form living chains, hooked together by their jaws and legs. After they have pulled the leaves into a suitable position, other workers arrive with larvae, which they use as shuttles to spin the silk that permanently binds the leaves together. The adult ants cannot spin silk themselves, but the larvae can (since they normally spin cocoons when fully grown). The use of offspring as tools in this manner is virtually unknown elsewhere in the animal world.

Weaver ants are not confined to Australia. A few years ago we visited the laboratories of Edward Wilson and Bert Hölldobler at Harvard University, where intensive studies of an African species are being made. The ants seem to have adjusted well to trees growing in pots in their laboratories. Colonies are highly territorial and fiercely aggressive against members of other colonies. When a worker meets an alien worker away from the nest, the two extend their legs as if walking on stilts, then circle one another with a jerky motion. Sooner or later they lunge at one another and grasp with their mandibles. The loser is pinned to the ground and his legs and antennae are clipped off—and often other parts of the body as well. In nature, colonies of weaver ants may contain half a million workers, and it is said that (at least in Africa) neighboring colonies may wage battles that last for days and leave the forest strewn with pieces of ants that have died in battle.

There are many other kinds of ants in Australia, well over a thousand in fact, including the notorious "meat ants" that are pests in houses and food-processing plants. By far the most conspicuous nests, however, are the work of termites (often called "white ants," though not at all related to ants). Tourist safaris out of Darwin invariably include these in their itineraries, for it is in northern Australia that the really big ones occur, some as much as twenty feet tall. These are nests of *Nasutitermes,* actually very tiny insects in which the soldiers have a snout from which they are able to squirt a substance that repels and entangles predators.

Even more remarkable are the nests of *Amitermes meridionalis,* the so-called magnetic termite, which builds slab-shaped nests that are always oriented with the long axis north and south. It has

This termite nest, not far south of Darwin, may have been started before the arrival of Western man on the continent.

been said that this orientation subjects the nests to less direct sunlight during the hottest months, when the sun is more directly overhead, and more warmth when the sun is lower in the sky. We are not aware that anyone has proved that this is in fact the function of these odd tombstone-shaped nests. In our experience, it is never anything but hot in Darwin!

Predictably the world's most primitive termite, *Mastotermes darwiniensis,* is also Australian, and common in Darwin, as the name suggests. These are large termites having several features in common with cockroaches, from which the termites are believed to have evolved—another not-so-missing link. Primitive though *Mastotermes* may be, it is nevertheless highly destructive of anything made of wood, and has even been reported to eat through lead sheeting to get at the wood beneath. In Darwin, telephone poles are made of concrete or metal, and houses are built on similar pilings or at least constructed so that no wooden parts are readily accessible to these voracious creatures. Thriving colonies of *Mastotermes* may contain a million or more individuals.

While social insects such as ants and termites tend to be conspicuous because of their nests and their huge populations, there are many nonsocial kinds that attract attention because of their bizarre form or brilliant coloration. Several books have been written about Australian butterflies, which rival in beauty and numbers those of any continent. So abundant are they in parts of Queensland that even the unromantic Captain Cook was led to remark on the "incredible number of butterflies, so that for the space of three or four acres the air was so crowded with them that millions were to be seen in every direction."

There are many beautiful beetles, especially the jewel beetles, which are large, wood-inhabiting insects that sparkle with various colors. These brilliant colors obviously play a role in sexual behavior. Darryl Gwynne, while a visiting fellow

A caterpillar from the vicinity of Brisbane is the larva of a swallowtail butterfly. Its horns are everted scent glands. (Allan Hook)

This glittering weevil is an inhabitant of eastern Australia.
(Allan Hook)

at the University of Western Australia, found several male jewel beetles mounted on "stubbies" with their genitals extended—stubbies being small, brown beer bottles (Australians rival Americans in their propensity to litter roadsides with empty bottles and cans). Evidently the shiny brown color of the glass is similar to the color of the female, and rows of knobs around the base of the bottles reflect light in a way similar to sparkles on the wing covers of the female.

Of course, the bottles are much larger than the female beetles—perhaps, according to Dr. Gwynne, an example of the "supernormal stimulus theory," whereby animals are more attracted to a stimulus larger than normal than to a more rewarding natural stimulus. When four additional stubbies were placed on the ground, two were promptly occupied by male beetles, but a wine bottle of another color was ignored. All of this was duly reported by the Perth *Daily News*, with the advice that "next time you discard a stubby bottle . . . spare a thought for the frustrated jewel beetle."

One of the strangest of beetles is the pie-dish beetle, a fairly large, black beetle that occurs in deserts and sand dunes at night. It is rather flat, nearly round, and has the thin sides of the body curved upward all the way around—hence the name "pie-dish." What function could this possibly serve? It almost looks as though they might collect rain water on their backs to tide them through droughts, but a little inspection reveals that there are several "holes in the pan." A more likely suggestion is that the thin, upturned flanges around the body serve to give predators a bite of expendable tissue to chew on before the beetle can bring into play the secretions of its powerful defense glands.

Even some very small insects sometimes put on spectacular displays. When we visited O'Reilly's Guest House, in Queensland's Lamington National Park, we were told of a "glowworm city" along the banks of a ravine in the rain forest. Although we were a bit put off by the word "city," we hiked there one evening along a trail made eerie by the cold, greenish light of luminous mushrooms, scarcely prepared for the spectacle awaiting us. It was a dark night, and the vertical, rock wall of the ravine sparkled with hundreds of lights which, at the top, seemed to merge with the stars of the sky. It was rather like visiting a planetarium, and we could even imagine the glowworms forming constellations because of their irregular distribution on the bank.

These glowworms [colorplate 18] are the larvae of tiny midges, each one occupying a crevice and living behind a veil of sticky, silken threads, which it spins to entrap insects that are attracted to the light. The larvae are slender and wormlike, less than an inch long, and only the tail end is luminous; nevertheless, on a dark night the light they produce is considerable. It seems odd that so many would occur together, seemingly competing with one another for prey, when vast areas of the forest have none at all. The Waitomo Cave of New Zealand is said to have even more spectacular displays of glowworms. In the Northern Hemisphere, the term "glowworm" is generally applied not to midge larvae but to wingless fireflies (which like other fireflies are beetles, not flies). True fireflies do occur in Australia, and as elsewhere use their luminescence not to attract prey but for the subtler art of sexual communion.

Speaking of catching prey with silken threads, Australia's spiders are also worth a few comments (though spiders are not strictly insects, of course, being eight-legged and without antennae). We had been in Australia only a few days when we encountered one of the most formidable-looking kinds, the giant huntsman spider that occurs commonly under the loose bark of gum trees. These gray, rather crablike spiders are not nearly as fierce as they look, and like most spiders show little inclination to bite.

There are only two kinds of poisonous spiders native to Australia, the funnel-webs and the redbacks. The latter are closely related to the black widow of North America and occur in much the same places: wood piles, outbuildings, and trash piles. The symptoms of the redback bite are severe, but antivenom is available, and bites by this retiring spider are rare indeed.

A much more notorious poisonous spider is the funnel-web (actually a group of related species). These are ebony-black spiders up to an inch and a half long (not counting the long, hairy legs). Funnel-webs occur in various places in eastern Australia, chiefly in rocky, scrubby country, where they build funnel-shaped silken tubes in crevices, with supporting lines on nearby sticks and stones. They are aggressive creatures and will bite with little provocation, striking downward with their fangs and injecting quantities of venom. The bite is said to be extremely painful and to cause muscle spasms and paralysis. About 50 percent of bites to humans are fatal, causing death in from one to twelve hours. Fortunately, researchers at the Commonwealth Serum Laboratories have apparently developed an antivenom for funnel-webs—at least it has been effective in initial tests with monkeys. But while we were in Sydney, a youth died in a hospital there as the result of a bite by a funnel-web, inciting a wave of fear of all spiders, most of which are harmless, beneficial, and thoroughly fascinating creatures.

There seems to be something about spiders that attracts women investigators. In the United States, much pioneering work was done by Elizabeth Peckham of Milwaukee; more recently, Jocelyn Crane, of the New York Zoological Society, has looked deeply into the lives of jumping spiders. In Australia, Valerie Davies of the Queensland Museum is a leading spider authority, and in Western Australia, Barbara York Main has long been intrigued by these animals and has recently published a book called (what else?) *Spiders.*

Dr. Main's specialty is trap-door spiders. These animals live in the soil in vertical burrows covered by a lid that is closed except when the occupant is out hunting. Some of the spiders never leave the burrow completely, but are able to rush part way out and grasp beetles or other insects that are passing. They do this by arranging a fan of twigs outside the entrance; these serve as "feeling lines," allowing the spider to sense the passage of potential prey over the twigs and to act accordingly. The major enemies of these spiders are centipedes, which are able to penetrate the trap doors. But the spiders have a defense against them: within the burrow they have a collapsible silken sock that can be pulled down to form a barrier across the burrow. One species even retains a pebble in a little pocket on the wall of the burrow, and when the sock collapses, the pebble falls into place to block the burrow.

In the dry, hot summer, female trap-door spiders of many species seal their doors tightly to protect the spiderlings which are developing within the nests at that season. Species that live in areas likely to be flooded build thick trap doors (like bath plugs, says Dr. Main), beneath which they are able to wait out the flood in their silk-lined tunnels. Australia has many kinds of trap-door spiders, which are among the most primitive spiders known, but unfortunately many of them lead a rather precarious existence, for the hoofs of sheep and cattle quickly render the soil unsuitable for their nests.

One of Australia's most unusual spiders has been variously called the "magnificent spider" or the "fishing line spider," the two names being equally justifiable. Keith McKeown, in his book *Australian Spiders,* waxes eloquent on this species, which is said to have a body "about the size of a large Barcelona nut" and to be cream-colored above, with a bluish-white cast "reminiscent of skim milk," covered with pink dots, brown lines, and a pair of tubercles "of a delicate primrose yellow."

These spiders suspend a silken line from their retreat, and on the end of the line is a sticky globule. When a moth approaches, the line and globule are twirled like a bola to strike the moth, which is then drawn up stuck to the globule, wrapped in silk, and eaten. Oddly, only certain kinds of moths are taken, and these seem especially attracted to these globules. There is evidence that actually the spider produces a chemical which mimics a sex attractant of the moths, luring them to their death. Evidently the twirling of the "fishing line" occurs in response to the beat of the moth's wings, for it sometimes twirls in response to the passage of aircraft or the plucked strings of a guitar.

Since we seem to have strayed a bit from the insects, we may as well digress still further and mention Australia's giant earthworms. Some of these are more than six feet in length and well over an inch in diameter, with a record specimen measuring more than eleven feet in length. These remarkable worms are said to produce a "gurgling, sucking sound" as they move through their burrows. We have never seen these giants, and evidently few people have, as they are confined to restricted areas in the Southeast away from cultivated land. There are plenty of "ordinary" earthworms in Australia, many of them immigrants from other continents.

There are certain relatives of the earthworms that we have encountered somewhat more often than we would have preferred, namely, the leeches, or, as they are often called, the bloodsuckers. Most rain forests have plenty of leeches that live in damp places and climb onto vegetation, especially after a rain, ready to move onto any passing source of blood. Even though their bite is painless and they carry no diseases, it is a bit disconcerting (even to a biologist) to find one's legs and feet streaked with blood after a hike in the forest. Since leeches inject an anticoagulent as they proceed to gorge themselves, the wounds may bleed for some time after the animals have dropped off. We were amused to find that Indooroopilly, the Brisbane suburb where we lived for several months, is an aboriginal word meaning "gully of leeches." Fortunately, they had long since been banished to distant forests.

Earthworms and leeches are legless creatures, but related to insects by way of an intermediate group known chiefly to specialists, who call them Onychophora, or more commonly by the name of one genus of the group, *Peripatus.* These are indeed ancient animals, known from fossils dating from 500 million years ago, and sometimes regarded as ancestral to insects, centipedes, and crustaceans. These soft-bodied, caterpillar-like animals have no distinct head, and their stubby legs are unjointed. Some are black or brown, others streaked or speckled with blue, red, or orange. All of them are unable to stand drying out, so they remain in damp places and come out chiefly at night. Although they are seldom seen and little studied, they occur widely in the more humid part of the continent. Because the species occurring in Australia belong to a group with a characteristic Southern Hemisphere distribution, it would seem that these delicate, damp-adapted creatures must have dispersed in this manner when Gondwanaland was a single land mass.

But such things as giant earthworms and *Peripatus* are not easily seen unless one is looking specifically for them. It is the insects that dominate the scene. Many of the insects are in fact unusually conspicuous because of their brilliant colors, especially shades of orange—one of the most conspicuous of colors, of course, which is why hunters and members of road crews use it to advertise their presence. In insects it is almost always associated with some noxious property, such as a sting, stink gland, or distasteful tissues, or with insects that are mimicking other insects which have one of these properties.

Many Australian wasps have orange wings or body markings, and a variety of nonstinging flies have adopted similar patterns, as well as various beetles and sucking bugs. Lycid beetles, which are notoriously distasteful to predators, are mainly orange in color, and their colors are copied precisely by beetles of at least four other unrelated groups, as well as by small moths. It is not surprising that one of the major contributions to theories of mimicry was made by an Australian, A. J. Nicholson, who brought forth many examples to support the belief that warning coloration and mimicry provide superb examples of natural selection.

We well recall the day we first became acquainted with the mountain grasshopper, *Acripeza reticulata*. Actually, our children first spotted it among dried leaves in the Brindabella mountains, and we brought several back to Canberra to photograph and to admire further. These large grasshoppers (really katydids) have a brown, crinkled appearance as they rest on the forest floor, where they are almost invisible among the leaves. But disturb one and a transformation occurs: an orange collar is puffed out behind the head, and the wings are lifted to reveal brilliant bands of red and blue on the abdomen [colorplates 19 and 20]. Presumably, mountain grasshoppers escape predators mainly by remaining concealed among fallen leaves; but if a predator molests them: Beware! You will not enjoy eating me!

We have often wondered why so many Australian insects have warning colors or are mimics of such insects. Perhaps it is related to the severity of the environment, especially in the Outback, where prolonged drought may be accompanied by wind storms and occasionally broken by sudden deluges. Under these conditions there must be much mortality among the insects from physical stress, and if predators were also highly successful there might be little chance for surviving at all. By "turning off" birds and lizards, at least some of the time, perhaps sufficient numbers are able to survive and reproduce their kind.

So much of Australia receives sparse and unpredictable rainfall that it is not surprising that insects have evolved many adaptations for survival under these conditions. As in desert areas throughout the world, many spend the day in hiding, emerging at night to take advantage of cooler temperatures and whatever dew is available. Many also time their emergence to coincide with rain. That is, the same heavy rain that triggers the germination of the seeds of annual flowers, or the blooming of perennials, also triggers the emergence of many kinds of insects from their resting stages. Some are able to spend two or more years in a dormant stage if sufficient rainfall is not received. Others employ alternate strategies: some individuals are programmed to emerge the following year, others two or more years hence; presumably one or the other will find optimal conditions.

On a trip to the Tompkinson Ranges, deep in the northwest corner of South Australia, we visited areas that had evidently received no appreciable rain for many months, perhaps years. It was hard to find any insects at all! Yet in other places not too far away, local showers had been heavy enough to transform the landscape: myriads of bees, flies, beetles, and other insects swarmed about patches of white daisies and lavender parakeelyas.

Another way in which some insects cope with patchy rainfall is by nomadism, followed by rapid population increase when favorable areas are found. A migratory grasshopper called the Australian plague locust provides a good example. These voracious creatures sometimes devastate crops and grasslands in inland New South Wales and Queensland, but their appearance in plague proportions is usually quite irregular, although there were particularly severe outbreaks in 1933–34, in 1953–54, and in 1973–74. Once they have built up a large population and have laid bare much of the vegetation, they tend to move off in swarms on relatively calm days, flying upwind fairly close to the ground. Swarms move like a conveyor belt, those in front landing to feed while those at the rear of the swarm are taking off and flying to the front.

In November 1979, we drove through such a swarm of locusts near Mitchell, in southern Queensland, and the front of our car was left in rather a mess. All of the locusts were moving north, and when we had occasion to drive along the same stretch of road the following day, they were still passing in the same direction in great numbers, presumably still part of the same swarm. Government teams were about, plotting the course of the swarm and prepared to take action when and where necessary.

Major migrations of locusts occur at night, however, and are associated with unstable air resulting from the passage of frontal systems. At these times many millions take flight just at dusk, sometimes ascending up to as much as 5,000 feet, flying downwind and being carried hundreds of miles, depending upon wind velocity. This response to changing atmospheric pressure tends to carry them into areas where rain has fallen or is about to fall and where there is likely to be abundant vegetation. Plotting of these nightly swarms by radar has made it possible to predict (sometimes) where they are likely to descend and to provide suitable warning to farmers and graziers.

These locusts have still another neat adaptation for survival in environmental extremes. The egg pods are laid in the ground and will die if subjected to unduly high temperatures or low humidity. In the spring and summer the pods are laid vertically rather deep in the soil, where it is somewhat cool and moist. But with the decreasing day length of late summer and fall, they are laid obliquely near the surface. Here some are programmed to respond to fall and winter rains, so that the hatchlings may develop on green plants, while others remain as eggs until spring. Thus there is double assurance that there will be locusts around to build up populations the following summer.

It should be confessed that Australia has its share of insects that, like locusts, are neither beautiful or particularly likeable. At times and places there are plenty of mosquitoes and sandflies, and the buffalo fly is a serious pest of cattle in the North, causing sores, loss of blood, and general debilitation of the herds. However, insect-borne diseases such as malaria and filariasis are rare in Australia. The most notorious and widespread pest of man is the bush fly, which we mentioned earlier. Bush flies breed in the dung of animals such as kangaroos, dingoes, emus, and, of course, man and his domestic animals. Development of the maggots in dung is rapid, especially when it is hot and somewhat humid. Consequently, bush flies are most prevalent during the rainy season in northern Australia, where there may be several rapid generations.

The adult bush flies often live a month or two, and may be carried hundreds of miles a day by strong winds. Thus they occur all over Australia, even at times and places that are too dry, or too populated for them to breed effectively. Because the flies prefer warmth and sunlight, people can avoid them to some extent by staying indoors or in the shade. Their attraction to humans and to other warm-blooded animals is explained by their need for water and proteins, which they find in tears, sweat, and saliva. Although bush flies do not bite or carry disease, only a few hours in the bush are enough to convince one how very pestiferous they are. Entomologists have been studying the bush fly for many years, and now know a good deal about it—but getting rid of an insect that breeds in animal dung scattered all over the countryside is another matter.

It would seem likely that the advent of Western man and his livestock has made life much easier for the bush fly, which has vast new sources of dung in which to breed. Perhaps this is so, although many of the early explorers seem to have found flies plentiful enough. At present there are some thirty million cattle in Australia, each producing an average of twelve dung pads a day. Not only do bush flies and buffalo flies breed in dung, but the mere accumulation of so much dung can ruin vast areas of pasture land. On other continents a variety of dung beetles are on hand to bury and consume much of it, but since Australia has no native herbivores that produce large, moist droppings, there are no native dung beetles capable of handling them. True, there are many native dung beetles, but they are adapted to using the dry, fibrous pellets of kangaroos, wallabies, and the like. Some of these beetles actually ride about on the fur of kangaroos in the anal region, waiting for them to defecate, whereupon they drop off quickly and make off with the dung. The adage "first come, first served" seems to apply regardless of the menu!

The Hungarian-born Australian entomologist George Bornemissza was the first to suggest that it might be possible to introduce beetles from other continents to reduce at least partially the amount of accumulated dung. He looked especially to Africa, which has a somewhat similar climate but a diverse fauna of large herbivores. Beginning in 1967, Bornemissza and his group at CSIRO (Commonwealth Scientific and Industrial Research Organization) released 275,000 beetles of four species in

Australia, all from stocks obtained from Africa. Some of these thrived in their new home and did much to clear pastures of dung.

CSIRO has prepared an educational motion picture of this unusual program, appropriately called "Dung Down Under," showing the various steps in the process of shipping, rearing, and releasing beetles, including the unattractive procedure of hand-rolling dung balls in which to rear the beetles in the laboratory. There have been problems, of course, some of them unexpected. For example, the cane toad, which had been introduced many years earlier to control beetles that attack sugar cane, found the imported dung beetles much to its liking. Bornemissza is now experimenting with some very large dung beetles, which toads cannot swallow readily; or if they do swallow them, the beetles are strong enough to dig their way out of the toad's body.

The introduction of beneficial insects is by no means a new thing for Australians, who have been leaders in the field of biological control of pests for many years. As early as 1895 Western Australia began a program of exchanging lady beetles and other useful insects with other states and other countries. The green vegetable bug, an Asiatic pest that appeared in Australia in 1916, has been effectively controlled by a small wasp imported from Egypt. More recently, an elegant tachina fly appropriately called *Trichopoda* (literally, hairy-foot) has been released for control of this pest. The accidental arrival of the European woodwasp a few years ago posed a threat to the timber industry, but progress is also being made in finding effective parasites of this insect.

The most strikingly successful example of biological control involves not a pest insect but a weed. Cacti are not native to Australia, but they are often grown there as a curiosity. In 1840 a physician immigrating to Australia brought with him a potted prickly pear, from which cuttings were eventually made and distributed widely. Over a period of time the cacti escaped and proved well adapted to the Australian climate. In fact, they grew much taller than usual, up to ten feet in height, and came to form impenetrable, spiny jungles. By 1925, sixty million acres of eastern Australia were covered with prickly pears.

Efforts to destroy the cacti failed or proved too impracticable: burning, cutting them up mechanically, spraying them with poisons, and so forth. Beginning about 1912, the Queensland government, and later the Commonwealth government, began to study the idea of using plant-feeding insects to control the cacti. Eventually, about fifty species were introduced from countries as diverse as the United States, Mexico, Ceylon, and South Africa. It was a small, poorly known moth from South America that eventually proved most valuable, and in a few years this moth, suitably named *Cactoblastis cactorum,* had reduced the prickly pears to a few scattered stands. One still finds a few cacti here and there in southern Queensland, but it is unlikely that the prickly pear will ever again become a major pest.

The success of this program has prompted a number of other efforts at the biological control of weeds. St. Johnswort was brought into Victoria many years ago by a German immigrant to the gold fields because his wife longed for the beautiful yellow flowers of her homeland. It quickly became a pest, proving to be poisonous to sheep as it took over valuable pasturelands. From 1930 to 1940 several kinds of leaf beetles were introduced from England, and these have effectively reduced the stands of weeds. St. Johnswort has more recently become a pest in California, where it is called Klamath weed, and Californians are finding the same kinds of leaf beetles useful in its control.

Parts of pastoral southeast Australia are covered with another imported weed of European origin, which is also a weed in North America, where it is called viper's bugloss. In Australia it is called Paterson's curse, after a gardener of Albury, New South Wales, who is said to have imported it to enrich his plantings. When the plants are in bloom, vast areas of pastureland are turned a beautiful blue, but native grasses and wildflowers are crowded out. Since there seemed to be no other way to control this pest, scientists at CSIRO set to work to find and import insects that would feed on it. After much effort, several kinds of leaf-feeding and stem-boring moths and beetles were found, and some of these were released in infested fields. But now the Federal Council of Australian Apiarists (bee-keepers) has obtained a temporary injunction against the further release of these insects. It seems that the Australian honey industry, worth about thirty million dollars a year, has come to rely on Paterson's curse as a major honey source. If they win their case in the courts, perhaps they should try to change the name of the weed to "Paterson's beauty," to allay further prejudice against it.

So there are quite a few problems in trying to manipulate nature's balances. Many times, introduced insects fail to become established or to control the pest in question. Any introduction has to be made with great care and after extensive research. Too many mistakes have been made in the past—prickly pears, St. Johnswort, green vegetable bugs, and of course rabbits and foxes! Pests such as the codling moth and the Oriental fruit moth, well known to American fruit growers, have been in Australia for many years and have resisted efforts to control them biologically. The growing of cotton in the Ord River Irrigation Project of Western Australia was stymied by the cotton boll worm and other alien pests.

It often seems that entomologists must spend so much time combating pests introduced from other countries that they have little time or funds to study their own, native species. As the human population increases and more land is devoted to agriculture, mining, and suburbia, habitats available to native plants and animals decline rapidly. The loss of any species is a loss to man—but that is particularly true if the species is part of a delicately balanced fauna that has evolved apart from other faunas for a long time, as has that of Australia. Considering that only about half of the Australian insect species are believed to have been described, there is a real problem that some will become extremely scarce or even extinct before they are discovered. And one of them might be just the one we need to fulfill an urgent need—just as we needed *Cactoblastis*!

8

THE GREAT BARRIER REEF AND OTHER AQUATIC LIFE

"Too much for the imagination"

Rachel Carson's expression "the sea around us" seems nowhere more fitting than in Australia, with its coastline (including Tasmania) of approximately 16,700 miles. With a population of about fifteen million, and with about 80 percent living in the green "fringe" around the edges of the continent, a quick calculation shows that something like twelve million people are within at least a few hours' drive of the ocean. Certainly whenever a holiday occurs, vast numbers of Australians will be found in holiday flats or "camped" literally side by side in trailer parks located in the coastal dunes or on headlands overlooking the ocean. Swimming, surfing, sunbathing, fishing, and boating are favorite pastimes.

Although today Australia has a number of excellent ports, the waters around it have always been considered treacherous for ships. The offshore reefs and rocks seem littered with wrecks, dating back into the sixteenth century when Portuguese and Dutch merchant sailing ships were looking for spices and gold in the Far East. In the Fremantle Museum, not far from Perth on the west coast, we saw some fascinating displays of cargo recently recovered from some of those old wrecked ships—vases, spoons, dishes, jewelry, and coins, which have been on the ocean floor for three hundred years or more. And even before any European ships found Australia, the Chinese and Indonesians came to the north coast fishing, mainly for sea cucumbers, which were dried and taken home to be used as a soup base (and some say as an aphrodisiac).

The loveliest port, Sydney harbor, surprisingly was overlooked by Australia's best-known explorer, Captain James Cook, although since its discovery it has been the main entrance port to the country. One of our most delightful remembrances of the island continent is of a sunset departure through Sydney harbor, when the sky was a myriad of changing colors reflected in the water, and the hills and the famous bridge were darkening shadows against those colors and the twinkling city lights.

Captain Cook did not overlook, however, another beautiful but treacherous area on Australia's east coast. He found and named many of the parts

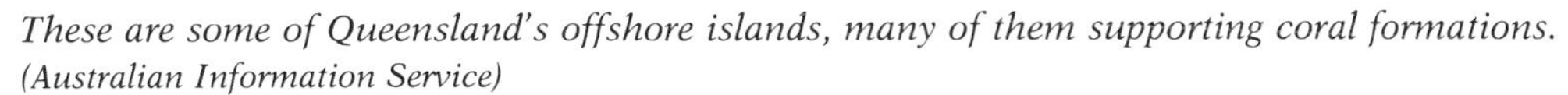

These are some of Queensland's offshore islands, many of them supporting coral formations. (Australian Information Service)

of the Great Barrier Reef, and today this area is probably better known around the world than any other part of Australia. "There are," wrote Elspeth Huxley in 1967, "some things that are simply too much for the imagination, like the Milky Way, eternity and the dimensions of the universe. The Great Barrier Reef is another."

The Great Barrier Reef, neither a single reef nor a barrier reef in a technical sense, is a conglomerate of drowned hills and coast lines, various coral formations, much sea water, and all of the associated plants and animals. It extends for 1,200 miles along the northeast coast of Queensland, limited by temperature requirements and the depth of the continental shelf. It covers an estimated area of 100,000 square miles, and is said to contain more than 2,500 identifiable reefs, all washed by the warm waters of the Coral Sea, part of the southern Pacific Ocean.

This is not an easy area to penetrate by sea, as Captain Cook discovered when he damaged his ship, the *Endeavour,* near a point he named Cape Tribulation, located south of today's Cooktown. Interestingly, the cannons he had thrown overboard to lighten his ship after it struck a reef were raised in the late 1960s by some Americans (without permission, to the understandable displeasure of Australians). Fortunately, one cannon was eventually given to Cooktown, where Britain's Queen Elizabeth II later came to formally open a new museum housing mementos of Captain Cook, as well as of others, both seamen and gold miners, who once swelled the population of this now sleepy little town (the highway north up the east coast turns into dirt before it reaches Cooktown).

Today most people go to the nearer islands and reefs by small boat, or by helicopter to the more distant ones, and although there is a navigable channel up the "inside," more than five hundred wrecks on the Reef attest to the fact that such a route is difficult at best, and can be fatal.

There are a number of resorts on the Great Barrier Reef (some on offshore islands, a few on coral islands), and we chose to stay at Heron Island, a coral island located on the Tropic of Capricorn about fifty miles from the mainland. A helicopter from Gladstone makes a trip across easy, but although we were scheduled to make our first trip by air, the helicopter developed electrical trouble on the flight just before ours, and so we went by boat. It was not a very large boat, carrying one other family and some supplies for the resort, and in the course of seven hours we became pretty thoroughly rocked by the waves, soaked in spray coming across the deck, and increasingly uncomfortable before reaching Heron. (But perhaps we did feel a bit closer in spirit to Captain Cook, to say nothing of Captain Bligh, who successfully navigated across the Reef in a small boat!)

From the air on our second trip, we had a better overall view of Heron Island and its neighboring reefs [colorplate 21]—appreciating the tiny speck that previously had loomed as a large haven to us from a wet boat. The reefs can be seen at great distances as spots of turquoise in deep blue, and these striking colors become delineated, as one approaches, by lines of white where the waves break across the outer edges of the coral. The shallow waters over the coral become much lighter in color and may even show white sands above the water at low tides as the business of island building begins. Heron Island stands out near one end of its extensive reef as a tiny black dot that slowly turns dark green with a glistening white border. When we emerged from the helicopter, we were almost blinded by those white sands at midday, and only too thankful to get into the shade of the pisonia trees, even though their branches were full of nesting noddy terns, which occasionally "noddied" on us as we passed beneath them.

Heron Island is a typical coral island, or cay. It rises a few feet above the water and is covered with various trees and herbaceous plants, which become so numerous in the island's center that it is almost impenetrable. Over the years, enough sand and debris accumulated on its coral base so that seeds brought in by birds, wind, and water could germinate. A leisurely walk around the island on the beach takes almost thirty minutes—if one does not make too many stops, which one usually does. In addition to the tourist resort, there is a marine biological research station run by the University of Queensland—making the island and its reef one of the best studied in the entire world. There are a number of other places where marine research is being conducted today, of course, but certainly much of what is known about the Great Barrier Reef (and coral reefs in general) has come from work done on Heron Island.

One description of coral reefs that we like especially says that they are gardens where all the plants are animals. Arthur C. Clarke, who is best known for his science fiction, said in his nonfictional *The Coast of Coral* that in the reef there is "an alien element filled with outlandish shapes so that we feel none of the sympathy, none of the kinships, which often link us to the creatures on land." Reefs are formed from interlocked and encrusted deposits and skeletons of corals, algae, molluscs, worms, and other organisms [colorplate 22]. The interrelationships are varied and complex, so much so that they are far from being fully understood even today.

The reef-building corals, mainly staghorn and brain corals, begin when tiny larvae float down and become attached to solid surfaces on the continental shelf or to the edges of submerged mountain tops. These young corals then grow into adult polyps, which may be anywhere from an eighth of an inch to half of an inch or so in length. The body of each polyp is a hollow sack with an opening on top that is surrounded by tentacles—a bit like an upside down jellyfish, which it more or less is. During the day the tentacles are contracted, but at night when feeding occurs, the tentacles protrude like a blossoming flower and entangle and sting passing microscopic animals. The prey is then taken in through the mouth opening and digested in the body cavity. The colony is formed when a polyp grows buds, which soon break off to form new individuals. As the colony expands, each member secretes a limestone skeleton around itself—the skeletons being the hard formations we usually think of when we think of coral. A piece of dead coral, such as we might find when we are looking for shells on a sandy beach, is usually white and full of small holes. In a living coral reef, the polyps project themselves through those holes when they are feeding, and those living bodies also give the coral its color.

A white-capped noddy tern sits on her nest among the pisonia trees of Heron Island. (Allan Hook)

The continental shelf, on which the Great Barrier Reef mainly rests, slopes down and away from the Queensland coast for a distance of approximately two hundred miles and to a depth of about six hundred feet. It is not a smooth, evenly tilted structure, but like any land form consists of valleys and ridges and faults and terraces, which are never stable for long. Thus the depth of the water above the shelf has never been constant, a result in part of the uneven surface of the shelf, but also of the raising and lowering of the ocean level over the centuries. Since coral can grow only in waters warmer than sixty-eight degrees Fahrenheit that have plenty of light, conditions above the shelf are ideal, but once the shelf gives way to the tremendous depths of the Pacific, coral can no longer grow or survive. Imagine, however, the surprise when some recent borings (by crews searching for oil) showed old coral reefs, that is, the dead skeletons, extending down for 1,800 feet to a volcanic rock base. The explanation involved changing sea levels and geology, for the old coral now at such depths must have sunk very slowly from the ocean surface (or the ocean risen slowly) so that the new coral could continue to grow on top of the old.

As the top layer of the ocean has the greatest population of organisms, it is the best place to feed. This would seem to be a sufficient reason to explain growth requirements, but there is another quite remarkable explanation for the need of light for reef building. In the tissues of the little animal polyps live hundreds, perhaps thousands, of tiny, one-celled organisms called zooxanthellae. Most people consider them to be simple plants (algae) because they are green and can manufacture their own food. (They can also develop tails and swim like animals, but inside the coral polyp cells they remain more plantlike.)

When some experimental polyps had their zooxanthellae removed, the polyps did not die, but their growth rate was greatly reduced. Since it was known that the polyps did not eat their algae, what exactly was the relationship between these two different organisms? After more experimentation, observation, and thought, the researchers decided that the algae served the polyps by removing their wastes (carbon dioxide, nitrogen, phosphorus, sulfur) when they utilize them to make their food. So with a built-in garbage disposal, the polyps had more time to devote to growing and reproducing. Further, although biologists had long known that coral polyps were carnivores, the scientists showed, by using radioactive tracers, that the algae contributed nutritional molecules to the polyps, as well as some basic elements to the surrounding carboniferous skeletons. But there was a price: the algae had to have light to make their foodstuffs from those waste products. A fair exchange, and so good coral growth occurs in warm, well-lighted waters.

Coral animals are considered to be among the most productive organisms known. Not only do they build massive bastions of limestone, which provide homes for hundreds of other creatures, but they produce many kinds of organic compounds of interest to biochemists. Some of these substances are quite novel, while others are known to occur elsewhere but for some reason are produced by corals in large amounts. Certain soft corals, for example, are as much as one percent prostaglandins—hormonelike compounds found in all living cells, but usually in small amounts only. Not only corals but algae, sponges, and other reef dwellers produce a variety of chemicals (some antibioticlike in that they restrict growth) that evidently serve to deter predators and competitors. Since so many of the reef organisms are sedentary and thus cannot defend themselves actively, they must rely on the subtle effects of these substances for survival.

Similarly, these organisms must rely on chemicals for communication. It is important, for example, that sperms and eggs be released into the surrounding waters at the same time by members of the same species to insure fertilization. Hence a variety of chemical "releasers" are employed by diverse organisms of the reef, but only recently have biochemists begun to identify these compounds. Thus the coral reef would seem to offer some tantalizing prospects for ecological biochemistry (or is it biochemical ecology?), as well as being a rich source of potential drugs for human use.

Coral reefs are of several kinds. There are true barrier, or ribbon, reefs on the outer edge of the continental shelf; platform reefs supporting the coral cays; and fringing reefs, which encircle the rocky islands located mainly in the northern part of the Great Barrier Reef. The atoll islands found farther out in the Pacific do not occur here.

Living coral reefs are not solid, as anyone knows who has tried to walk over one. At low tide around Heron Island such ventures are common, but require a certain amount of care, both for the walker and for the reef inhabitants. Brain and similar solid corals do not break readily, but staghorns and other fragile ones will break if stepped on or hit with much force. And a reef walker or swimmer who chances to brush against the hard coral structures will come away with cuts and abrasions that are quite painful, especially in saltwater. To avoid this, we wore tennis shoes and carried a "reefing" stick (an old broom handle is ideal) to help maintain balance and to search out the holes in front of us. Such a walk is most rewarding, and can be taken day after day without becoming dull or routine.

Corals come in many shapes and colors, including pink, lavender, various greens, yellow, and blue. Not all have hard skeletons, either, but may be soft and leathery. Algae are common on the reef, and in fact contribute to the reef formation by cementing it together more securely. Also found attached or buried in the reef are sponges, tube-dwelling worms, giant clams, and sea anemones. Among the most striking inhabitants are the featherworms that thrust out bright red, blue, or yellow plumes at the open end of their tubes to feed. We enjoyed touching them, and some of the anemones, too, and watching the quick retraction.

The clams in the reef, which at Heron Island are not really giant clams (being only a foot or so across), "sit" in the reef with their shells open a little and their colored mantles partially extended. These mantles are of a different color in each clam because each one has its own combination of algae within its tissues, giving the mantle a uniquely patterned hue. A quick tap with a reef stick on the clam's shell causes it to shut so quickly that it shoots up a spray of water over the stick carrier.

On top of the reef in the shallow water are many more animals, most of them hidden under debris. Most conspicuous are the sea cucumbers (also often called bêche-de-mer or trepang), which sprawl in great numbers over the reef, quietly feeding. It is said that they move more ocean bottom rubble than any other animal as they eat their way through the silt and debris. A sea cucumber looks like a rather large and rotting vegetable cucumber, can be black or perhaps mottled brown, and is a relative of the attractive starfishes and sea urchins. Most reef walkers prefer to leave sea cucumbers alone, but if you do finally overcome their repulsive appearance and pick up one, it spins fine, colorless strings around your arm and hand which tighten and pinch as they dry off—a good defensive mechanism against predators, including human ones.

Although we never saw it, the sea cucumber has another "trick," namely, the expulsion of its internal organs. This was long thought to be a "last resort" defense against a potential predator, but more recent studies have thrown doubt on that explanation. Biologists now believe that visceral expulsion occurs only when the oxygen content of the surrounding water is poor. Evidently this act serves to reduce body metabolism at a critical time, for the organs regenerate when environmental conditions improve.

Less common on the reef are the starfishes,

Coral—seen through the water at low tide at Heron Island.

The tentacles of featherworms extend from a coral base. At the slightest disturbance, the bright red tentacles will be retracted quickly.

The crown-of-thorns starfish is an ugly and destructive member of the reef community.

which may be dark red, royal blue, or, more often, light brown. In addition to the typical five-arm stars are pincushion stars and basket stars to add variety. The crown-of-thorns starfish, which has many arms and is credited with gnawing away other parts of the reef, does not seem to be a problem around Heron Island, and we never saw it while reef walking.

Also present on the reef are sea urchins, and although they are not abundant on top of the reef, they can inflict a wound on the unsuspecting who might step on one, leaving a splinter under the skin to cause an inflammation. Incidentally, tropical sea urchins tend to be darker (a lovely "deep purple") and to have much longer spines than those we used to find along the coast of Maine. And by turning over old coral boulders out near the edge of the reef, as we did at Heron, you may also find flat worms, small crabs, and various mollusks including a wide variety of snails, clams, limpits, chitons, and the incredible nudibranchs or sea slugs.

Nudibranchs are endowed with the most marvelous colors, each species being patterned differently, and when they swim they move through the water like gently waving scarves. The Spanish dancer is among the largest, perhaps five inches long, and displays its "scarf" of dark red and cream with a graceful rhythm that is a delight to watch.

Australian waters, like those everywhere else in the world, contain the more modern bony fishes as well as the more primitive, cartilaginous sharks and rays. And because there are no places richer in these marine creatures than coral reefs, fishes can be seen in abundance when one is snorkeling, diving, or looking down through a glass-bottom boat. One can also see them in the shallows on top of the reef, especially a flat sole or a small coral shark, both of which blend in with the sand and move only when about to be stepped on—much to the surprise of the stepper.

There is another fish, the clown fish, which hides in the tentacles of a sea anemone—a marvelous adaptation whereby the fish is not ensnared by its particular anemone while it lures other fish into the poisonous tentacles of its hungry host. Surprisingly, a clown fish is not born with immunity to the stings of the anemone, but must acquire it gradually—a hazardous and painful childhood, one assumes. Cardinalfishes tend to take refuge in branching corals, but some of the smaller individuals hide among the spines of sea urchins and thus gain protection from their enemies. Some even have longitudinal stripes that enable them to blend in better with the spines that surrounded them.

Altogether, some 850 species of fish have been identified from the reefs and seas near Heron Island, and these are most diverse, belonging to over eighty different families. That so many kinds live here successfully reflects the diversity of the reefs themselves, the innumerable niches and crevices, inhabited by a varied array of organisms that can serve as food. The patchwork nature of the reefs provides homes for all these fish, many of which remain in hiding part of the time. Some recent studies have shown that there is a "day shift" and a "night shift."

In evening, about dusk, members of the day shift seek shelter, while various nocturnal fishes take their places. At dawn the shifts change again, but in neither case does it all happen at once. Rather, a group of one species will appear and

One of the many gaily patterned coral fish is the angel fish. The tubular mouth is used for nibbling off bits of coral and algae. *(Australian Information Service)*

begin to feed in certain places, then a few minutes later another group, followed by another. Evidently, this succession of species, each responding to a different light intensity, insures that each will occupy its niche with a minimum amount of aggressive competition.

Many of the reef fishes remain quite closely attached to one particular home territory, usually a space among coral boulders where ample food is available. Richard Low, then at the University of Sydney, followed several yellow-tailed damselfishes at Heron Island over a period of five months. Each time he checked them they were in the same place, an area of about two square yards, where they browsed on the algae and drove off other fishes that entered their territory. He found that members of some thirty-eight species were attacked—all of them herbivores that might compete with the damselfishes for the available algae. Quite a few other kinds of fishes were not usually attacked, and these were mainly kinds that do not feed on algae and thus were not competitors for food.

It has been known for some time that many reef fish aggressively defend a home territory, and it has been claimed that the splashy colors of these fish play a role in this. That is, the colors may enable members of a species to recognize quickly from a distance other members of their species, individuals who might usurp their territory or attack their eggs or young. The noted behaviorist Konrad Lorenz devotes the first two chapters of his widely read book *On Aggression* to reef fishes. He exclaims: "But what colors, and what incredible designs: one could almost imagine they were planned to create a distant effect, like a flag or a poster."

Experiments have shown that fish do respond more quickly to brightly colored models than to drab ones. Dr. Lorenz observed reef fish (off the coast of Florida) driving away other members of their species, and in aquaria where there was no escape, they often killed one another. The colors, he believed, serve to inform fishes from a distance that a territory is occupied or about to be invaded, thus avoiding bloodshed. There are several reasons for believing that he was overgeneralizing, however. Damselfishes, as we have noted, drive away fishes not only of their own species but of many different kinds; and many fishes with spectacular "poster colors" are not territorial. At one point Dr. Lorenz comments: "It is a good morning exercise for a research scientist to discard a pet hypothesis every day before breakfast. It keeps him young." So perhaps he welcomes the fact that this hypothesis has been at least in part set aside.

Nonetheless, the brilliant patterns of these fish must have evolved to fulfill some function in the crowded life of the reef. The reef is full of predators, chiefly larger fish, and there is no doubt that many perish before reaching maturity. Perhaps these colors serve to deceive predators. The prominent banding may be disruptive, that is, it may serve to break up the profile as seen from the side. Then, too, these are often very thin fish, so that when they turn to flee from a predator their colors suddenly disappear, leaving the would-be assailant confused by their sudden transformation into a thin and colorless wraith. It has been claimed that these fish are distasteful; stomach analyses of predatory fish suggest that they do rarely consume angelfish.

Quite a few reef fish have large spots of black or bright colors near their tails. These may serve as "false eyes," causing a predator to nip at the tail rather than the head, or they may serve to frighten off some predators. One researcher has found that a spotted fish with a pair of black eye spots near its tail end actually lives in a hole with its back end protruding—looking like nothing so much as the head end of a moray eel, one of the most dreaded fish of the reefs.

So perhaps the curious colors and forms of reef fishes serve various functions. Some fish are not brightly colored at all, but blend with the background, like the soles and stonefish. One of the most curious inhabitants of the reef is the pipefish or trumpetfish, a very slender creature that drifts back and forth among the coral branches as if it were a piece of seaweed, then darts out suddenly to swallow a smaller fish. Then there are the rays, which spend a good deal of their time in the sea but often rest on the reef at high tide, partially buried in the sand. When snorkeling, we were sometimes startled by groups of rays emerging from the bottom and gliding off like strange, aquatic birds. The shovel-nosed ray, in particular, looked a little too much like its relatives, the sharks, to make us comfortable. But none of these creatures attack man.

In deeper waters, the fishes tend to travel in schools. These fishes are mostly streamlined and lack the gaudy colors of the reef fishes. Generally, they are not much bothered by snorkelers or divers, passing like silvery ghosts, at times almost close enough to be touched. At the edge of the reef, where it falls off into deeper waters, one may see great numbers of both free-swimming and reef-dwelling fishes, including the strange wobbegong or carpet shark, a shaggy-looking beast that may grow up to twelve feet in length.

These sharks are blotched with brown and gray and blend beautifully with the bottom. They have been known to nip a diver if disturbed. More dangerous is the stonefish, a nasty inhabitant of the reef, whose skin is covered with warts and protrusions that cause it to blend with the algae-covered rocks and coral boulders, among which it hides. A reef walker unfortunate enough to step on a stonefish will find that the creature has raised its dorsal spines, punctured his foot, and then injected a poison into the wound. The pain will be immediate and intense, breathing can become irregular, and death may result. There are recommended treatments to counteract the venom, but fortunately we never had occasion to find out about them.

Attacks by sharks are not uncommon along the Australian coast, but they occur chiefly farther south, where the excellent swimming and surfing beaches along the main coast attract great numbers of people. Most of these beaches are protected by large nets placed well offshore, and these have greatly reduced the incidence of shark attacks. Unfortunately, the nets do not protect swimmers from various stinging jellyfish. One of these, a box jellyfish called the sea wasp, is so prevalent in the waters of northern Australia during the summer months that swimming is discouraged at that season. The bluebottle, a colonial jellyfish of the type called "Portuguese man-of-war," runs a close second. The attractive blue, air-filled floats of these creatures belie the fact that several long, stinging tentacles dangle below. Bluebottle stings have been reported as fatal, but when one of our party tangled with one in the waters off Stradbroke Island, a sand island not far from Brisbane, the stings were slight and faded within the hour. But maybe those specimens in the surf were not in good health.

Perhaps we make it sound as though Australian waters were dangerous: bluebottles, sea wasps, sharks, stonefish, jagged coral rocks, and so forth. In fact, one rarely hears of injuries from these sources; drownings from incautious swimming or boating are far more commonly reported. The most common complaint of visitors to Australia's shores is a familiar one in similar places everywhere: sunburn.

One of the most unusual fishes is an inhabitant of freshwater: the Australian lungfish. These fish are seldom seen by tourists, though there was a live one on display in the Queensland Museum in Brisbane when we were there. The lungfish belongs to a very ancient group called the fleshy-finned fishes, one branch of which is considered to have been the ancestral line of the first land animals. All of these fishes lived in areas subjected to seasonal droughts, and consequently developed a lung that enabled them to survive dry periods, although they also retained gills for normal breathing. They continued to be successful, and were common in fresh water two to three hundred million years ago.

Interestingly, the fossil bones of these ancient lungfishes are difficult to distinguish from those of the Australian species living now, although the other two living species (one in Africa and one in South America) look quite different, having become eellike so that they can burrow deep into mud to survive long dry periods, something the Australian lungfish cannot do. The Australian species originally occurred in only two river systems, the Burnett and the Mary near Maryborough, 130 miles or so north of Brisbane. One of the small towns there is quaintly named Ceratodus, the old name of the genus to which the lungfish belongs. Recently, the lungfish has been successfully introduced into several other rivers, including the Brisbane River.

Presumably, many millions of years ago some ancestral fleshy-finned fishes moved onto the land, progressing on their modified fins, and became the first amphibians. While we can only read about that in books, we can see "in the flesh" another group of fishes creeping from the water on their fins and even climbing on low, exposed roots of the mangroves among which they live. Common to tropical mangrove areas, these are the mud-skippers, or mangrove fish, strange little fish with huge "goggle-eyes," which are directed forward rather than to the side as in most fish. Their generic name, *Periopthalmus,* meaning "encircling eyes," seems apt.

Loren Eiseley, in his book *The Immense Journey,* humorously describes a friend of his who was pushing a dugout up a creek in northern Australia when he hit a mangrove and things came tumbling down. His friend then asked: "What were they doing sitting up there in bunches? I ask you. It's no place for a fish. Besides that they had a way of sidling off with those popeyes trained on you. I never liked it. Somebody ought to keep an eye on them." Perhaps, but those eyes do enable the mud-skippers to actively seek and feed on flies, crabs, and other small creatures they find out of water, and when disturbed, they do skip off across the mud with remarkable speed. They breathe not by lungs, but by gills, which extract oxygen from water held in enlarged "cheek pouches." Perhaps the ancient lungfishes came from the water for the same reason: to find new sources of food.

One of the joys of living on a continent with such a fondness for the sea is that fresh seafood is almost always available. On Heron Island we were treated to reef fish at every meal, each better than the last. In most coastal cities the English dish of "fish and chips" (chips being French fries) is available at innumerable quick-food stands. We found this "dish," especially if wrapped in newspaper and carried to the beach and shared with the sea gulls, to be the ultimate in tasty dining. Australian fishing fleets provide the seafood, and game fishing is an important aspect of the tourist industry, especially in the waters off Cairns in northern Queensland. Marlin, albacore, and sailfish are among the prizes. Understandably, a recent government sale of offshore fishing rights to allow commercial Japanese fishermen to take some of these game fishes has led to some hard feelings and bitter

The coral cod, a large reef fish, is much used as food. (John Cancalosi)

words among Australians. In spite of this seeming indifference (or perhaps from a guilty conscience), the government recently issued a set of postage stamps featuring game fish. As for us, we especially recommend barramundi, coral trout, and sweetlip: tastier fish are not to be found anywhere.

When in Sydney one should try Sydney rock oysters, a special delicacy of that part of the coast. Oyster beds flourish off many of the shores, but most commercial oysters are grown for the market on specially prepared platforms in protected bays along the coast.

At one time, pearling was an important industry in parts of Australia, and pearling trawlers sailed out of Thursday Island off the northeast coast and from Broome off the northwest coast. They were searching for pearls, true, but the most money was made from the large shells, which were cut into buttons and other mother-of-pearl items. Occasionally, a large and beautiful pearl was found, and there are many stories (probably very few true) of murders, intrigues, and treachery having to do with the pearls and the pearlers who found them. One of the best fictional portrayals, we think, is the book *Come Away, Pearler,* by Colin Simpson and first published in 1952. The best divers were Japanese, and many eventually moved permanently to Australia—creating a problem during the Second World War from which the industry never fully recovered. In any case, plastics have now replaced pearls and mother-of-pearl for many uses. This is perhaps fortunate, since exploitation and pollution have devastated the natural beds.

Crustaceans are also harvested in numbers off many Australian shores. We enjoyed sand crabs, mud crabs (much tastier than their prosaic names imply), prawns (shrimp), and crayfish. When we were in Wooli, a small coastal town in northern New South Wales, we bought a "kilo" of prawns off a fishing boat that had just come in. The prawns varied considerably in size and were still warm from a brief boiling; they were well worth the hour it took us to shell them, dip them in melted butter, and devour them at our camp. In front of a fire in the elegant Fox and Hounds Restaurant not far from Eaglehawk Neck on the windblown, rocky coast of southeastern Tasmania, we treated ourselves to a "cray." That large crayfish, unlike the smaller ones found in our own creeks and rivers, is marine, and while tasty, it did not seem to us to be worth the rather high price. The price, we were told, was due to increasing scarcity, as many are harvested for export.

True freshwater crayfish occur in many Australian streams. Called "yabbies," they too are esteemed as food. They range in size from an inch-long midget occurring in Queensland to a Tasmanian giant crayfish said to reach fourteen pounds in weight: together the smallest and the largest crayfish in the world. Some of these crayfish travel considerable distances overland, either seeking food or moving from one stream to another. Our major acquaintance with them came about rather abruptly, when we were hiking a trail in the rain forest of Lamington National Park during a rain. Suddenly a crayfish about ten inches long, red, white and blue in color (we were cold sober!) appeared in the trail before us, challenging us with its pincers. Later we saw several more, all equally gaudy and equally prepared to defend themselves.

When the salt lakes of the Interior fill with water, they are often the home of shield shrimps or "tadpole shrimps," odd-looking olive-green shrimps with a carapace remotely like that of the extinct trilobites. The eggs of these shrimps are drought-resistant, and when the lakes dry out they persist in the soil or may even be blown about in dust storms. When the lakes fill, they hatch and develop rapidly, often filling the lakes with countless millions. Shield shrimps belong to a primitive group of crustaceans called the branchiopods, literally "foot-breathers," since parts of their legs are modified for respiration. They are by no means confined to Australia; in fact, similar species abound at times in some of the temporary lakes of our own Southwest.

Australia's most unusual crustaceans are the mountain shrimps of Tasmania. They have no carapace and are one to two inches long, brownish in color, with fully segmented bodies and many leglike appendages, almost suggesting a centipede. Mountain shrimps belong to a group first discovered in 1865 as fossils in Illinois coal-bearing strata, something like 250 million years old. No one suspected there were members of this ancient group still living until 1893, when they were found in some of the lakes of western Tasmania. Here they have apparently survived unchanged for many millions of years through isolation in clear, cold waters containing few predators. Will they survive the introduction of trout, and the various hydroelectric projects completed or planned in Tasmania? So far they have managed, after a fashion.

Shrimplike creatures abound in the Great Barrier Reef. Some are nearly transparent; others have spindly legs much longer than their bodies; others are striped and spotted in incredible patterns. Perhaps the most striking is the harlequin shrimp, also called the elegant coral shrimp and the painted prawn. This is an animal about two inches long, with strange, leaflike appendages, its body light pink and covered with large orange-brown or purple spots. These coral reef inhabitants almost always occur in pairs and feed exclusively on starfish, including the formidable crown-of-thorns. We have seen these remarkable creatures only once, in the excellent public aquarium in Noumea, New Caledonia.

The harlequin shrimp has been of special interest to the German biologist Wolfgang Wickler, a colleague of Konrad Lorenz. Dr. Wickler finds them an unusual example of monogamy in a group not noted for prolonged associations between the sexes. It appears that the male and female cooperate in subduing their large and tough-skinned prey. Their courtship is interesting, too. When the female molts, the male begins to court her energetically, and after extended foreplay the two become locked in a tight embrace, their bodies tangled in a ball of brightly spotted carapace and protruding appendages.

Among the many Australian crabs, we were especially impressed by the soldier crabs, small, brightly colored animals that move forward rather than sideways like most crabs. When the tide is going out, these crabs emerge from the sand and move toward the water like a troop of soldiers, sometimes hundreds of them or even thousands,

A pair of harlequin shrimps, their curious antennae and stalked eyes facing the photographer.
(Wolfgang Wickler)

feeding on detritus left by the receding tide and apparently preferring to do so socially rather than by themselves. When the tide returns, they break ranks and once again corkscrew into the sand.

Beachcombing in Australia is probably unequalled anywhere in the world, and we indulged in it, too, no matter on which beach we found ourselves. Although most of us concentrate on shells, there are other interesting items around for observing, if not collecting. On a hot, fly-infested beach on Phillip Island southeast of Melbourne, we found the remains of a small whale.

At Yeppoon, Queensland, just north of the Tropic of Capricorn, the beach at low tide appeared to be covered with tiny pebbles, which upon closer inspection turned out to be pellets of sand formed by a crab belonging to the ghost crab family, a species delightfully called the sand bubbler. The crab dashes into its burrow if anything approaches, but we lay quietly on our stomachs and waited, and soon out came the little creature, about the size of the tip of one of our little fingers. With its spoon-shaped chelae it began to scoop up sand and push it into its mouth, and soon a small ball of sand formed above the mandibles and was brushed off if it did not fall off. It seems that any organic material found in the watery sand is allowed to settle out and is then swallowed; the inorganic remains are then "balled" and discarded as the animal moves along—leaving behind long lines of pellets radiating from the burrow entrance. This constant forward movement and pellet formation keeps the crab from refiltering the same sand over and over—a very efficient procedure! As one surveys the enormous expanse of covered beach, one gets the impression that the crab population is tremendous, or that the food-gathering activity of the crabs present is inexhaustible, or both.

On Kemp beach, a few miles south of Yeppoon, there were no sand pellets, but that beach was unusual with its shell debris above the high-tide line. It was a mixture of small cone shells, clam shells, bits of coral, and so forth, and so thick that the beach seemed to be covered with macaroni. So shell collectors can find much to be happy about on almost any Australian shore, but there are some who have become such fanatics that they have taken up scuba diving in order to collect the fresh shells where they grow and before pounding surf and other collectors reduce the choices. It seems to us, though, that nothing can replace the exhilaration of long beach walks through wind, spray, sun, crowds of gulls, and scattering crabs. Consequently, we have collected shells here and there, not systematically but simply as mementos of beaches we have enjoyed and of the remarkable colors and shapes these organisms have so mysteriously evolved.

Our shelves are crowded with boxes of cowrie shells in delicate patterns of red and brown and yellow, pastel butterfly shells like fallen petals, grey-blue moonshells, orange scallops, murex spirals looking like nothing so much as decorated castle turrets, whelks for listening to the ocean, hard worm castings, bits of coral, sand dollar and sea urchin shells. We even have some cone shells which, had we found them with the animal alive within, we might have regretted collecting. There are a number of cones that obtain food, such as fish, by injecting the prey with poisonous venom, and if a person unsuspectingly picks up a live cone by the narrow end, he or she may be seriously and perhaps fatally wounded.

The sea beach to many people is more than the sum of its sand, shells, and sun; it is a place where the mysteries of the sea at times lie exposed, reminding one that beyond the shore is a world in which man is a stranger, a world he has hardly begun to understand. Rachel Carson put it well in her book *The Edge of the Sea:*

> To understand the life of the shore, it is not enough to pick up an empty shell and say "This is a murex," or "That is an angel wing." True understanding demands intuitive comprehension of the whole life of the creature that once inhabited this empty shell: how it survived amid surf and storms, what were its enemies, how it found food and reproduced its kind, what were its relations to the particular sea world in which it lived.

Life on a coral reef, or along a coastal beach, is complex and interdependent—almost beyond comprehension. In tropical waters, as on tropical lands, food chains are expecially long, mainly because there are so many organisms involved. And because population numbers are so great and species so diverse, a tremendous variety of adaptations have developed among these creatures to enable each one to avoid being eaten while increasing its chance of getting food and surviving to maturity and producing young. We know about the adaptive value of color, shape, stinging cells, and venomous darts, symbiotic algae in jellyfishes and clams, a fish that can walk on its fins, and many other such factors, but there are probably even more adaptations we have not as yet discovered.

Yet in spite of current knowledge, many of our plants and animals are being destroyed, often not deliberately, but by indirect pollution or changing of habitats. The natural beds of the Sydney rock oyster in the estuaries of the Hawkesbury River became silted and polluted almost to the point that oyster growing and harvesting there were nonexistent. Today artificial beds and better pollution control have changed that dismal picture. Tasmanian crayfish have become scarce (and expensive, as we mentioned) because of over-fishing. Barra-

One of Australia's beautiful and largely empty beaches. This one is near Kempsey, New South Wales.

mundi, the most popular food fish in Australia, is thought to be having similar problems in northern waters.

But perhaps the greatest tragedy in Australian waters is the mistreatment of the Great Barrier Reef. In the northern part, where it is closer to the coast, it has received runoff from rivers polluted with agricultural wastes, including insecticides, herbicides, silt, and fertilizers. Mining wastes have added to the problem, as have direct wastes from city sewers and various coastal industrial plants, such as the aluminum refining plant in Gladstone, "the gateway to Heron Island" (which fortunately is fifty miles off the shore).

A still more serious threat is posed by limestone mining and oil drilling on the reef—activities that are still limited in scope but likely to become extensive as the scramble for resources accelerates with increasing world population. The tourist industry must take some blame, too, for the presence of resorts with hotels, underwater observatories, and people who collect shells—all causing changes on the Great Barrier Reef. The Queensland state government has tended to favor the developers over the conservationists and scientists. It has also granted permits for building refineries and developing mines on or near the coastal waters, with little attention to adequate pollution controls. One of the most amusing, but at the same time frightening, bumper stickers we saw in Brisbane said: "See Queensland first before [the premier] sells it."

Into the middle of these controversies came the crown-of-thorns starfish in the 1960s. It seemed that in areas near the center of the Great Barrier Reef, where the coral had been disturbed most by drilling and heavy pollution, the crown-of-thorns increased greatly in numbers and proceeded to eat the coral polyps at phenomenal speed—thus devastating vast areas of the reef. Some people maintain that the population explosions are cyclic, and that the numbers will drop in time and the reef recover. However, the starfishes do seem to be working their way south, and although, as we said, we never saw any while walking on the reef around Heron Island, they have been reported there in increasing though not epidemic numbers.

Under Australia's peculiar national park system, wherein all "national parks" are financed and managed by the state governments, certain islands on the Great Barrier Reef, including Heron, are Queensland national parks. Thus some protection exists, but most conservationists are hoping that the federal government will take over the entire area and create a Great Barrier Reef Marine National Park. In 1975 an act was passed to create the machinery to do this, but to date no suitable legislation has resulted, mainly because the Queensland government is opposed to it. Concern for the reef increases steadily all across Australia, however, and we believe that increased pressure from Australian voters and concerned internationalists will finally bring about suitable protective laws. At least we hope so.

To persons long associated with the east coast of Australia, the effects of man's disregard for this complex watery realm are all too apparent. For many years Percy Trezise was a pilot for Ansett Airlines, and his interest in saving Queensland's rain forests and the Great Barrier Reef (and also aboriginal art sites) developed as he flew over these areas and noticed changes he did not like. In his 1973 book, *Last Days of a Wilderness*, he wrote of the reef:

> I had discovered many years before that the Reef was best seen from an aircraft flying about five hundred feet above it. In those days when flying the DC3 from Cairns to Cooktown we used to fly out to the huge spread of Batt Reef, then proceed along a string of reefs up to the Hope Islands, past Endeavour Reef and on into Cooktown.
>
> On a sunny morning the colours of the reef were breathtakingly beautiful—the stuff that dreams are made of. In the clear water we would see sharks, schools of dugong and fish, large stringrays and turtles which dived in fright when the shadow of the plane passed over them. In the winter months we often saw whales, huge black shadows underwater which would suddenly surface to blow white spumes high in the air.

Later Trezise added:

> We made the same flight later in a Fokker Friendship but it was much less interesting than in former days. The sea and reef were just as beautiful but many of our old friends had gone. Many whales had been slaughtered when passing Tangalooma whaling station and now none ever came north again to give birth to their calves in warm tropic seas. Occasionally a solitary old dugong could be seen patrolling over Batt Reef, but most of his kind, along with the turtles, had been drowned in the shark-meshing operations in Trinity Bay.

Any serious intrusions into these complex webs of life are unthinkable to a scientist, too. In 1980 the marine biologist A. J. Domm, in his essay "The Future of the Great Barrier Reef," wrote as follows:

> After eight years of living and working on the Great Barrier Reef I still find it an exhilarating experience to stand alone on a reef, assailed by the thunder and spray of ocean waves. I am always overcome by a sense of wonder that the reef underfoot, so gigantic and durable against the relentless sea, is the product of tiny plants or animals as delicate as flowers. I have often asked myself sadly whether these reefs and their delicate architects, which for thousands of years have withstood the forces of nature, can possibly survive the activities of man in the future.

In his conclusion he said:

> The Great Barrier Reef is still relatively pristine and it is one of the last untouched wilderness areas left on earth. We can only hope that Australia will set a good example to the world in the way it manages this wonderful asset. This will only be achieved by combining an understanding of how reefs function biologically with a realistic appraisal of the dangers that lie ahead. . . ."

9

THE ABORIGINES

"The Earth . . . furnishes them with all things necessary"

When white Europeans first discovered Australia in the eighteenth century, they found a land already populated—with black men who appeared to be, to quote William Dampier, "the miserablest people in the world." That they were without clothes, or permanent homes, and used stone and shell tools, seemed to indicate that they were indeed "Stone Age" relics, left behind by a changing world because they were so isolated on their island continent.

Aborigines are thought to have been in Australia for at least 30,000 years, probably 40,000 or perhaps more, and to have come across from southeastern Asia when the level of the ocean was lower and sailing distances between islands were shorter and less dangerous. No one knows for sure how many times such trips were made, or exactly which route or routes were used. Was it through New Guinea (most probable), or across from Java and Timor (more dangerous in little boats), or some other way? And why did these people migrate? Were some of their trips accidental—boats or rafts blown off course? Did some move out because it was too crowded at home? Were some men just curious about distant shores, or perhaps just running away? The questions cannot be answered with any certainty.

For some time scholars had thought there were three distinct types of aborigines, and so they must have come from three different places. Another theory, never taken seriously by most, was that they were direct descendants of Java Man, or his immediate ancestor, and survived only because they were isolated in Australia. Today all agree that the Australian aborigines are true modern men, members of *Homo sapiens*, as we all are. Further, as more and more archeological evidence appears, and more linguistic and blood group studies are made, it becomes difficult not to believe that the first Australians were people of a common origin, that they entered the continent through Cape York in the northeast, and then spread out slowly across the land as their numbers increased—first around the coasts and up the river valleys, and finally into the sparse, arid areas of the Center.

One interesting side problem in this story has been the aborigines' dog, the dingo, which every aboriginal family on mainland Australia has seemed to own in abundance since long before 1788, but which (as we have mentioned elsewhere) was never in Tasmania. The missing dingo, plus some apparent differences in the physical features of the Tasmanian aboriginal people, caused some anthropologists to theorize that Tasmania had been settled by people coming from a different place than those who first settled in mainland Australia—perhaps Melanesia or India. This may continue to be argued for some time, especially as there are no more full-blooded Tasmanian aborigines, but the most acceptable explanation seems to be that the first people to reach Tasmania came across from mainland Australia before Tasmania and Victoria were separated by the sea, or at least barely separated, and that they had no dingoes to bring with them. It was on one of the later migrations from the East Indies that the dingoes entered Australia with their masters, and these later migrants (dog and man) never made their way across Bass Strait to Tasmania.

In 1788, before white settlement, 300,000 or so aborigines are thought to have been in Australia. They were not evenly distributed across the land, but, as might be expected, tended to be concentrated in areas with better food supplies. They were divided into about six hundred tribes at that time. The tribes varied in size and consisted of groups that had a common language (more or less) and whose members shared their hunting grounds and religious beliefs. Early students of human history in Australia were puzzled by the variety of languages spoken over the continent and by the fact that members of one tribe really could not converse easily with anyone from another tribe. But as it became more and more evident that the aborigines had been in Australia much longer than first thought, these diversities of language and of physical appearance became easier to understand.

Australian aborigines are often called "blacks," though in fact their features are quite different from those of blacks of African or of Melanesian or Polynesian origin. Their skin is dark brown, their noses broad, their eyes brown and deep-set beneath prominent brow ridges; their hair is wavy and generally brown. Although their bodies are well proportioned, they have relatively thin arms and legs, so that their hands and feet appear large. The children are most attractive, and young adults often strikingly handsome.

Before the advent of whites, the aborigines wore little or no clothing, although in southern parts of the continent in winter they sometimes used skins of kangaroos or possums for warmth. Their bodies were, however, often decorated with cicatrices cut into the chest or back, or with head bands, earrings of shell or bone, nose pegs, or in times of ceremony, paints applied to the skin in elaborate patterns. Those near white settlements or mission outposts were taught very early to wear Western clothing, and nowadays virtually all of them do. We were told that the first use of clothing in some of the missions was accompanied by outbreaks of tuberculosis among the aborigines, perhaps partly from continued wearing of clothing that was damp and dirty. So the "rules" were relaxed, as long as they came to church fully clothed. Living as they did close to the soil and in areas where water was at a premium, they were not accustomed to bathing, and even today many of them have not adopted the Western custom of hypercleanliness.

In the spring of 1972, we had an opportunity to travel to an aboriginal preserve deep in the Center, near the point where South Australia, Western Australia, and Northern Territory meet. Here we spent several days camping with some of the Pitjantjara people. Our aboriginal guide, Jimmie Mujanji, had taken us to meet his parents, his uncles and his aunts, and his brother, who lived in the open, far from any white settlements. His father was a most impressive old gentleman who wore only a single garment, a tattered shirt which did not quite reach far enough to cover his genitals. The women wore dresses of a sort, and spent their days gathering edible plants (where they found them in this desolate country was beyond us). The men spent their days hunting, carrying spears and spear throwers, but they did not catch much except lizards, although part of a kangaroo hung from a mulga tree near their camp.

Our party carried a rifle, and Jimmie urged us to shoot an emu for his father, which we reluctantly did. This the aborigines placed in the coals of their fire and covered with dirt; after a while it was removed, half-cooked and dirty (by our standards), and was devoured eagerly by all the family—with help from their dogs. We impolitely declined to join them. Jimmie sometimes ate canned Western food with us, but he obviously preferred "bush tucker."

At night Jimmie's family slept around a campfire, protected from the wind by a small lean-to; their dogs crowded close to the fire, too, providing extra warmth during the cold night. We could not communicate with them, and even Jimmie knew only a few words of English, but we gathered that from time to time they moved their camp, but only rarely had any contact with whites. By our standards these people appeared shabby and dirty, yet they laughed readily, and seemed alert, intelligent, and happy.

At the headquarters of the Preserve, a village called Amata, many miles to the east, there was a commissary and a small hospital. Burns, we were told, were the major problem among these people—burns from having rolled into the fire during the night. Respiratory problems were also common, and many of the children had runny noses, which rather spoiled their cheerful good looks. There were young families with children living around headquarters. Many of the children would receive something of an education, after which most of them would migrate to population centers, leaving only the older people to preserve some remnant of their former way of life.

When we were in the Northern Territory in 1979, we spent several days in the area between the South and East Alligator Rivers, an area newly opened up to tourists because of a recently improved road to a uranium mine on the edge of the Arnhem Land plateau. We had no chance for direct contact with the aborigines there, but outside of the recently built motel and pub they gathered in groups and seemed to chatter and argue constantly, usually at the top of their voices (or so it seemed to us as we could not understand their language). They evidently lived in the bush nearby, and gathered here to socialize and to indulge in a soft drink or beer now and then. In the Border Store at the East Alligator just outside of the Arnhem Land Aboriginal Reserve, however, we saw aboriginal families quietly buying groceries, and we enjoyed watching their smiling children as much as they seemed to enjoy watching us. Today, in the 1980s, there are said to be no aborigines anywhere in Australia who have not at least sampled the white man's tea, sugar, flour, and tobacco; nor many adult males who have not sampled his alcoholic beverages.

As long as white people considered black people

to be inferior, as long as they considered them merely primitive or, worse, savage, they made little or no attempt to know or to understand them. If they showed any interest in the aborigines, it usually was only to teach them to be "civilized," or to take advantage of them as cheap labor. It appeared inconceivable to them that aborigines were men and women with daily routines, family ties, a complicated system of marriage codes, a history, a religion, and a profound knowledge of the environment. But their culture has turned out to be more complex than Australia's white founding fathers could ever have imagined had they tried.

As no one land area could support large numbers of people at one time, at least for long, the daily gathering of food was done in smaller groups (two or three families), the whole tribe coming together only for special occasions. These family groups would set up a temporary camp near a water hole and stay there until the area's foods and/or water began to give out. Each morning the women and children took their digging sticks and coolamons (a slightly rounded piece of smooth bark or wood for carrying food as well as babies) and went out to forage mainly for plant foods—roots, tubers, seeds, leaves, berries, nuts. They also looked for insects and other smaller animals that they could catch with their hands. Termites, honey ants, and "witchetty" grubs were among their favorites, as were bird and lizard eggs, and honey. If they were near water, they collected mussels, clams, oysters, and crayfish, although sometimes it was the men who brought these back to camp.

Most mornings the men went hunting with their spears and clubs, looking for fish, lizards, snakes, ducks or other birds, kangaroos and wallabies or any meat that would sustain the group for a day or two. There were times when the men were not too successful, and the women's "tucker" was the only food. The meat was normally cooked (barely, as we have already indicated) over the fire, but many of the plant foods were eaten raw. Some, however, were ground into flour and baked, while others, those which contained poisons, were soaked in water first for several days, and then eaten directly, or dried, ground, baked, and then eaten.

Some days, especially when food gathering was not urgent, the men stayed in camp to prepare for coming ceremonies, or to make or repair their tools and weapons. Spears were probably the most important of these because they were used for hunting, although sometimes they had ceremonial uses, too. Spears varied considerably in shape and size, but usually they were six to eight feet long and were tipped with stone, bone or hardwood. The tips were fastened on with sinews (usually kangaroo) and sometimes also by sticky gum, often obtained by pulverizing, winnowing, and heating spinifex grass or something similar. A spear thrower (woomera) was frequently used with a spear to give it more force. In addition to these, men might carry clubs and nonreturning boomerangs, which were also hunting implements. The returning boomerang, much more curved than the nonreturning kind, was used mainly for amusement and only in certain areas; it was hardly the centerpiece of aboriginal life that it is sometimes made out to be.

In addition to these basic items, many aborigines made axes, shields, baskets and dilly bags for carrying food items, and ornaments for the body, such as arm bands, necklaces, and hair "pins." Some even made canoes and rafts. These were often intricately decorated by carving or painting, as too were the more basic tools and weapons. Much has been said about the aborigines' primitive way of life, but the fact that most survived with comparative ease in an environment white men later found extremely harsh points to the fact that their technology, though simple by today's standards, was finely attuned to the requirements of the land in which they lived.

Except in times of serious drought, aboriginal life was not too taxing to individuals. Hunting and food gathering usually took only three or four hours a day and it was a happy, social time. Evenings were spent around fires, as shelters were seldom erected except to keep off bad winds or rain. Wars, that is, armed attacks, were not common, and were committed by avenging parties (in most cases) out to right real or imagined violations of tribal laws, usually about women, or perhaps unexplained killings. Most aborigines had few material possessions,

Porcupine grass, or spinifex, often grows in concentric rings. It was once highly valued by aborigines, who obtained a gum from it useful for fastening the tips on spears.

mainly because they were nomads, and when they moved they took only what they could carry. Some authorities feel that this way of life also kept families small, for a nomadic woman would be handicapped if she had too many small children. But the children they did have were loved and pampered.

While the children were growing up, they accompanied the women on their food-foraging trips, but much of their time was spent in play modeled on adult activities. The girls cared for the babies and gathered such food as they could reach, while the boys had little spears and spent hours learning how to throw them successfully. Once an aborigine became an adult, however, he or she was expected to live by strict tribal laws and codes. For example, marriages were arranged, usually while the girl, at least, was still a baby or perhaps not yet born.

Within a tribe were various kinship groups based on family relationships, and marriages could be arranged only between different groups (to prevent incest). There were some variations across tribes, but usually the wife went to live in her husband's household at puberty, often joining other wives. Older men often had several wives, insuring their chances of being well cared for in old age. Most men did not marry young (wives were not available to them), but spent their time learning the tribal lore from their elders. If any of these codes or laws were broken, as for example, if a younger man stole one of the wives of an elder, he was severely punished, perhaps banished or even

killed. Revealing tribal secrets was certain death.

Central to aboriginal life was religion, and traditional aboriginal religion begins with "The Dreamtime." Once long ago, according to the tribal elders, the world was without shape and without life, much like a flat, barren plain. Then out of this arose the ancestral spirits, who roamed the earth, sometimes in the shape of men, often as goannas, or snakes, or emus or bandicoots, or any other native animals, or plants, or even as elemental forces. The stories of their escapades are plentiful, and while they vary with different tribes in different localities, there are many similarities in these myths of The Dreamtime.

These ancestral spirits created mountains and valleys and rivers, the stars and the moon, caves and pools, trees, crows, kookaburras—all things, including men. They were not human, yet they behaved like humans—hunting, dancing and singing, fighting, marrying. Nor was there one spirit more important than any other. The Dreamtime came to a sudden end, however, when the ancestral spirits disappeared, some into the sky, others into water holes, or caves, or similar landmarks, which were left behind as signs of their former earthly existence. These places became the sacred places, and could be visited only by those properly initiated into tribal lore.

The Dreamtime, though gone, survives into the present, not only by the constant physical reminders, but also by the inherited laws, taboos, customs, and material possessions (fire, tools, and weapons) of the modern tribe. In addition, the spirits persist, though unseen, and give form to all new plants and animals. When a human dies, the aborigines believe the spirit escapes the body (after the proper ceremonies) and is free to roam or assume a new body. A woman's pregnancy is recognized only after it has been shown that a spirit has entered her when she was at a suitable site, or if she or her husband have had a suitable dream. So the past and present as well as the future are all linked through the lore of The Dreamtime.

One of the most articulate men to study aboriginal religion and interpret it for us is W. E. H. Stanner, Emeritus Professor of Anthropology at the Australian National University in Canberra. He finds The Dreamtime, or The Dreaming, as he calls it, to rank philosophically with the world's best metaphysical thought. He says:

> In my own understanding, The Dreaming is a proof that the blackfellow [aborigine] shares with us two abilities which have largely made human history what it is.
>
> The first of these we might call "the metaphysical gift." I mean ability to transcend oneself, to make acts of imagination so that one can stand "outside" or "away from" oneself, and turn the universe, oneself, and one's fellows into objects of contemplation. The second ability is a "drive" to try to "make sense" out of human experience and to find some "principle" in the whole human situation. The "drive" is, in some way, built into the constitution of the human mind. No one who has real knowledge of aboriginal life can have any doubt that they possess, and use, both abilities very much as we do. They differ from us only in the directions in which they turn their gifts, the idiom in which they express them, and the principles of intellectual control.

The Dreaming is, he states, "a kind of narrative of things that once happened; a kind of charter of things that still happen; and a kind of *logos* or principle of order transcending everything significant for aboriginal man."* The tales of The Dreamtime make little sense to an outsider, he points out, because they are heard not only out of context (away from the people and the land to which they

*Stanner's remarkable essay has been reprinted several times, but first appeared in 1956 in *Australian Signpost*, edited by T. A. G. Hungerford (Melbourne: Cheshire), pages 51–65. We found it in *Reader in Comparative Religion: An Anthropological Approach* (1972), edited by W. A. Lessa and E. Z. Vogt (3d. ed. New York: Harper and Row), pages 269–77. The most recent reprint is in Stanner's 1979 collection of essays, *White Man Got No Dreaming*, published by the Australian National University Press in Canberra.

belong), but also in ignorance of their poetic, symbolic philosophy.

A "corroboree," in modern Australian parlance, is an evening of aboriginal singing and dancing and general good time. The term, probably a corruption of some dialect name, may but does not usually distinguish between the sacred religious rituals restricted to the adult men (or, in some cases, women) of a tribe and the secular merriment enjoyed by all. To the aborigines, however, there was a great difference; the religious ones were serious and exact, while the secular fetes depended on the mood of the participants at the time. There were two types of serious ceremonies, one having to do with the initiation of the young into adulthood (probably the most sacred), and the other, called "increase," having to do with insuring the fertility of various plants and animals so that there would be plenty of food in the coming seasons.

The religion of the Australian aborigines has been called "totemic," and although the exact meaning has never been too clear (at least to us), we do know that it implies a close relationship of a person or persons to specific natural objects. These objects were then their totems, and had a special meaning. If a man's totem was a crocodile, then all crocodiles were his brothers. Families could have a totem, or the women or the men of a family group could belong to a particular totem, but different one from another. As all natural objects had been created by the ancestral spirits, either in The Dreamtime or since then in ways made possible by those spirits, then the people, the land, the plants and animals were all interdependent, though some were closer than others. And if a person brought up in such a religion was removed from his home area, he would be as bewildered as we might be in a foreign country whose language we did not understand and whose landmarks and heritage we did not know or appreciate.

The aboriginal tribal heritage was entrusted to the care of the elders of each tribe, much as it was to those of the Indian tribes in our country. It was slowly revealed by those older men to the younger ones as they went through the initiation rituals, which might last from a few months to several years. One of the first initiatory actions usually was a marking of the boys by knocking out a front tooth (or some similar defacement), by circumcision, and in some tribes, subincision. These were obviously painful, but, according to most anthropological reports, endured stoically and silently by each initiate to prove his worthiness. Once these were over, the revealing of the tribal secrets began.

Tribal lore was not told in everyday language, but dramatically danced, usually to the accompaniment of songs and chants rendered in rather archaic but poetic language learned especially for these rituals. The initiates learned the meanings of the sacred landmarks, as well as of previously hidden sacred objects or "tjurunga," which could be stones, often decorated, shells, feathers, and other small objects, many of which also worked important magic. In some tribes, for example, the boys soon knew that the terrible shrieking of the bullroarer (a piece of flat wood on a string whirled over the head) was really the cry of an ancient spirit keeping away the uninitiated. Later they might learn that revenge could be sought through the magic of the pointed bone (the victim merely lay down and died unless a more powerful sorcery was worked) or by the kurdaitcha man, who tracked his victim stealthily while he wore his kurdaitcha shoes (made of emu feathers stuck on with blood) to leave no tracks.

Very few white men learned any tribal secrets in the eighteenth and nineteenth centuries, but as more and more tribes were dispersed, annihilated, or assimilated into white society, many of the remaining tribal elders decided (against the threat of death) that the only way to keep their rich lore from being lost forever was to give it to those white men who were interested. So, secrets kept orally by only a few properly initiated elders for centuries were finally written down for posterity. As Dr. Stanner pointed out, the lore does lose much of its meaning when separated from tribal lands and people; nonetheless, a good translation of the songs, and especially the sacred ones, should give any reader or listener a better grasp of the emotions involved—of the poetic and musical appeal of the words.

Pidgin English, used by so many white settlers when dealing with aborigines, though originally not meant to be so, became a "put-down," and by its continued use white men lost out, too, by failing to learn and appreciate the native languages, and consequently the native oral literature.

The songs and accompanying dances presented to the young initiates on the sacred site were really musical dramas. The participants, the older, already knowledgeable men, were costumed to represent the totemic ancestral spirits—perhaps with gaily painted and feathered headdresses, maybe with masks or with their bodies painted in intricate designs. Sometimes feathers might be added (held in place by dried blood), or beads, or shells. The women had ceremonies, too, to initiate the girls into womanhood, at least in some if not all tribes; but either the women's rites were not very theatrical or less is known about them (because, some say, most anthropologists have been male and so the women's stories have not been told to them). Most tribal legends were apparently familiar in a general way to all members of a tribe, but the details as well as the specific sacred sites and objects (and the sacred songs and dances about them) were reserved for the initiated only.

The myths of one tribe were quite different from those of another, generally speaking, but one legend that seems to have been present pretty much across the continent was that of the Rainbow Serpent. In some tribes, the Rainbow Serpent was a female, a "mother-earth" type figure; in other tribes, probably the majority, the Rainbow Serpent was a man, old and revered for his wisdom. He could live in winding rivers (hence the snakelike shape), or in waterfalls showing rainbow colors as they fell, or up in the sky as a rainbow, or as a human. He showed many human foibles, especially anger if he did not get his own way. He once swallowed all of the tribal ancestors because they displeased him, and then, just before disappearing into the river, spit them all up and left them strewn around like bodies after a flood. He had two wives, according to another version, and one was stolen by the man who belonged to the Bat Totem. The Rainbow Serpent chased the pair, and as in any good chase scene in a modern movie, tellers of this tale could make a marvelous, exciting drama for an appreciative audience. Eventually the Rainbow Serpent and the Bat Man killed each other, and their spirits went back to their old homes, the Rainbow Serpent into the water hole, and the Bat into the sky. (We did not hear what happened to the erring wife!)

Still another story of the Rainbow Serpent reminded us of Wagner's Rhine maidens: the Rainbow Serpent had several daughters and they all lived in a big pool. Occasionally one of the daughters would come out, change herself into a beautiful woman and lure a lover to the pool, where he would plunge in and disappear forever.

There are many of what we might call "how-and-why" stories in various tribes, and one typical one (which happens to come from Arnhem Land) is about a turtle and a spiny anteater, or echidna. Once Echidna Woman and Freshwater Tortoise Man, in their human shapes, quarreled over a snail, which both wanted to eat. The quarrel continued until finally Tortoise became so angry he picked up a bundle of bamboo spears nearby and threw them at Echidna. They stuck in her back and became quills. She then retaliated by hurling a large flat stone at Tortoise, and it stuck to his back like a shell. That is how they became as they are today.

These tales can be paraphrased and retold innumerable times by us or other outsiders, but these shortened versions could not in any way convey the feelings, the magical mood that must have been created by the aboriginal artists in their proper outdoor "theater." Fortunately, there have been some attempts to make poetic translations, particularly of nonsacred songs. These are long, and like our own chorales, have many repetitive lines. Here is a sample of one we think particularly lovely:

> The "swallow" approaches, flying through the west wind and the rain clouds.
> The "swallow"—its feathers blown by the wind—
> It is always there, at the wide expanse of water—

Flying through the west wind, and the dark storm clouds,
Flying through the wind, close to the clouds—
It flies through the wind, close to the wide expanse of water—
All over the country, the bird flies low:
To the place of the Clouds, and the Sea-Eagle place, to Goulburn Islands, and Milingimbi Point,
All over the sky; to the place of Coloured Reflections, the place of the Western Clouds—
Bird, with its feathers blown by the wind—
The "swallow," flying through the west wind and rain clouds—
Winds from the west calling, like sacred singing.*

Most aboriginal singing was unaccompanied, except by the clapping of hands or sticks. In parts of northern Australia, however, there were also simple drums, and a special instrument called the "didjeridu." The latter was made by hollowing out a sapling or large tree branch, which was about a yard in length and perhaps two inches in diameter. It was played by blowing into it, and an expert produced two very vibrant low notes to accompany the singers. Perhaps a simple trumpet might be the best comparison, although we found the didjeridu much harder to blow, and really not like any trumpets we have heard or tried to play. We have a didjeridu and prize it, although we cannot play it. It has been prepared and hand painted in the traditional way, and as each artist (like artists everywhere) has his own style, our didjeridu is not exactly like any other.

Aboriginal art until fairly recently was pretty much restricted to paintings on rock surfaces, on tools and weapons, and on dancers about to perform. Obviously, little was permanent, although some rock chipping (sculpture rather than painting) has survived. The paintings were done with a limited palette of natural dyes of red, yellow, and brown ochres, white and black, and with brushes made from twigs which had been chewed on each end. The paintings at ceremonial sites, usually on walls of caves or on rock pinnacles under large overhangs, were frequently repainted, especially just before important ceremonies. However, once the tribe came under the influence of the white settlers, and the old ways faded, so did the paintings, and today many are indiscernible, others barely visible, and often nothing is known about them.

In Carnarvon Gorge National Park in Queensland are some aboriginal paintings and rock carvings on a cliff not far above a popular trail along the river. They are supposed to be protected, but parks in Australia are greatly underfinanced and inadequately staffed, and vandalism is evident. Far worse, perhaps, is the fact that little if anything is known about the people who created this art. The self-guiding booklet for the park says that within fifty years of the first white man's visit to Carnarvon, the aboriginal culture of the area had been totally destroyed.

Our most exciting view of aboriginal art was on our previously mentioned trip to the Alligator Rivers near the Arnhem Land escarpment. There, a few miles from Cahill's Crossing bordering the Aboriginal Reserve, we visited Obiri Rock, a sandstone pinnacle about fifty feet high, with a large overhang on the west side. The wall at the back of this "open room" was covered with paintings—mostly huge fish, but also kangaroos, goannas, emus, long-necked turtles, human figures, and the ubiquitous hand prints. The fish, barramundi common in local waters, and most of the other animals, were x-ray pictures, which show not only the external features, but also the internal structure—all done with complicated cross-hatching, stippling, and subtle use of the few colors.

Our photographs of these paintings did not come out (our camera developed an allergy to heat), so we were happy to learn that they have been much photographed and studied by experts, who are greatly concerned over their preservation. The

*From Song 22 of "The Goulburn Island Cycle" in *Love Songs of Arnhem Land,* transcribed by R. M. Berndt, (Chicago: University of Chicago Press, 1978), page 68.

Aborigines at a corroboree, an evening of singing and dancing. The man in the right foreground is playing a didjeridu, while the one at left is using music sticks.
(Australian Information Service)

paintings are considered to be some of the finest in the country, but are rapidly fading. That, plus the increasing probability of vandalism as more and more outsiders come into the area, makes their future rather bleak. In 1979 the Australian Institute of Aboriginal Studies published *Australian Aboriginal Art: The Art of the Alligator Region, Northern Territory,* by Robert Edwards. The book includes many photographs of this magnificant art and the art sites (there are many sites in addition to Obiri Rock), and describes what is happening to these paintings—with a plea that the government or some interested party in some way prevent further damage. The paintings have been compared to the frescoes painted 20,000 years ago in the caves of Europe, which also show the animals hunted for food, stick human figures, hand prints, and enigmatic geometrical designs. Edwards tells how England, France, and other countries have preserved their antiquities, and says that it is the duty not only of Australia but of the international community to keep the Arnhem Land art safe.

Aboriginal art today has taken some new twists, and these may preserve it in a more permanent way. Included are sand paintings (done now on artist boards) from central Australia, and bark paintings done mainly by artists from Arnhem Land. On carefully prepared pieces of bark (or on boards), the aboriginal artists paint in the same careful and stylized way their favorite totemic plants and animals, or perhaps a geometric design [colorplate 23]. Like the tribal legends, these pictures, though artistically pleasing, may mean little to outsiders, and can be understood only when explained by the painter. Today, where these paintings are sold, a short explanation usually accompanies the picture.

Also, in central Australia, some aboriginal art-

A rocky overhang in Arnhem Land is covered with a variety of images, including that of a ship, perhaps reflecting contact with trepangers. (Australian Information Service)

ists are expressing themselves in a different way—through a technique long familiar to us, watercolor landscapes. Not far from Alice Springs, a member of the Aranda Tribe, who had worked with and for white men, observed a visiting white artist at work, liked what he saw, and asked to be shown how to paint in a similar way. The aboriginal man was Albert Namatjira (1902–1959), and although his personal life was tragic, his pictures of rugged red cliffs and blue-shadowed mountains behind startling white ghost gums—the brilliant sunlit Center—are world renowned and bring high prices today, and many imitators.

Albert Namatjira's sons, some of his relatives and friends, and now many other Arandas are painting watercolor landscapes and selling them to the tourists through various art galleries. Some are exquisite, some are not, but one wonders how much of the money paid for those pictures reaches the artists. We could not help but notice the many poorly dressed aborigines in Alice Springs, the terrible litter on the roadsides, and the make-shift "houses"—although we were told that many aboriginal families do have permanent dwellings in Alice Springs, Hermannsburg Mission to the west, and other places nearby.

When we arrived in Australia for the first time in 1969, we were not aware of any aboriginal problems. In fact, we were scarcely aware of the aborigines, because in Canberra, where we lived, we did not see any. When we finally asked about aborigines and how Australia seemed to cope with racial problems, we were told by our white neighbors that there were no problems. Too bad the United States could not do as well!

Today in the 1980s aborigines are much more visible. Many have gone to the cities looking for work, their children are in city schools or on city streets, and their activities are apt to be chronicled in local newspapers and on television. Many remain on reserves, of course, but Australia can no longer ignore its problems with its aborigines—the culmination of two hundred years of mistreatment and lack of understanding, beginning with killings and beatings and usurpation of tribal lands, continuing through poverty and disease, discrimination in education and employment, and subjection to a government policy of assimilation (including conversion to Christianity) instead of having equality under the law and control of their own destinies.

Today the black people of Australia, as so often in our own country, are second-class citizens, although their situation is probably more like that of our Indians than any other minority. Many have been put on government reserves or church-affiliated missions, where they may receive food (many are taught to garden or run cattle), medical care, schooling (teachers are usually white and seldom bilingual), and, in the case of missions, spiritual leadership according to the dictates of the particular sect in charge.

Aboriginal leadership, up until very recently, has been virtually absent, or at least not encouraged by the white supervisors. Further, reserves were not necessarily on former tribal lands, and even if they were, the aborigines located there had no control of the land. During World War II, for the first time aboriginal men serving in the army were able to escape these restrictions and receive equal pay with whites for equal work. Once the war was over, however, the old prejudices seemed just as prevalent.

In 1946 aboriginal stockmen from several different tribes in the Pilbara region in northwestern Australia went on strike for better pay and working conditions. The strike was not judged successful, but it did mark the first time that any aboriginal people had organized and done something to fight for their own rights. Not until the 1960s, however, did major changes begin to be made, when for the first time aborigines were included in the national census, and consequently it became obvious that they were not a dying race whose passing needed to be made peaceful. Daisy Bates, the controversial white woman who had abandoned her own family to nurse aborigines from her tent in the bush, had encouraged this attitude of "smoothing the dying pillow." But now the aborigines were not dying (in the 1976 census there were about 160,000, more than one percent of the total population) and had to be dealt with, and so assimilation became the official attitude. Educate the aboriginal people so they can become part of white society; let them learn to be mechanics or secretaries, speak English and join a Christian church. Forget the old ways, the old pagan religion, and the old ties to the land.

But suddenly in the 1960s there were aborigines who stated flatly that they did not want to lose their cultural identities. In 1966 members of the Gurindji Tribe near Darwin struck for better working conditions and the return of their tribal lands. Conditions for tribal members began to improve with better wages, better housing, better health care, and better education, but the government refused to give them land. Not until 1972–73, after much more pressure, did the government finally return at least some of their lands.

In 1977 an aboriginal land rights bill was passed—the first Australian law to recognize that aboriginal cultural values were different and needed to be recognized. The law was not ideal (mining rights remained a problem, and still are), and it only existed in the Northern Territory, but it was a beginning. Further, the national government was to provide money to help aborigines buy pastoral or agricultural lands if desired. The aboriginal "tent embassy" on the lawn of the Parliament House in 1972 did much to publicize the plight of the aborigines, not only to white Australia, but to the world.

Early in 1980 in Alice Springs we had the good fortune to meet and talk with the secretary (white) and two board members (black) of the Central Land Council. They told us about some of the work done by the council in the Northern Territory (southern section), and what they hoped could be accomplished. The aboriginal men also talked about their own lives: one, the president of the council, had studied with Albert Namatjira and still painted, while the other, although he had not had much formal schooling, was very articulate and regretted, he said several times, that he had never had a chance to study English literature.

Both men felt that their people needed to be taught not only vocational training, but also better health procedures and better English so that they could communicate fully with all of the tribes through a common tongue and could live together in settlements without despoiling them with trash. Both men apparently believed that assimilation was inevitable, but that assimilation should not deprive them of their cultural heritage, including the sacred sites on their tribal lands.

There have been white Australians who abhorred the mistreatment of the aborigines, and one of these was Don McLeod, who taught the Pilbara aborigines how to organize a strike, and who also encouraged them in a home industry, mining, where they could use their coolamons (also called yandies) to separate mineral ores much as they winnowed seeds. Patsy Adam Smith, whom we have quoted before, visited Don McLeod at an aboriginal camp, where he lived in a windowless, tin shanty. He showed her around the area, and she wrote of the experience:

> Walking ahead Don missed nothing. He climbed a dead tree and put his hand down a hole in a limb and brought out a baby parrot, naked and squawking; he raised a hand as a signal for silence so we could creep by a flock of budgerigars feeding on seeds in the wild flowers. Once we came on a hollow in a rock, filled with the soft white silky down of the puff-balls. "Did you say there are no fairies?" he said to me. "Put your hand in there. You'll feel the warmth where they slept last night." And again, farther on, in a cradle of blue, bell-like flowers. "Spirit babies. You can't laugh at the Aborigines' talk of spirit babies when you see a cradle made of bells as blue as the sky they fell from."
>
> As we edged our way through this square mile of garden he said, knowing he'd surprise me, "Ever see a mine site as beautiful as this one?" I waited. "This whole area has been yandied by the people." There were no scars. "This is why a yandy is unbeatable for selective mining. They can go through an area of small deposits without tearing up a valley as large machinery would."
>
> That was in 1961. In 1964 I walked again among the flowers that rioted across the valley and up the hills among the rocks. From that date on the Pilbara was in the news. The foreign mining companies had moved in, and buried

> beneath the rubble and turmoil of their passing are the blue-bell cradles of spirit babies and the white silky beds where fairies had slept the night before.

In the 1980s, mining of uranium, coal, diamonds, and many other minerals still threatens the natural landscape, including many sacred sites.

Alan Marshall, another journalist, wrote a book called *These Were My Tribesmen*, which is a collection of stories of his visits to Arnhem Land and Cape York in the 1940s. He said that aborigines could be saved if the government wanted to save them.

> It is a task that must not be delayed. It is above politics, above missions, above the interests of station owning companies, above the interests of buffalo shooters and trepangers, above all interests bent on making profits at the expense of the people who once owned this country.
>
> Any plans for the future of the blackfellow must grant him dignity as well as legal equality, and be based on the fact that all human blood is the same, that skin colour has no connection with intelligence, and that Racism is a myth superstition.

Although Marshall's book was first published in 1948, and went through three editions before coming out in paperback, his advice as given here went largely unheeded.

What is to become of the aborigines and of their needs, especially for land? Professor Colin Tatz, who is director of the Centre for Research into Aboriginal Affairs at Monash University in Melbourne, wrote:

> When people talk about Aborigines they often ask: "What's the solution?" "Solution" suggests there is a "problem" and those who discuss the "problem" infer that somehow Aborigines are a naughty, deviant and difficult bunch who have saddled *us* with a problem. If one begins with the idea, as most people do, that Aborigines must be or should be assimilated or integrated, that they must or should adopt our way of life, outlook, culture and values, then there is some truth in the concept of "problem": the problem of how to change Aborigines, how to devise programmes of social change by what is hideously called social engineering. From an Aboriginal point of view, *we* are the problem: outsiders engaged in trying to re-shape their lives, their attitudes, trying to make them not just plain citizens, but model ones. The way to social and equal acceptance into the Australian mainstream, perhaps, is to be clean, neat, well-dressed, well spoken, Christian, educated and skilled dark Australians.*

Although missions and missionaries were generally involved with the assimilation policy, there was an ardent pastor who is remembered not for his conversions but for his understanding of "his" people. He was Carl Strehlow, a German who came to the Hermannsburg Mission in 1894 to work with the Arandas. His son, the late Professor T. G. H. ("Theo") Strehlow of the University of Adelaide, was born and raised at Hermannsburg, and he spent his life studying and writing and recording Aranda language and beliefs. In his book *Journey to Horseshoe Bend*, which is a tribute to his father, Professor Strehlow wrote (using the formal third person):

> Though Theo [at fourteen] possessed only a vague knowledge of Aranda mythology, he was fully aware that every hill and mountain, every river and creek, every spring, rockhole, and waterhole, every plain and clay-pan, and all the highest dune crests in the sandhill areas, bore names of their own, and that they derived these names from the sacred myths and songs of the Aranda people. Theo also knew that every man, woman, and child, including himself, was linked indivisibly with one special site in the country of his birth. He knew that his father had preserved many of the Aranda

*Quoted from *The Aborigine Today* (1971), page 77.

sacred myths and songs in his scientific writings. . . .

The Aranda folk of Central Australia had always lived and died secure in the belief that their immortal totemic ancestors, too, were living and sleeping in their very midst in this Eternal Land whose geographical features they had created at the beginning of time. To the Aranda, Central Australia had been the Land of Altjira, the Land of Eternity. . . .

Men, animals, and plants might indeed die and turn into dust; but the earth which absorbed their dust yielded new grasses and flowers, new trees and shrubs, fresh food for men and all other living creatures; and, according to Aranda belief, the second souls of all unborn children, too, emanated from the sacred soil of Central Australia.

Carl Strehlow was buried in the land he had come to love, as he had the Aranda people, who belonged to the land. Could we do no less for those modern aborigines, or anyone today, regardless of the color of their skin, who wish to keep their ties to the natural world that they know? As long as there are those of us who love the mists on mountain tops, the wind rustling the leaves, waves breaking on the beaches, an eagle gliding on an updraft, or a butterfly flitting through the shadows to another flower, there will be a need for land untouched by cattle, plows or parking lots—a land that remains as it has always been. And the Australian aborigines, as do all of us, have just and equal claims to this untamed world.

The following poem, "Oration," was written by Kath Walker, a poet who also happens to be an aborigine. This was read on the steps of Parliament House in Canberra in 1970—a tribute to all the aboriginal tribes now gone.

Here, at the invaders talk-talk place,
We, who are the strangers now,
Come with sorrow in our hearts.
The Bora Ring, the Corroborees,
The sacred ceremonies,
Have gone. All gone.
Turned to dust on the land,
That once was ours.
Oh spirits from the unhappy past,
Hear us now.
We come, not to disturb your rest.
We come, to mourn your passing.
You, who paid the price,
When the invaders spilt your blood.
Your present generation comes,
Seeking strength and wisdom in your memory.
The legends tell us,
When our race dies,
So too, dies the land.
May your spirits go with us
From this place.
May the Mother of Life,
Wake from her sleeping,
And lead us on to the happy life,
That once was ours.
Oh Mother of Life,
Oh spirits from the unhappy past,
Hear the cries of your unhappy people,
And let it be so.
Oh spirits—Let it be so.*

*Quoted from *The Aborigine Today* (1971), page 64.

10

EXPLORATION AND SETTLEMENT

"A big, thirsty, hungry wilderness"

"Australian history," wrote Mark Twain, "does not read like history, but like the most beautiful lies. And all of a fresh sort, no moldy old stale ones. It is full of surprises, and adventures, and incongruities, and contradictions, and incredibilities: but they are all true, they all happened."

The story of Western man in Australia is nearly as full of anomalies as the continent's natural history, and it is particularly fascinating to Americans because of the parallels to and departures from our own history. In any case a book on natural history would not be complete without it. The landing of the first boatload of Englishmen at Botany Bay began a transformation of Australia infinitely more rapid and revolutionary than any past changes in climate or position of the continents. Ships, planes, and communication networks have diminished its isolation and its uniqueness, substituting sheep for kangaroos and cricket fields for the site of native corroborees. But were this not so, the continent would scarcely be as accessible as it is!

As we have said elsewhere, Australia was first discovered by man almost 50,000 years ago; but the first recorded landfall by Western man was less than four hundred years ago. Dutch, Spanish, and Portuguese vessels bound for the Spice Islands (the East Indies) tried to take advantage of the westerlies to cross the Indian Ocean. Once across, they could then steer north to their destination. But as they had no chronometers, and the winds were unpredictable, they found themselves now and again abreast of an unknown shoreline, or worse, wrecked on one of the treacherous offshore reefs or islands.

For a long time little was known of these early voyages, and only as modern treasure hunters have uncovered the sunken remains have we learned more about them. We have already told of our trip to the Fremantle Museum, where many of the recent findings are displayed. One of the strangest and bloodiest tales is that of the Dutch ship *Batavia*, one of a fleet of four commanded by Francis Pelsaert. All were carrying money and families of the Dutch East India Company to Java, and Pelsaert was aboard the *Batavia*, although he and the captain did not like each other.

Somehow the *Batavia* became separated from the other ships and one night in June 1629, ran aground on a reef off the west coast near the present city of Carnarvon. In the morning all of the crew and passengers (250, including women and children) went ashore on two nearby islands. When it was discovered that there was no water, Pelsaert and some of the crew rowed twenty-four miles across to the mainland. They spent almost two weeks looking for water without success, then decided to head for the city of Batavia (now Jakarta) for help. After a long and perilous journey in a small, open boat, they eventually arrived, and Pelsaert was given a small vessel, the *Sardam*, in which he was to return and rescue the survivors.

As Pelsaert approached the Australian coast he was intercepted by one of the former crew members, Wiebbe Hayes, who warned him of a threatened mutiny and told a gruesome story. One of the officers, Hieronymus Cornelisz, had taken command by force and had persuaded some of the crew to join him, perhaps with offers to share the women. It was his plan to overcome the rescue ship when it arrived and to use it for piracy. Anyone who opposed his scheme was shot. Before the carnage was over, only 124 people were still alive, some of them (including Wiebbe Hayes) by managing to escape to another island.

Thus forewarned, Pelsaert captured the mutineers and hung the leaders on the spot. Two more of the mutineers he marooned on the mainland and they were never heard from again. Then he sailed back to Batavia with the survivors and the company's money chests. Confirmation of this story came rather recently, when a number of skeletons were found with bullet holes in them.

The Portuguese discovered and settled Timor and explored other islands north of Australia, but they failed to find the continent itself. Dutch trading parties, sailing from the headquarters of the East India Company in Batavia back to Amsterdam, touched on the north and west coasts, and as a result the first outlines of Australia began to appear on maps. But these were bleak and unfriendly coasts, apparently without water and (more important) devoid of spices and gold.

Finally, in 1642, Abel Tasman, a seaman of note, was given two small ships by the East India Company and told to explore southern waters. The company hoped, of course, that he would find new and richer sources of trade goods, and perhaps a more direct route to South American ports, where Spanish wealth might be plundered. Tasman sighted the west coast of Tasmania, which he called Van Diemen's Land after his patron, but he did not sail close enough to realize that it was only an island and not a peninsula. He continued on around New Zealand, again not approaching closely, then up past New Guinea and back to the East Indies, unknowingly skirting the Australian continent. His voyage was a disappointment to the Dutch, and they tended to ignore the area thereafter, leaving it to the English to chart the continent and eventually to settle it.

Although Captain James Cook is the man usually credited with discovering Australia, he was preceded by another, a very colorful Englishman named William Dampier. Born in 1652, Dampier had always wanted to go to sea, did join the British navy, where he served briefly in the West Indies, and then in his late twenties turned pirate and joined others who were harassing Spanish shipping and ports in the New World. Some years later he moved his activities to the South Pacific.

In 1688, while his ship was beached for repairs on the northwest coast of "New Holland," as Australia was then called, Dampier took advantage of the situation to go ashore and explore. Thus he and his companions were the first Englishmen known to set foot on Australian soil. While Dampier had been in the Caribbean, he began to keep a journal of his adventures, noting not only exciting sea fights, dangerous escapes, and other aspects of the life of a pirate, but also recording descriptions of the lands he visited, the people there, the plants and animals, and anything else that came to his keen eye and curious mind as being of interest. From a part of this journal, much revised and rewritten, Dampier published in 1697 *A New Voyage Round the World,* a book that made him famous. In many ways Dampier was a product of his age, for such travel books were common, but his work far excelled the others. Professor P. G. Adams from Louisiana State University wrote of him (in the introduction to a 1968 Dover edition):

> From the appearance of *A New Voyage round the World* in 1697, Dampier was admired and imitated by scientists, mariners, and writers. The Royal Society immediately placed a digest of his book in its *Philosophical Transactions.* Defoe borrowed his facts, parodied his title, and studied his style. Swift, in order to build on the famous writer's prestige, let Lemuel Gulliver follow in his footsteps and call him Cousin Dampier. Sir Hans Sloane, a foremost scientist, became the traveler's personal friend, had his picture painted, and borrowed from him when he wrote his own book about the Indies. Debrosses, compiler of one of the foremost collections of voyages in the eighteenth century, marveled, "Where is it possible to find navigators like William Dampier?"

A second volume of his journal was published two years later, and as a result of these successes, Dampier was taken back into the navy and given a ship, the *Roebuck,* for a voyage to New Holland and New Guinea. Although the ship was old and sank half way through the trip, he and his crew were rescued and returned to England. And through all this, Dampier kept his journal and published from it, in two parts, *A Voyage to New Holland.* In addition, he brought back a collection of plants, as requested by the Royal Society. He made other trips, too, but never again did he meet with as much success, either nautical or literary. He died in London in 1715. Nevertheless, he was unsurpassed as a writer of travel literature. To quote from Adams, again:

> Such accuracy and thoroughness, supported by colorful anecdotes, would cause the renowned scientist-traveler Baron Humboldt to say one hundred years later that illustrious savants such as Condamine had added little to the observations of William Dampier.

Although Dampier called the aborigines "the miserablest People in the World," he went to great pains to describe their appearance, their lack of body covering and of houses ("the Earth being their Bed and the Heaven their Canopy"), their apparent lack of worship, what they ate, how they probably obtained fire, how they were bothered by flies, and so on—all this in three or four pages. He also described the countryside and its plants and animals in similar sparse prose:

> The Land is of a dry sandy Soil, destitute of Water, except you make Wells; yet producing divers sorts of Trees; but the Woods are not thick, nor the Trees very big. Most of the Trees that we saw are Dragon-Trees as we supposed; and these too are the largest Trees of any there.

They are about the bigness of our large Apple-trees, and about the same height; and the Rind is blackish, and somewhat rough. The Leaves are of a dark Colour; the Gum distils out of the Knots or Cracks that are in the Bodies of the Trees. We compared it with some Gum-Dragon or Dragon's Blood that was aboard, and it was of the same colour and taste. The other sort of Trees were not known by any of us. There was pretty long Grass growing under the Trees; but it was very thin. We saw no Trees that bore Fruit or Berries.

We saw no sort of Animal, nor any Track of Beast, but once; and that seemed to be the Tread of a Beast as big as a great Mastiff-Dog. Here are a few small Land-birds, but none bigger than a Black-bird; and but a few Sea-fowls. Neither is the Sea very plentifully stored with Fish, unless you reckon the Manatee and Turtle as such. Of these Creatures there is plenty; but they are extraordinary shy; though the Inhabitants cannot trouble them much having neither Boats nor Iron.

We have mentioned Dampier's influence on Jonathan Swift, who mapped Lilliput far south of Sumatra. Gulliver's ship, the *Antelope*, was "driven by a violent Storm to the Northwest of Van Dieman's Land . . . in the Latitude of 30 Degrees 2 Minutes South." Evidently the Lilliputians lived on the Nullarbor Plain (are they still living there, deep in one of the limestone caves?). James McAuley, in a delightful satirical poem, calls Gulliver's landfall *The True Discovery of Australia.* McAuley pretends to have discovered a letter signed by Gulliver himself, and he uses it to deride the character of Australians of today:

. . . they smile
And sit on their verandahs taking tea,

Watching through the pleasant afternoons
Flood fire and cyclone in successive motion
Complete the work the pioneers began
Of shifting all the soil into the ocean—

The Southern Sea, my lord, in time to come
Will be the Bargain Basement of the earth,
With nations like demented women snatching
Remnants without enquiring what they're
worth.

Since *Gulliver's Travels* was a satire on English life of the eighteenth century, McAuley, a professor of English literature at the University of Tasmania who died quite recently (1976), is surely entitled to these few biting comments about his countrymen—and there is (we think) more than a grain of truth in them.

Almost fifty years elapsed between Dampier's last voyage and Cook's first one, but meanwhile a French explorer, Louis Antoine de Bougainville (whose name is immortalized by that beautiful tropical vine, bougainvillea, which he discovered in Brazil), touched briefly on the Great Barrier Reef as he was going west from Samoa and the New Hebrides. He decided the waters were too dangerous so turned northeast, going out around New Guinea, through the Solomons and then back to Java. Thus he missed touching the coast of northern Queensland by only a few hundred miles or so. It was Captain Cook who finally penetrated the coral reefs and at last discovered the east coast of mainland Australia.

In the Museum of Mankind in London is an impressive exhibit showing the many accomplishments of James Cook, who is considered to have been one of the best if not *the* greatest explorer, navigator, and cartographer. He was born in 1728 of "humble" parents, was a good student, but had to leave school early to help support the family. So at eighteen he entered the coal-shipping industry, and for nine years served aboard coal ships—studying mathematics and navigation in his spare time. When war broke out with France in 1755, he joined the navy. He rose rapidly through the non-commissioned ranks, and in 1758 went to Canada as a ship's master on the HMS *Pembroke.* While in Canada he learned about a portable surveying instrument used in land surveying. He adapted this for coastal surveying from a ship—a valuable asset for his later work. And incidentally, he helped defeat the French at Quebec by making soundings in the St. Lawrence River so that the British troops could make a safe passage. He then went on to survey the coast of Newfoundland.

In 1768 the British government, at the urging of the Royal Society, decided to send a ship to the newly discovered island of Tahiti to observe a transit of Venus crossing the sun. The best available naval man to lead the expedition was James Cook, so he was made an officer (almost unheard of in those days, when officers were considered to be gentlemen and everyone knew gentlemen were born and not made!). Cook was then given a small ship, the *Endeavour,* which had a shallow draught and so could come fairly close to shore, along with a crew of eighty-four and a scientific party of nine. The scientists were Joseph Banks, a wealthy young Englishman interested in natural history and already a member of the Royal Society; two Swedish naturalists, Dr. Daniel Solander (a student of the great Linnaeus) and Herman Spöring; two artists, Sydney Parkinson and Alexander Buchan; and their four servants.

The *Endeavour* sailed quietly out of Plymouth on August 26, 1768, made two brief stops for fresh supplies at Madeira and Rio de Janeiro (where the local authorities were less than cordial because they suspected the *Endeavour* was not a naval vessel but a pirate ship), and then reached Tierra del Fuego in mid-January. Banks led a party inland to gather plants and found many of interest, but he ran into trouble, beginning with unexpected snow. Next, Buchan, the landscape artist, had an epileptic fit, and had to be made comfortable temporarily by a fire; and then, while Banks was off botanizing, two of the servants froze to death, not primarily because of the cold, but because they drank up the expedition's rum supply. Buchan made it back to the ship, but died soon after reaching Tahiti.

The astronomical observations in Tahiti did not prove to be of much value (mainly because the instruments—not the observers—were inadequate), but the most amazing part of that long eleven-month trip from England was that the people on board maintained good health and did not get scurvy. This was because Cook had had the idea (when fresh fruits and vegetables were not available) of feeding sauerkraut to all hands—often, at least at first, over loud protests against that sour, foreign food!

Cook, under secret orders from the Admiralty, left Tahiti to sail south as far as latitude forty degrees in search of *Terra Australis.* Once he had satisfied himself there was nothing there, he headed for New Zealand, which Tasman had vaguely located more than a hundred years earlier. Cook circumnavigated it, proving it to be two islands and not part of a continent. He would have liked to continue east across the southern Pacific searching for the elusive continent, but winter was coming when he finished mapping New Zealand, so he decided to head west for New Holland, then to the East Indies, and eventually home around Africa. Because of strong southerly winds he missed Van Diemen's Land and Bass Strait (so he could not prove his suspicions that Tasmania was an island), and approached the mainland at the promontory on the southeast corner.

Cook turned north looking for a suitable harbor, and as he sailed along he could see rolling green hills and smoke from numerous fires. After a week he found a good harbor with suitable drinking water, plenty of fish to catch, and aborigines who were not especially hostile (or friendly). And Banks and his fellow scientists found plants beyond their wildest expectations, causing Captain Cook to change his mind about calling the area Stingray Harbour; instead he named it Botany Bay. Interestingly, Banks was not as impressed with the area as was Cook; it was Banks who was mainly responsible for the later sending of convicts to Botany Bay. Cook, although the son of a farmer and generally an accurate observer, overestimated the potentialities of the harbor and the surrounding soils, writing in his *Journal:*

> . . . the woods are free from under wood of every kind and the trees are at such a distance from one another that the whole Country or at least great part of it might be cultivated without being oblig'd to cut down a single tree; we found the soil every where except in the Marshes

> to be a light white sand and produceth a quant[it]y of good grass which grows in little tufts about as big as one can hold in ones hand and pretty close to one another, in this manner the surface of the ground is coated in the woods between the trees. Dr. Solander had a bad sight of a small Animal some thing like a rabbit and we found the dung of an Animal which must feed upon grass and which we judged could not be less than a deer, we also saw the track of a dog or some such like Animal.

Cook also noted that the Bay was "Capacious, safe and Commodius."

The *Endeavour* left Botany Bay on May 7, 1770, and headed northward without serious trouble for some five weeks, while Cook named hills, bays, rivers, islands and any notable landmark along the way. Once the ship had crossed the Tropic of Capricorn, it was, of course, inside the Great Barrier Reef, although Cook was not aware of that. In his *Journal* he wrote that the passage was "one continued safe harbour." Then one night while moving slowly through clear, deep water, the *Endeavour* struck a submerged reef and was held fast. The crew, by throwing overboard much of the heaviest cargo, including the cannons (and we have already told of their rescue in an earlier chapter), managed to float the ship and steer it into a protected bay where it could be repaired. This naturally gave the scientists an excellent opportunity to study the wildlife in what was to them a tropical paradise.

Banks, Solander, and the rest would gladly have stayed longer to collect plants and animal skins, and to make hundreds of sketches of unknown birds, flowers, butterflies, and so on, but Cook was uneasy about getting his patched-up ship away from the reefs and to the distant shipyards in Java. So they set sail in early August, managed to find a passage through the coral out to the open ocean, and then went around Cape York (which Captain Cook named, although he had intended that name for the north tip only—the remaining east coast he called New South Wales). They passed through the virtually unknown Torres Strait instead of going around to the east of New Guinea, and finally made Batavia in mid-October. It has been said many times since that no other navigator but Cook could have made it through those hundreds of miles of uncharted seas filled with so many hazards.

When the *Endeavour* again reached England after an absence of almost three years, it brought back news, not of *Terra Australis Incognita*, but of new Crown lands, New Zealand and Australia, and of exotic plants and animals such as the world had never known. Cook made two more long voyages of discovery, finally dying tragically at the hands of the natives of Hawaii. Joseph Banks was honored with a knighthood, served as president of the Royal Society for many years, and was England's most influential man of science in his time.

When England lost her American colonies, she had many problems, but one of the most troublesome was what to do about her overcrowded prisons. In 1779 Banks had suggested that Botany Bay would be a good site for a penal colony. Others began to support the idea, and in 1786 the government took action by appointing Captain Arthur Phillip, R.N., first governor of New South Wales. In the following year Phillip sailed with the First Fleet carrying convicts and officers to found the new colony. Once there, he quickly realized that the bay was too shallow and exposed, that the fresh water was inadequate, and that the soil was not good enough for growing crops. He explored the Port Jackson area nine miles to the north, and when he found an excellent harbor, plus good water and better land, he moved. This area he named Sydney Cove.

The accounts of the first years of transportation and settlement are filled with all manner of horror stories, involving sickness, cruelty, hunger, corruption, drunkenness, thievery, and prostitution, to name only a few. There are historians (probably Americans) who believe that the American trading ships that came to Sydney in those years deserve most of the credit for keeping the colony from dying of starvation. Although Governor Phillip was a compassionate man and tried his best, before his five years as governor were up he became ill and depressed and had to return to England. The governors that followed him were not of his caliber, and the penal colony deteriorated even further. Not even Captain William Bligh, the stern master of the *Bounty* and fourth governor of New South Wales, could reduce the power of the military clique tyrannizing the convict colony, and Bligh was forced to flee for his life.

During these first few years of dealing with convicted "criminals" and a corrupt military, little exploration was possible. Governor Phillip, in an attempt to reduce starvation when seeds would not sprout in the soil around Sydney Cove (and adequate supplies were not coming from England), had led or sent parties inland in search of richer soils. He found suitable acreage to the northwest (where Parramatta is now) and he successfully explored the Hawkesbury and Nepean River valleys. But inland exploration was limited during those first twenty years or so—one reason being that no one could figure out how to get beyond the seemingly impenetrable Blue Mountains (the section of the Great Dividing Range that passes about fifty miles west of Sydney).

Coastal exploration was another matter, and the two outstanding men involved in that activity were George Bass and Matthew Flinders, the latter having served (not too happily) under Captain Bligh. Both young men (in their early twenties) had arrived in Sydney with the second governor, John Hunter, in 1795, and within two months of their arrival were charting the harbor from an eight-foot rowing boat. Bass then tried unsuccessfully to make his way across the Blue Mountains by scaling the formidable cliffs, and he was also repulsed in his first attempt to find a sea passage between New South Wales and Van Diemen's Land (his boat was too small for the open sea). However, when he tried again with a twenty-five-ton sloop, and the aid of Flinders, the voyage was a success and they passed through the straits (later named for Bass at Flinders's recommendation). They continued on and became the first men to circumnavigate the island, thus proving Cook's suspicions of twenty-five years earlier. Bass became a trader in the South Pacific, and sailed out of Sydney one day in 1803, never to be heard from again.

Flinders, meanwhile, had gone back to England and told Joseph Banks about his desire to chart the entire coastline of New Holland. Banks was enthusiastic, persuaded the Admiralty to give him a ship, and then made certain that a good team of scientists and artists went on the expedition. Flinders's ship, the *Investigator,* was large but not very seaworthy; it barely made it to Australia, and never made it back to England. Nonetheless, Flinders did map the coastline, and the "scientific gentlemen" were highly successful.

The most important figure among the scientists was the botanist, Robert Brown, who brought back to England, when he finally returned over three years later (he remained in Australia after Flinders's work was finished), more than three thousand plant specimens, most of them previously unknown. His publications on Australian plants (part published in 1810 and the rest as an appendix to Flinders's *A Voyage to Terra Australis*) were not in any sense replaced for fifty years or more. Brown became secretary to Banks, and an honored scientist in his own right—best remembered perhaps for his discovery of the cell nucleus.

Flinders's fortunes did not prosper, sadly, for on his way back to England he suffered shipwreck (not on the *Investigator,* but another old ship), and then a six-year detainment as a prisoner of the French on the island of Mauritius (France and England were at war). When he finally did reach England in 1810, he was prematurely aged and ill, and he died on the day his book was published in 1814. Today Flinders is remembered as a sensitive though tragic adventurer. In the final chapter of his biography of Flinders, James D. Mack wrote:

> In a way he was a Romantic, for the spirit that caused him to weep over the distant bones of dead pelicans was not essentially different from that which produced Sir Walter Scott and Lord Byron. On the other hand, Flinders was secularist in the sense that he devoted his life, every breath of it, to the advancement of science, clearly a matter of this world, not of the next. He carried to it a deeply professional purpose, a purpose set alight by his own hope and

> passion. . . . His successors were able to build upon his work—which is the essence of science.

Flinders had wanted to title his book *A Voyage to Australia*, but Banks had said it would be confusing. Still, it was due to Flinders's influence that during the term of the fifth governor of New South Wales, Lachlan MacQuarie, the name of the continent was officially changed from New Holland (which after all was not really suitable for a British colony) to Australia. Governor MacQuarie was in New South Wales for eleven years and during his very able regime, many changes, most for the best, took place. Convicts continued to be sent to New South Wales, but their lives were generally not quite as pitiful. Instead of being kept in Sydney prisons, many were assigned as servants to free settlers, who were beginning to come from England to take up land, mostly for raising sheep. If a convict was fortunate enough to have a good master, he could do well and eventually become a free settler himself; if not, convict labor was little more than slave labor.

Although some pastoralists objected to losing free labor, public antagonism stopped the transport system into New South Wales in 1840, when some 27,000 convicts were reported to be there. However, England continued to send convicts to Van Diemen's Land until 1853. One of the most infamous penal colonies was at Port Arthur, located on the Tasman Peninsula to the southeast of Hobart Town. Port Arthur was founded in 1825, primarily as a place where the worst offenders could be sent. Distance plus dogs kept at the narrow neck of the peninsula made successful escape almost impossible. The only redeeming feature was the lovely setting, but it must have gone largely unappreciated by those forced to live there.

We visited Port Arthur and found the green hills and small, quiet harbor most attractive. Against those blues and greens were the remains of the old buildings of yellow sandstone, some partially restored, most just standing in the ruin brought on by sixty years of neglect. Many Tasmanians felt, as did many other Australians, that any reference to their convict past was best forgotten. After Port Arthur was closed in 1877, it was allowed to decay and be burned by bush fires. Today it is protected and administered by Tasmania's National Parks and Wildlife Service, and is one of the major tourist attractions in Australia. The loveliest and most photographed structure there is the church, which was built from the plans of a convict architect who had been transported to Port Arthur in 1829. Because it was used by all denominations, it was never consecrated.

Van Diemen's Land was politically separated from New South Wales in 1825, and its name changed to Tasmania in 1856. Also in 1856, the new state of Victoria was formed from the southern part of New South Wales, and the boundaries of South Australia were set up. Queensland was separated from New South Wales three years later. All this had come about mainly because new settlements were springing up almost everywhere as more and more settlers arrived in Australia, and these new areas were too far from Sydney to be governed properly from there.

The convicts and first free settlers had found Australian landscapes bizarre and alien, as suggested by quotations in our first chapter, and the main goal of many, it would seem, was to change or eliminate them as soon as possible. The forests needed to be cleared to make agricultural and pastoral land, and the bothersome natives needed to be moved out. Any new plantings should be made with trees, shrubs, and flowers from England, for everyone felt at home with those. War was declared on the native wildlife by the new Australians. But the people of England, France, and other European countries, scientists and laymen alike, were fascinated by the curiosities coming from Australia (and they still are). Perhaps this accounts for the fact that many natural history findings are recorded and preserved, not in Australian museums and libraries, but in those of England, Europe, and even the United States.

Preceding (usually) the early settlers inland were the explorers, who often were also looking for good agricultural land. One of the first of these explorers was Allan Cunningham, who was sent out from England in 1816 as a King's Botanist to collect plants for Kew Gardens, which were a

The church at Port Arthur, designed by a convict architect, is now a hollow shell.

favorite project of Joseph Banks. Cunningham first discovered Queensland's lush inland plains, and many plant species (such as the elegant hoop pine) are named *cunninghamii* in tribute to his botanical collecting ability. He stayed in Australia, became Colonial Botanist for a short time, and fittingly is buried in the Botanical Gardens in Sydney.

Another explorer who made extensive botanical collections, as well as detailed observations of plants and animals, geology, topography and the aborigines, was Major Thomas Mitchell. His discoveries as an explorer were not nearly as outstanding as his writings, but he did find the fertile valleys of western Victoria. Perhaps he spent too much of his time trying to prove that Charles Sturt, a fellow explorer, was mistaken in his theories of river drainage. Sturt was not wrong.

Charles Sturt had found the Darling River on his first journey in 1827, but the next year had shown that this and other west-flowing rivers did not drain into an inland sea, as he and so many others had supposed, but joined to form the Murray River. Sturt then sailed to the mouth of the Murray in a whaleboat with seven companions (three of whom were convicts), and found to his dismay that the river had no large exit to the sea where a port might be built. Instead, the Murray entered a vast, tidal lake. To reach the sea, one must cross sand bars and navigate narrow, treacherous channels. (We visited the mouth of the Murray in 1980; it is indeed no more than a sluice across sand bars, much as it must have been in Sturt's time.)

Sturt had hoped to be able to signal an ocean vessel that would carry the party back to Sydney, but instead they had to row back upstream for a thousand miles to their depot camp, which they found abandoned. That nightmare journey, in which the men were pursued by near starvation and exhaustion, is considered to be one of the epics of Australian exploration—one fortunately without a tragic ending, since no one was lost, and Sturt, though struck with blindness before he reached Sydney, did recover his sight.

Even further ordeals were ahead for Sturt. The center of Australia had long intrigued explorers, and its very inaccessibility seemed to be the major challenge. Sturt had tried to reach it (from August 1844 to January 1846), and had been repulsed by a combination of drought and heat. It was during the first six months of 1845 that he and his men became marooned far inland because the streams and water holes behind them (the ones they had used to reach the Center) had dried up after they had passed. Only an all-night downpour finally released them.

Wherever he went, however, Sturt took much interest in the animals and especially in the plants he discovered along the way. He collected plants for Sir William Hooker, director of Kew Gardens, with whom he had corresponded for many years. And once Sturt had retired and returned to England, he divided his time between the Royal Botanical Gardens, the Linnean Society, and the Royal Geographic Society. Sturt's discoveries include one of Australia's most beautiful birds, the pink cockatoo, and one of its most spectacular wildflowers, Sturt's desert pea.

A few years before Sturt's last expedition, Edward John Eyre had tried to penetrate the center of the continent from Adelaide, but when he could not get around the great salt pans blocking the way, he turned west (along the Great Australian Bight) seeking a route to Perth. He was the first to see the Nullarbor Plain, but he did not explore it because he could not go far from the coast, where water and provisions were brought to him by ship. During one long stretch, he and his party had no water at all except what they were able to collect from morning dew by soaking it up and squeezing it into pots. The one white man accompanying him was robbed and shot by two of the aborigines in the party, who disappeared and left Eyre to stumble on with only a single aboriginal guide. Fortunately, the two of them came upon a French ship anchored in a cove, and there they rested for a few days before completing their trip.

For a time thereafter, Eyre was the toast of the colonies—rather surprising, since he really had not discovered anything of importance. To his credit, however, he did a great deal later to improve relationships between settlers and aborigines. His name is preserved in Lake Eyre (which he never quite reached) and the Eyre Peninsula (which he was the first to explore).

Perhaps the oddest figure in the history of Australian exploration was a German mystic, Ludwig Leichhardt, who liked to be called "Dr. Leichhardt," although he had never earned that title. Leichhardt was reasonably well informed in the field of natural science, and he had a passion for discovering new plants and animals, new rivers and mountains. By sponging off friends in Germany and in Australia, he proposed to explore areas never before seen by white men, even though he had had no experience in the bush and could not take accurate bearings or read maps. His first expedition in 1844–45 was from Brisbane to Port Essington, on the north coast not far from where Darwin now is located. It was poorly organized, mismanaged, and succeeded, some think, only because of his aboriginal guides.

Leichhardt was a poor leader who would periodically wander off and have to be brought back by his guides; he was even caught stealing food from the general larder. He failed to discuss his next day's plans with his comrades, and in fact often had only the vaguest idea where he was. John Gilbert, an ornithologist who was collecting birds for John Gould (as we mentioned in chapter 5), was killed by an avenging party of aborigines who had caught Leichhardt's aboriginal guides molesting their women. But the remainder of the party struggled on to Port Essington, and Leichhardt became a national hero.

His second expedition, which was supposed to cross the continent from east to west, ended after the first eight months when the half-starved men refused to go any further and returned to Sydney. Never one to give up easily, Leichhardt launched a third expedition, which headed west from Roma, Queensland, in 1848. It was never heard from again, although several search parties were sent out after it. Legends persisted for many years that Leichhardt was living with the aborigines somewhere in the Center, but considering his ineptness, it is likely that the party perished from starvation or after skirmishes with the natives. Patrick White's novel *Voss* was inspired by this eccentric man, and although the novel's central figure is portrayed sympathetically, he meets a fate perhaps not unlike that of Leichhardt.

We have not mentioned the expeditions of the three Gregory brothers, mainly because they were so well organized and so efficiently run that there are no dramatic moments to relate. One of the brothers, Augustus, was leader of one of the search parties looking for Leichhardt, and all three were involved in explorations in Western Australia. Their expedition to the North in 1855–56 was the one that included Ferdinand Mueller as botanist, as we mentioned earlier.

In the 1850s the only line of communication between Australia and the rest of the world was by sailing ship. By 1860 news, at least, traveled a bit faster, coming by telegraph to India and from there to Australia by ship. Plans were being made to lay an underwater cable from India to some point on the Australian coast. But where? There was no agreement, so the South Australian government, hoping to hasten the decision to its advantage, offered a prize of 2,000 pounds for the first expedition across the continent from south to north. The result of this offer was a spectacular expedition promoted by the Royal Society of Victoria, one of whose members was Baron von Mueller. It was the best equipped and most expensive expedition in Australian history, with eighteen men, twenty-five camels (an innovation for desert travel), horses, and wagons.

A sergeant of police, Robert O'Hara Burke, was put in charge, with William J. Wills second in command. Burke, though flamboyant, was impatient and dictatorial, and had no practical knowledge of the bush; Wills was young and inexperienced, though he had some training as a surveyor. The expedition left amid great fanfare, and Burke and Wills succeeded in reaching the Gulf of Carpentaria. Both men died on the way back, however, mainly because of Burke's poor judgment and their inability to find wild food (in a countryside where aborigines appeared to be well fed). A third man, John King, was still alive when a search party arrived—primarily because he had been found by aborigines who fed and cared for him.

Burke kept no records, so what is known of the expedition comes mainly from Wills's notebooks, which he kept up as long as he could write—to within a few days of his death. They were recovered when Wills's body was found, and provide the basis for the many retellings of this tragic story, the best of which is in Alan Moorehead's book *Cooper's Creek*.

Meanwhile, John McDouall Stuart, who had been a draftsman on Sturt's 1844 expedition, was also trying to explore the Center. Before the Burke and Wills expedition, he had managed to get two to three hundred miles north of the Alice Springs area, but was turned back by scurvy and lack of water. Finally, in 1861–62, he successfully laid out a route that could be used for the Overland Telegraph from Adelaide to Darwin. Stuart was seriously ill from scurvy and exhaustion on the return trip, and had to be carried on a litter between horses for 400 miles. He was welcomed in Adelaide as a hero, and a fine statue has been erected to him in Adelaide's Victoria Square. But he died a few years after his return, without ever regaining his health.

Once the telegraph line was operational (in 1872), it became a lifeline in more than one sense. In addition to its main job, it also became a "point" of departure for explorers trying to penetrate the last unknown areas to the west. A number of men attempted to enter and map that country, but none did it as well as Ernest Giles, who not only went from the telegraph line to the coast of the Indian Ocean, but turned around and successfully came back again. In his biography, *Australia's Last Explorer: Ernest Giles*, Geoffrey Dutton begins:

> Of all the great unexplored regions of the world, none subjected explorers to more consistent humiliation than Central and Western Australia. An area the size of the whole of Western Europe lured these fly-tormented men on from waterhole to watersoak with promises of an inland sea, of great rivers, of plains where millions of sheep and cattle could run, but in most cases nothing more was achieved than a connection between existing settlements. . . . There is no Chicago, Kansas City or Dallas in the middle of Australia, only a small town called Alice Springs, and five hundred miles in any direction much the same emptiness that engulfed the first explorers. West of Alice Springs, despite all the excitements of mineral discoveries, there is still a thousand miles of red emptiness.

Giles, the most poetic of all explorers, left his stamp on the red emptiness, as Dutton, a poet in his own right, has indicated:

> But Giles adored poetry, and carried volumes of it around in his mind instantly available for response to every fresh, amazing sight. The names he gave these harsh realities are a wild Golden Treasury: The Vale of Tempe, Zoe's Glen, the Fairies' Glen, Titania's Spring, the Ruined Ramparts, Dante's Inferno. There are chapter headings in his narrative like "Extract from Byron for breakfast." Like Byron, he cheerfully admitted the sublime and the absurd, and often laughed that he might not weep. There are quotations from the poets scattered like auriferous stones across the country of his narrative, and sometimes there are odd outcrops of what appear to be his own verses. When he discovered something "truly wonderful" like Mount Olga his response is poetic, not scientific, his imagination leaps for comparisons: "it is composed of serveral enormous rounded stoneshapes, like the backs of several monstrous kneeling pink elephants."

As a young man, Giles had spent considerable time making short exploring trips for local pastoralists around the Darling River area, and as a result he became very adept as a bushman. But he developed a longing to make longer trips, especially into country that no white man had ever seen previously. He found a sympathetic friend in Melbourne's leading botanist, and Baron von Mueller not only encouraged Giles, but helped raise funds for him. As he prepared for his first expedition in 1872, Giles was thrilled as he considered the unknown:

> There was room for snowy mountains, an inland sea, ancient river, and palmy plain, for races of new kinds of men inhabiting a new and odorous land, for fields of gold and golcondas of gems, for a new flora and a new fauna, and, above all the rest combined, there was room for me!

When we visited Giles's country in 1980, there had been no rain in over a year, the desert had no flowers and most of the water holes were dry. But in twenty-four hours this changed! It started to rain, and it continued to rain as we visited the Finke River (which remained dry) and the Glen of Palms, as well as Ayers Rock. On this trip we did not reach the Olgas, because the road became impassable, but we had visited them on an earlier trip. The Finke River valley reminded us of Canyonlands in Utah, its red cliffs assuming strange shapes and forming a colorful backdrop for green bushes and golden grasses.

The sight of palms in such arid country comes as a shock, even though one is forewarned, and had the sun been shining we would have been able to appreciate fully Giles's romantic comment about his new-found watery glen "where dial-like to portion time, the palm-tree's shadow falls." The top of Ayers Rock was hidden in clouds, and waterfalls poured intermittently down its sides; yet when the clouds lifted the next morning, it loomed a purple

Water holes in the Interior, no matter how stagnant, were vitally important to the aborgines and to early explorers such as Ernest Giles.

giant over the desert, which was already speckled with green seedlings.

It is easy to understand Giles's love affair with this picturesque country, but it is less easy to understand his disdain for the natives. Although he seemed to mellow with age, he considered the aborigines less than human, and he thought their art, which he found in many rock outcrops, to be crude and primitive. He was not above firing on aboriginal parties if he thought they would become bothersome or dangerous. The fact that Giles had had contact with pastoralists during his early years, when the lands were being cleared of natives as well as forests, may have influenced his outlook. Nonetheless, he was an able explorer, deserving, says Dutton, "of the wonders and terrors he discovered, such as Mt. Olga or Gibson's Desert."

During these years of exploration, which we can scarcely do justice to in so few pages, other changes were affecting the country. England was beginning to realize that the best way to retain an empire was to let its colonies govern themselves, and so removed its autocratic, appointed governors. But it was reluctant to stop dumping its surplus criminals in Australia until the protests from the eastern colonies became too loud to ignore. However, Western Australia, which had been proud of being a free state since 1829, decided it needed free labor to develop effectively and so accepted convicts until 1868.

Under its own duly elected officials, the colonies continued to grow, not only in their capital cities but also inland, where great cattle and sheep "empires" developed. Many of the station owners (we would call them ranchers) in the rural areas were younger sons of British gentry—sons who would not inherit at home; their hired workers were either freed convicts or young people whose parents had been convicts. Wishing to forget or ignore dubious pasts and overcome loneliness across the great expanses of the Outback, these people developed a comradeship previously unknown in a class-conscious society. This "mateship," as it was called, entered the legends and literature of the country, and even today seems to color the attitudes of Australians, most of whom are second or third generation city dwellers. It even survived and was perhaps enhanced by one of the greatest upheavals in Australian history—the gold rush of the 1850s.

Gold was discovered first in western New South Wales, then in Victoria not far from Melbourne, and suddenly the population of those states doubled, then tripled and continued to soar as word of the rich gold finds spread. Crews deserted ships, merchants closed their doors, cattle and sheep stations lost their hired hands. Everyone was heading for the "digs" to get rich, although actually the first miners did not need to make deep holes or tunnels. The gold was on top of the ground, washed out from the ancient rocks over long periods in the past, and so these men needed only to pan for it. Eventually, of course, these sources began to give out, and then deep mines and more refined mining techniques were developed. Interestingly, Australian gold is thought to have had a greater impact on world economics than the gold mined in the United States, because Australian gold was almost all exported.

Ballarat, Victoria, is today a modern city, but it maintains much of the flavor of its colorful past. It was there that we first saw a Eureka flag (the Southern Cross in white on a light blue field), and when we asked about it we were told that it commemorated the Eureka rebellion, the only battle ever fought on Australian soil. The miners, resenting a licensing fee aggressively collected by soldiers and police, built a log stockade and defied the authorities in a gun fight. When the miners were routed, men were hurt on both sides. Our impression was that most Australians would prefer to forget that episode in their history. Some blamed the agitation in the gold fields on the Americans who had arrived fresh from the California gold fields. Many historians have doubted this, however, and indicated that American influence was felt more in transportation and not in politics.

At sea, American ships, sailing faster and faster, brought miners, occasional whalers, and many goods to the swelling flood of immigrants, who were mainly British. On land, Americans contributed horse-drawn stagecoaches. Until 1853, traffic to the gold fields was mostly on foot or horseback, or, when families were involved, by bullock-drawn, two-wheel carts. Freeman Cobb, an American, came to Australia, imported light-weight coaches from home, and hired American men for good wages to drive them. He soon sold out and returned home, but Cobb and Company coaches became the main transport in Victoria and New South Wales, replaced only much later by river boats and trains, which came in with the growth of the wool industry.

In retrospect, the years of the gold rush probably did not have as much of an influence on Australia as was once thought. Positive effects included improved transport, formation of the first trade unions, and increased mateship among the middle class as their numbers increased. A less desirable result was the development of racial prejudice, which previously had not been noticeable (if attitudes toward the aborigines were not considered). Violence began to flare with the influx of thousands of Chinese—many brought by American ships, as they had been taken to California (a profitable business for the shipping companies). The Chinese were generally law-abiding and inoffensive, certainly not involved in riots or the Eureka rebellion, but because they seemed so different, they were not liked or trusted by whites. As Russel Ward, the historian, says: "People did not fear them, but feared that more and more would come to live in Australia until they became the majority when, naturally, they might do as they had been done by."

Bushrangers, or highwaymen, increased in numbers during the gold-rush years, too. They predated those times, of course, for convicts who managed to escape often became bushrangers to support themselves. The bushrangers of the 1850s and 1860s, however, tended to be "wild colonial boys," sons of poor free settlers, born to the bush, and with contempt for the authorities, whether deserved or not. The best known of all was Ned Kelly, who has become part of the Australian legend, but whose real character remains controversial. Some think of him as a Robin Hood who defied corrupt police and robbed the rich to give to the poor; others doubt that he was anything more than a ne'er-do-well, who was in trouble as a teenager, went on to be a killer, and deserved to be hung.

Australia has a rich tradition of "bush ballads," dating from the days of settlement and of the prospectors and bushrangers. Many are anonymous, others the work of "bush poets" like Henry Lawson and "Banjo" Paterson. They tell of swagmen and stockriders, of mayhem and mateship, of bush flies, goannas, and wallaby stew. One anonymous ballad begins:

> By the sluggish River Gwydir
> Lived a wicked red-backed spider,
> Who was just about as vicious as could be.

The spider, we are told, held forth not far from a shearer, who was "snoozin'," having been "on beer and boozin'," and conveniently bit a passerby who was intent on cleaning out the shearer's pockets. A tall tale, no doubt, but told with a lilt and good humor, like most of the bush ballads.

Gold was also discovered in Queensland and Western Australia in the 1880s, and in the 1890s at Kalgoorlie, several hundred miles east of Perth, the yield was so high at one site that it became known as the Golden Mile. Not many Americans went to Western Australia, but one exception was a twenty-three-year-old mining engineer, Herbert Hoover, who arrived in 1897 and was in and out for the next ten years.

The 1890s saw some other interesting developments in Australia—the most important being the first development of a feeling of self-identity. Easterners (as well as Londoners) suddenly realized that the western half of the country was valuable, and should not be allowed to develop as a separate colony. Australian literature and painting were beginning to show Australian themes and techniques, instead of merely reflecting British tastes. Museums, libraries, and colleges appeared in the cities. The cattle and sheep "industries" continued to boom, and the workers there, traditionally conservative bushmen, joined the new unions to insure good working conditions on the huge, impersonal stations of the Outback. And then, during the great depression of 1890–94, the idealism and optimism (especially as expressed by the unions) developed along new lines: a wish to form a federal union of the colonies.

The Commonwealth of Australia was proclaimed on the first of January 1901, and Melbourne became the temporary capital until a new capital could be built. This would be Canberra, of course, a lovely city built on plans designed by an American architect (see page 190). Meantime, a parliament was formed, common tariffs were introduced, a foreign policy for the Commonwealth was enunciated, and a high court was established; but for most Australians there was little change in their daily lives. The various states were reluctant to give up any more rights than they had to, and each continued to administer its own public health, educational, transport, and judicial systems. In fact, as we watched national and state pronouncements during our stay in the country, we became more and more aware of how strong today are states' rights (compared to ours), and how loose is the Australian federation.

The trade unions are a case in point, and the constant inconveniences resulting from work stoppages seem uncontrollable even by the federal government. There seem to be no federal laws that can be evoked or federal troops that can be sent in to keep the mines open, or the electricity generators running, or to meet whatever emergency arises. Nor is there an overall federal program regarding

Australia's natural resources, including their parks, forests, and wildlife. The CSIRO (Commonwealth Scientific and Industrial Research Organization), now over sixty years old, is perhaps the closest one comes to such a federal agency, but it was formed primarily to deal with technological problems and those dealing with pest plants and animals. We have talked about it from time to time in earlier chapters.

Today Australia is a modern country clearly in the mainstream of international affairs, primarily because it is rich in oil, coal, many minerals and other raw materials. When we first visited Australia in 1969–70, we found it reminiscent of the United States of our childhood. In the following ten years it matured rapidly, and we found life there in the 1980s very much like life at home—and only the "odd" pronunciations of some of the English words reminded us that we were in a foreign country.

"The tyranny of distance," which Geoffrey Blainey analyzed so well in his interpretation of Australian history and development, is no longer serious. Australia's innumerable war memorials, which we first found morbid, we came to realize are tributes, not to violence, but to Australia's participation in world affairs. And while Australians remain part of the British Commonwealth, their attention and affection have been diverted to a considerable extent to the people of the United States. They felt deserted by England during World War II, when the Japanese threatened their security and their very lives, when they bombed Darwin on the nineteenth of February 1942, four days after the fall of Singapore. Later, they also bombed Broome, Wyndham, and other ports. Two Japanese submarines even penetrated Sydney harbor, but were sunk before doing any damage.

When the "Yanks" arrived, they came as saviors, bringing men, supplies, and technical capabilities to build defenses. On Darwin's beaches one may still see the remains of bunkers, and beside the north-south highway are crumbling strips of pavement built as runways for planes bringing supplies. Currently, American satellite tracking stations dot the landscape here and there, and there is almost daily talk of increased American military presence in Australia.

Today the American halo is a bit tarnished, in part by too many American television programs (often ones we ourselves would not have watched when they were first presented in our country), but more fundamentally perhaps because of America's diminished role as leader of the free world. But America and Americans still provide goals many Australians hope to attain. And a fair number of "Aussies" dream of visiting our country sometime. It is our hope and belief that the traffic will also be the other way, for Americans could learn much from Australia.

There are many obvious parallels in the history of the two countries, as well as some interesting differences. Both have been populated by a mixed lot of Europeans (but mainly English) who have usurped the lands of a native population that is becoming increasingly vocal. Both are dedicated to freedom of thought and action in a world where freedom is becoming less possible as a result of gross population growth (and Australia's relatively small population—about fifteen million, or less than that of the New York metropolitan area—is perhaps its greatest asset). Both are beset with problems of energy and development versus the preservation of an environment that is worth living in. Australia today is a most livable country; one may follow the routes of many of the explorers in relative ease, and take as much delight in their discoveries as did Charles Sturt and Ernest Giles, without suffering their travails. These words, written in 1794, are almost as true today as they were then:

> To a philosophic mind, this is a land of wonder and delight. To him it is a new creation; the beasts, the fish, the birds, the reptiles, the plants, the trees, the flowers are all new—so beautiful and grotesque that no naturalist would believe the most faithful drawings, and it requires uncommon skill to class them.*

*Quoted from *Land of Wonder: An Illustrated Anthology of the Best Australian Nature Writing,* selected and edited by A. H. Chisholm (Sydney: Angus and Robertson, 1979), page 16.

11

FINAL IMPRESSIONS

"Australia is, in the most literal sense, unforgettable"

Australia today is one of the most urbanized countries in the world. About 85 percent of its fifteen million people live in cities, most of them in the five major state capitals. A visitor traveling by air is invariably impressed by the sea of red tile and metal roofs surrounding each urban center—suburbs splashing over wide areas, in the current pattern of Western man. The cities, too, conform to pattern, the advantages of modern, high-rise buildings, shopping malls, and cultural centers at least partially offset by congestion and the hustle-bustle and impersonality of cities everywhere. (And yes, there are Pizza Huts, McDonalds, and Kentucky Fried Chicken establishments!)

The results of Australia's vigorous immigration policies are easily seen in the major cities, where it is common to hear Italian, Greek, Slavic, and various other languages spoken on the street. Nearly a fifth of today's Australians were born elsewhere, and almost a quarter of Australia's children have at least one parent who was born overseas. While the British Isles continue to contribute many immigrants, southern European countries also supply a large number (Melbourne claims to have more Greeks than any city outside of Greece).

It would be a mistake to assume that each capital city is stamped in the same mold, however. All are worth visiting. Sydney is a turbulent—some would say grossly materialistic—metropolis clustered about one of the most beautiful harbors in the world. The opera house is a marvel of imaginative architecture, ready, it seems, to take off into the stratosphere. Melbourne strikes one as a more staid and dignified city, conservative (and wise) enough to have preserved its trolley cars ("trams"). Sydney and Melbourne each have well in excess of two million people, while none of the other three major cities has quite made it to one million.

Adelaide was laid out carefully in 1837 by Colonel William Light, who died two years later after his plans had been initially rejected, leaving it to posterity, as he said, "to decide whether I am entitled to praise or blame." The ring of attractive parks surrounding the spacious and well-ordered city center leaves no doubt on that score.

Perth, too, is noted for its parks, particularly Kings Park on a hill overlooking the city as it embraces the shores of the broad Swan River. Perth feels its isolation from other capitals and its responsibility as capital of a state nearly four times the size of Texas.

Brisbane is the most tropical of Australia's major cities, where life proceeds at a more leisurely pace in a setting of lush vegetation and flowers that bloom in all seasons of the year. There is a saying in Australia that when a stranger arrives in Perth he is asked: "Where do you come from?"; in Adelaide he is asked: "What church do you attend?"; in Sydney: "How much money do you make?"; in Melbourne: "What school did you attend?" But in Brisbane: "Come and have a drink, mate!"

There are still three smaller capitals to be accounted for. Hobart, Tasmania, was founded only a few years after Sydney, on the banks of the Derwent River below imposing Mount Wellington. It grew less rapidly than the other capitals, and still retains some of the atmosphere of a nineteenth-century seaport. On Battery Point can be seen stone buildings dating from the 1830s and 1840s, carefully preserved and still in use as homes and offices.

Darwin, the capital of the Northern Territory, has recovered remarkably from the devastation of Cyclone Tracy on Christmas Eve of 1974, thanks to the injection of federal funds on a large scale. It has a flavor quite unlike that of any other Australian city, very much a multiracial tropical port, and gateway to scenes of water buffalo, giant termite mounds, and swamps teeming with waterfowl.

Canberra, the national capital, was planned as a compromise in a dispute between Sydney and Melbourne as to which should be the center of state. In 1913 the design of the city was put in the hands of Walter Burley Griffin, an American architect who had been an associate of Frank Lloyd Wright. Griffin proposed damming a local creek and building the city around the lake in a series of circles connected by broad avenues. Like Colonel Light seventy-five years earlier, Griffin was dismissed and his plans were greatly modified, though the beautiful city that arose owes a great deal to his vision. Canberra is a curious city, with elegant buildings and tree-lined avenues, but with no real center—"sixteen suburbs in search of a city," in the words of one critic. Canberra has grown rapidly, and we found it had changed a great deal (and grown still more diffuse) between our visits there in 1970 and 1980.

Aside from the capitals, there are a number of other sizable cities. Newcastle, New South Wales, exceeds both Canberra and Hobart in size, and there are several other important cities—all on the coast or near it. As of 1961, 83 percent of Australians lived within fifty miles of the coast; but by 1971 the percentage had increased to 84.7. Clearly, there is truth in James McAuley's lines (from *The True Discovery of Australia*):

. . . though they praise the inner spaces,
When asked to go themselves, they'd rather not.

But there is much to be said for places away from the well-known population centers. Study of a good map is enough to stir one to action. Toowoomba, Katoomba, Borroloola, Wollongong, Mittagong—Coolangatta, Cootamundra, Cunnamulla, Kununurra—Innamincka, Illawarra, Oodnadatta, Orroroo—in the southwest, Yallingup, Balingup, Beedelup, Cowaramup—locality names that roll off the tongue like music, aboriginal music, that is.

Then there are romantic place names: Mary Kathleen, named for the wife of the discoverer of major deposits of uranium in Queensland. (She died a few weeks after the discovery, but "Mary K," as the town is affectionately called, lives on.) Darwin and Beagle Gulf, named after Charles Darwin and the ship that carried him to unforeseen horizons. (But Charles never came anywhere near Darwin, although the *Beagle* did, on another voyage.) The Fitzroy River, named for the captain of the *Beagle*, who did not like the shape of Darwin's nose, or his book. (But Fitzroy Island was named by Captain Cook for Augustus Fitzroy, the British Prime Minister at the time of his departure from England.) Cooktown, on the Endeavour River, named for Captain Cook, who beached his ship the *Endeavour* after damaging it on the Great Barrier Reef. (Cook himself proposed no end of fascinating names, still in use: Cape Tribulation, near the spot where his ship grounded on the reef; Magnetic Island, where his compasses acted strangely; Mount Warning, where breakers warned him of danger; and many others.) Alice Springs, named after Lady Alice Todd, wife of the gentleman responsible for the completion of the Overland Telegraph Line that first linked Australian cities to those of the Northern Hemisphere. Katherine, on the Katherine River, named by its discoverer, John McDouall Stuart, after the daughter of James Chambers, one of the major backers of his expedition. (It was rumored that John was secretly in love with Katherine.)

Australia's towns are commonly evaluated by the number of pubs. A one-pub town "isn't much account," though its one pub may be a lifesaver to a traveler. The one pub in Birdsville, Queensland, has become something of a legend, situated as it is in one of the driest and most remote places on the continent. When it burned down in 1979, the proprietor set up the bar outdoors until it could be rebuilt. Birdsville without beer? Not possible.

On the other hand a town with two or three pubs is a bit more of a town, and if there are five or six it is a thriving community, almost a city. (We especially remember Mitchell, Queensland, which has five pubs but seemed to have trouble justifying them. But we liked Mitchell.) The closing of a pub can be a traumatic experience, a sure sign of decline, while the opening of a new one is a cause of rejoicing. We were much taken by Port Douglas, just north of Cairns, situated on a peninsula projecting into the Coral Sea, a two-pub town that is said to have once had twenty-five. But the mines in the nearby mountains gave out, and the town faded rapidly many years ago, to be revived at least partially, we suspect, when tourists fully discover the beauties of the North Queensland coast.

Pubs, by the way, are called "hotels" and are required to keep a few rooms for transients. They provide an inexpensive place to stay in many towns if one does not mind the noise from the bar, and sometimes a lumpy mattress and a five-watt bulb hanging from a cord over the bed. These become much more tolerable if one remembers the cost of staying in the luxury hotels in the big cities!

Australian towns vary from charming to dismal, though doubtless even the latter have something to be said for them. It would be hard to find a more desolate and depressing place than Coober Pedy, built on a broad gibber plain in central South Australia, completely treeless and baked in summer temperatures consistently over one hundred degrees Fahrenheit. The few dreary buildings and rough-looking inhabitants do little to suggest the riches of the town—for most of it is underground, where temperatures are more tolerable and where some of the finest opals in the world are mined and processed for shipment to the cities. Even the aborigines disdained this country, and were puzzled at the hordes of whites digging holes madly in this stark environment. Coober Pedy, they called it, "white man digging holes in ground." We had one cold drink there; it was enough.

At the other extreme, we would have loved to have spent more time in Coonabarabran, New South Wales (it takes at least three days to learn to pronounce it; we stayed six, and learned to admire it). Situated in rolling hills clothed with cypress pines and eucalypts, it is large enough to have all necessary services and still small enough to have a cozy, village atmosphere; high enough to avoid much of the intense summer heat, but not so high that the winters are really cold. Not far away are the Warrumbungles, a lumpy range of small mountains topped by Wambelong Peak (there are some names for you!).

Australia has more than its share of ghost towns, most of which reflect the faded dreams of gold and silver miners. We especially remember Wiluna, deep in Western Australia, where great masses of mining machinery rusted in the sun beside huge, jumbled slag heaps. Wiluna—a beautiful name. It is said to be based on the aboriginal word *weeluna*, in imitation of the call of the bush curlew. Once it was a town of major importance, at the southern terminus of the Canning Stock Route, over which cattle were driven from the Kimberleys, and the northern terminus of a rail line to Perth. Neither the stock route nor the rail line has been in use for many years, and there is little left of Wiluna: a store, a petrol station, a pub, and a few houses separated by blank spaces or tumbled ruins. Not far away the government has an agricultural experiment station, where various crops are grown successfully, using drilled water and soil additives—a remarkable oasis in desolate, semidesert country.

One hot spring day we drove into Milparinka, in far northwestern New South Wales, and were so thirsty we drank a bit too much cold beer and had to sleep it off under a coolabah tree. Milparinka is really just a pub without a town, the "town" being reduced to stone chimneys, parts of old stone walls, and rusting sheets of iron roofing. But in 1886 Milparinka had a courthouse, several stores, banks, a newspaper, and several prosperous hotels. Two other towns sprang up not far away: Mt. Browne and Albert, each with pubs and stores of their own. Gold was, of course, the lure. Now Mt. Browne and Albert have vanished without a trace, and Milparinka survives thanks to a single family that provides refreshment for travelers and for local graziers.

Actually, we profited a good deal from our brief stop in Milparinka (and not just from the beer). Here we first saw the School of the Air in operation, for the pub-keeper's children were at their lessons by radio. Here, too, we saw historic Mount Poole, near which Charles Sturt and his party were isolated for six months in 1845 at a water hole, unable to advance or retreat for lack of water elsewhere and because of heat that split their fingernails and made the lead drop out of their pencils, the bolts fall out of their carts. James Poole was a member of the party who died during this ordeal, hence the name Mount Poole.

A number of old mining towns have become tourist attractions, and a few have been restored to some semblance of their former state. This includes perhaps the most famous mining town of all, Ballarat, Victoria, which we visited on a summer day in 1980. Gold was discovered there in 1851, and a previously quiet little town in the center of grazing country suddenly found itself a wild mining town of fifty thousand. When the gold began to run out, the city declined, but it has come back and has a population of over sixty thousand. Ballarat maintains much of its old flavor with wide streets, extensive plantings, and beautiful old buildings still enhanced with the lovely iron grillwork so common to nineteenth-century structures in Australia.

In addition to the city itself, visitors can absorb much of the past glories of the area by visiting Sovereign Hill, a reconstruction (near the site of the first gold strike) of the town and the "digs" as they were in the period from 1850 to 1860. This is one of the better "old cities" that we have seen, and visitors can even go down into Sovereign Hill through the narrow, dimly lighted, damp tunnels to see and feel the conditions under which the miners had to work. Above ground are working displays of various ore crushers (including one large crushing stone powered by a handsome Clydesdale horse), a stream and equipment (large pan) for panning, and, most intriguing (to us), sails that caught the wind and shot it down the shafts to keep the miners from suffocating (we wondered how many had!).

The dusty streets are lined with small shops, run by suitably costumed local citizens, and include a blacksmithy, a bakery, a copper and brass shop, a pottery shop, a sweets store, a hotel with a running vaudeville act, and a small but colorful Chinese temple for the many Chinese miners. And periodically through all this goes a Cobb and Company stagecoach, treating its passengers to the dust and bruises of a bygone age—a nostalgic ride we declined.

The days of the gold rush are long since over, but active mining towns still dot the landscape in mineral-rich Australia. Most are deep in the Outback, and provide intriguing stopping points for travelers. Broken Hill, in western New South Wales, is a sizable city on the site of one of the world's largest deposits of lead, silver, and zinc ores. Discovered in 1883 by Charles Rasp, a boundary rider on a local sheep station, the mines still flourish and are now highly mechanized, the ores being shipped to South Australia by rail. The company founded by Rasp and others, called Broken Hill Proprietary (BHP), has evolved into a mammoth conglomerate of companies that dominate the mining and chemical industries of Australia.

Silver, lead, and zinc are similarly the major products of mines at the flourishing city of Mount Isa, Queensland. A number of reservoirs nearby supply water and recreation for residents in this arid, rocky area. Water for Kalgoorlie, Western Australia, is piped all the way from Perth, some 375 miles to the west. Kalgoorlie's broad streets are lined with supermarkets, hotels, and night spots, for the city has become something of a minor Las Vegas as well as a center for the mining of gold and nickel. Australia also has its share of coal, iron, and bauxite mining towns, and uranium mining centers are doing business in the North.

But these mining towns, important though they are to the economy, are sparsely distributed, and there are vast areas in the Interior where there are few if any settlements. Road maps are deceptive, for they show spots with names—these are the names of homesteads, or "stations," many of which are far from the nearest village and connected with it by miles of dirt tracks that are at times impassable.

The wide dispersal of these stations (one never says "ranch" in Australia) is a result of the fact that, because of the semiarid and unpredictable environment, relatively few sheep or cattle can be run per acre. Some of the cattle stations dwarf even the famous King Ranch of Texas. Alexandria Downs, in the Northern Territory, covers 11,262 square miles—about the size of Belgium. Of course, not all stations are that large, but by and large Outback families are extremely isolated and only now and then have a chance to visit neighbors or run to town for supplies. Many have air strips, and virtually all have two-way short-wave radios (most are well out of the range of television stations, although television may be coming soon via satellite).

The invention of a two-way transmitter that could be powered by foot pedals was a tremendous boon to Outback families, who had previously communicated by telegraph (or not at all). These radios came into use about 1940, a result of the efforts of two men, Alf Traeger and the Reverend John Flynn, who were dedicated to improving the lot of isolated families. Too often they had seen persons who were ill or injured fail to reach medical assistance in time. Thanks to the efforts of Flynn, who was not only a visionary but a persuasive writer and speaker, successful experiments with a "flying doctor" had begun in 1927, using a Qantas biplane out of Cloncurry, Queensland (near Mount Isa). But full fruition of the idea awaited the development of a two-way radio that could be powered and operated by most homesteaders. The RFDS (Royal Flying Doctor Service) is now well established, with centers in Alice Springs, Mount Isa, Broken Hill, Kalgoorlie, and several other cities.

Medical advice can be given over the radio. Every station is supplied with a cabinet of standard medicines, each bearing a number, so when a person is ill, his symptoms can be described by radio to a doctor, who might reply by saying something like: "Take two of number seven every four hours, and call me back tomorrow." In emergencies, a modern plane with a pilot stands ready to take the doctor to the site and, if necessary, to take the patient to a hospital. Itinerant doctors, dentists, and nurses also visit stations from time to time. Station owners are given instructions on maintenance of the air strip, and are told to drive up and down the strip as the plane approaches—to drive off any cattle or kangaroos or emus. The RFDS receives some government support, but it is largely supported by contributions from individuals, service clubs, and private companies. Many outback towns stage rodeos or other sporting events to raise money to support the service.

The widespread availability of two-way radios makes it possible to carry many other messages to neighbors or to villages and cities—planning trips, ordering supplies, or just saying "hello." The most inspired use of this network was the brainchild of an educator named Adelaide Miethke, who had also been associated with the establishment of the RFDS base at Alice Springs. Why not set aside a few hours each day for children to attend class by air? Previously, Outback children had taken correspondence courses, with little or no contact with other pupils or with teachers other than their parents. Later, when they left home for boarding school, as many did, their problems of adjustment were formidable.

On June 8, 1951, the School of the Air was initiated from Alice Springs with a spelling test and a reading from *Tom Sawyer*. Teachers took a roll call of their classes, dispersed as they were over hundreds of square miles, and were able to address individual students, who of course could also talk to their teacher, join in songs, and so forth. Schools of the Air now operate from about a dozen centers in Australia, supplemented by correspondence courses and by occasional visits from teachers. Pupils include, in addition to whites, a good many aborigines and children of mixed blood. Often it is possible to bring pupils together briefly during holidays in school camps, where they meet their fellow pupils for the first time.

While transition to boarding schools and colleges is still more difficult for these pupils than it is for city children, graduates of Schools of the Air tend to do well in universities, for they have learned to study by themselves. Although Flying Doctor services operate in several countries, the School of the Air is a uniquely Australian institution and has done a great deal to improve the lot of persons brought up far from settlements.

Considering the growing world population, it is perhaps inevitable that a large part of the interior of Australia be used for grazing, even though much of the land would have to be classed as marginal for any use whatever. Graziers often seem to be taken by surprise by drought, and plead for government help, though in fact ample rainfall is more the exception than the rule. Life deep in the Outback will always be difficult, despite the many bores that have been sunk (often producing water that is hot or mineralized) and despite the Flying Doctor Service and School of the Air.

There are parts of the Outback, of course, where grazing does not occur, including some of the aboriginal reserves and major deserts such as the Great Victoria and the Great Sandy. There will always be areas of Outback wilderness, but it is a desolate, inaccessible, and unpredictable land, with little spiritual refreshment except for hard-bitten "desert rats." Still, it is good to have the wilderness there, good (we think) that there are crested bell-birds singing where there is no one to listen to them.

A number of national parks have been established in parts of the Center, and these are generally accessible, at least by four-wheel-drive vehicles. Ayers Rock and the Olgas provide a major tourist attraction, with motels, camping areas, stores and conveniences. Palm Valley on the Finke River north of Ayers Rock is well worth the long, difficult drive. Other parks should be established in the Center and Far North and made accessible to visitors, who far too often judge Australia by its cities and its beaches.

Most of Australia's national parks and faunal

preserves are in the "wet rim" of the continent, as indeed they should be, for this is by far the most scenic part of the continent and the most rewarding in terms of wildlife. By choosing one's itinerary carefully, the visitor may experience at close range kangaroos, platypi, goannas, lyrebirds, the riotous vegetation of rain forests—or the delight of the unexpected. Dogs and cats are not allowed in such areas, and all plants and animals are protected, so the wildlife often becomes quite tame. There are attractive parks near several of the major population centers. Sydney, for example, is flanked by Royal National Park to the south and Ku-ring-gai Chase to the north, to say nothing of the Blue Mountains a few hours drive to the west. Even the most casual tourist should not miss these.

Americans should be warned that the term "national park" in Australia means something different than it does at home. First of all, parks are administered by the states, and thus are more analogous to state parks (each state has its own "National Park Service"). Also, many of them have few facilities other than a picnic spot and a few trails, though most of the larger ones have camping facilities of variable development and sometimes kiosks. Many of the smaller or less developed parks have no full-time rangers. And many are small, sometimes only a few acres, far too small to provide a habitat for much wildlife. Often they are plots left undeveloped because they are too steep or rocky for anything else.

Mount Tamborine, near Brisbane, was once covered with beautiful rain forest. It deserves to have been made a national park, but in fact it is seven tiny ones, each separated by pastures and outposts of suburbia. Some parks have limited scenic and recreational value. We well remember our introduction to Kakadu National Park—one of Australia's newest and largest. The park sign greeted us from a perfectly flat, treeless plain that had just been burned over—as desolate a scene as one can imagine (more about Kakadu later).

But far be it for us to belittle Australia's growing park system. It is absolutely vital to the survival of much of the native flora and fauna, and as a site for research on species rarely found elsewhere. Some of our finest days were spent in national parks! We found the rangers genuinely friendly, helpful, and well informed. And, we might add, we encountered none of the entrance and camping fees that are the blight of American parks.

A few comparisons may be in order, based on figures in the World Directory of National Parks and Other Protected Areas, published in 1975 by the World Wildlife Fund and UNESCO. As of that date, 1.2 percent of Australia was in parks and other protected areas, as compared to 1.5 percent in the United States. (Since that date Australia has added Kakadu, and the United States is adding parts of Alaska, so both may be approaching 2 percent.) On a per capita basis, as of 1975, Australia had 1.75 acres of parks and protected areas per person, as compared to 0.07 acres in the much more densely populated United States. So Americans are hardly in a position to be critical!

The battle to protect Australia's natural heritage has often been bitter and is not likely to be less so in the future. Some battles have been lost. Not many years ago, the boundaries of Mount Field National Park, in Tasmania, were altered so that some of its finest stands of mountain ash (*Eucalyptus regnans*) could be harvested to insure a continuing supply of wood chips for the Japanese paper pulp industry. Efforts to make the entire Great Barrier Reef a national park have been opposed over the years by interests that would like to mine the reefs for limestone or offshore oil. Some of Queensland's lovely coastal islands have dunes that provide valuable sources of zircon, titanium, and other metals; to date, only a few bits and pieces have been saved from the sand miners.

Curious distortions of the national park concept also sometimes occur. Queenstown, Tasmania, is a small community set in hilly country and devoted to the mining and processing of copper. For years the hills were denuded of wood to fuel the furnaces, and quantities of sulfur and other waste products were released in the air, causing further destruction of the vegetation and coloring the naked soil yellow, pink, and purple. Queenstown receives more than a hundred inches of rain a year, and the resulting erosion of the bare slopes produced huge gullies, creating a "badlands" so spectacular that Queenstown became a major tourist attraction. Tourist brochures described the landscape as "moonlike," and a television program about the area used background music from Richard Strauss's *Also Sprach Zarathustra* (as in the movie *2001*). But now that more modern methods of smelting copper are being used, there is less pollution, and the hillsides are becoming covered with wattles and small eucalypts. The city fathers would like to have the area declared a national park, so that it can be preserved as it is, or was; otherwise, Queenstown will no longer be a tourist attraction. A novel approach to conservation: down with the trees, up with pollution.

The development of holiday resorts for Australians and for overseas tourists is spelling the doom of many of the lowland rain forests, the coastal heathlands, and the mangrove swamps (which are the breeding grounds of much marine life). But many of the people who inhabit such resorts also enjoy seeing wildflowers and pelicans, and eating seafood, so perhaps a balance will be achieved. A more serious problem is posed by the fact that Australia's prosperity is seen to reside in the exploitation of the country's natural resources for the benefit of other nations.

"Australia's Booming Future," scream headlines in *The Bulletin*, one of Australia's most widely read magazines. "Australia is entering the greatest development boom ever imagined ... for every man, woman and child in Australia, the big investors—most of them multi-national corporations—are committed to putting up the equivalent of $2000 a head in new capital investment in this country."

These investments involve such products as coal, zinc, lead, iron ore, bauxite, uranium, woodchips, wheat, wool, and beef. Exports in 1977–78 exceeded twelve billion dollars, with coal, wheat, wool, iron ore, beef, and aluminum ores leading the list, in that order. And exports to Japan approximately triple those to any other country—Japan with its population of 704 people per square mile, as compared to Australia's four. But evidently Australia's future depends upon its being carried off bit by bit—a "willing quarry" for the rest of the world, as Maximilian Walsh puts it in his book *Poor Little Rich Country*.

Fortunately, Australian natural history has its champions, its equivalents to Aldo Leopold and David Brower. In 1966 a shocker appeared on the market, a book before its time, fated to be ignored, questioned, reviled—and to stir some thought and action. This was *The Great Extermination*, edited and partly written by A. J. ("Jock") Marshall, a professor at Monash University near Melbourne. Marshall lost an arm in an accident when he was young, but went on to become a captain in World War II and to lead his troops in combat. As a zoologist he taught himself, one-handed, to skin and dissect animals, and he spent much time "roughing it" in the Outback. He was an outspoken, flamboyant person, and this is reflected in his no-holds-barred prose. But he was also a warm-hearted man, a characteristic nowhere better reflected than in the book he wrote with artist Russell Drysdale, *Journey Among Men*. Jock Marshall was an outstanding researcher, and his untimely death in 1967 was a loss both to science and to the cause of conservation.

But there were others, such as the Serventy brothers, Vincent and Dominic, and Harry Butler, whose television program "In the Wild" was watched by millions. Even stage and television entertainers such as Rolf Harris and Spike Milligan became involved in the cause of conservation. From time to time in these pages we have quoted poet Judith Wright, whose poems and essays display a contagious love of the Australian environment—and a mixture of hope and despair for its future. Judith Wright was brought up on a cattle and sheep station in New South Wales. One of her great-great-grandfathers joined one of the expeditions that went in search of Leichhardt's missing party. Her forebearers, she says, "must have accounted for many thousands of trees over many thousands of acres. With settlement, no doubt many of these trees had to go ... after all, they were only *Australian* trees, thought of as ugly, monotonous, hostile."

As a girl, Judith Wright helped with the family chores and wandered through the countryside. An understanding schoolteacher encouraged her in her writing, and at the University of Sydney she haunted the library. One of her fellow students was James McAuley, another poet whom we have sometimes quoted. Since writing poetry is scarcely a way to make a living, Judith Wright worked as a cook, stock musterer, secretary, and statistician.

To Judith Wright, being both a poet and a spokesman for conservation was perfectly natural, for "the movement to change our attitudes toward 'nature' or 'the environment' . . . is not primarily scientific or political; it is a matter for everyone who cares either about the world he sees and lives in, or about its future welfare and his own." To her, the central problem is "how to stay human in our times." "We can rejoin ourselves in creative responsibility and participation with what we call 'Nature'—which is also ourselves—or we can die with it. Perhaps we have time to choose the first alternative."

Judith Wright was cofounder and president of the Wildlife Preservation Society of Queensland, and for a time edited their magazine, *Wildlife in Australia*. She is a member of the Council of the Australian Conservation Foundation, and an active member of the Citizens to Save the Reef Committee. She has authored the influential book, *The Coral Battleground*, and many essays on poetry and poets of Australia, as well as on conservation issues. But above all she is a poet, speaking with a soft, lyrical voice, as in her 1970 poem "Wings" (in *Collected Poems, 1942–1970*):

> Between great coloured vanes the butterflies
> drift to the sea with fixed bewildered eyes.

Or with bitterness, as she writes a few pages later, in "Australia 1970":

> Suffer, wild country, like the ironwood
> that gaps the dozer-blade.
> I see your living soil ebb with the tree
> to naked poverty.
>
> For we are conquerors and self-poisoners
> more than scorpion or snake
> and dying of the venoms that we make
> even while you die of us.
>
> I praise the scoring drought, the flying dust,
> the drying creek, the furious animal,
> that they oppose us still;
> that we are ruined by the thing we kill.

With voices as eloquent as this being heard, there is surely hope that space will be left for generous samples of the real Australia (as opposed to Australia as a copy of London, or Wales, or Miami Beach). Here is a continent whose past history is such that it has acquired a gathering of plants and animals so different from the rest of the world that, as Charles Darwin remarked, a different creator might be supposed to have been at work. No nation, and surely no corporation, however multinational, owns the trees, the birds, the sky. Conservation is the business of everyone who has any sensitivity or any vision of the future.

So, as visiting Americans, we did not hesitate to become involved in Australia's problems (without forgetting how we have decimated our redwoods, our bison, our eagles). We attended some of the meetings of the Queensland Littoral Society, as dedicated a group of young conservationists as one will find anywhere. We even wrote to the premier of Tasmania—a state that is fully 7 percent in national parks, yet is beset with special problems. These relate to the fact that the wild, well-watered mountains of the western part of the state are heavily forested and filled with lakes and with torrents racing to the sea—a landscape scarcely duplicated anywhere else in Australia, but one admirably suited for the development of hydroelectric power.

Tasmania already has more than enough power to serve its citizens, but it would very much like to become a major center for the processing of aluminum ore—a very power-hungry industry. The continent is rich in bauxite, but poorly provided with sources of waterpower. That Tasmania should go all-out to harness its mountain streams seemed most reasonable—except to fishermen, to backpackers, to canoers, to those who find inspiration in the mountains and forests; and, of course, to biologists.

In 1967 the Tasmanian Hydro-electric Commission planned a series of dams on the Gordon River and its tributaries, threatening to flood mountain valleys whose plants and animals had been little studied. Despite an inquiry by the federal government and protests by the international scientific community, a dam was built that greatly increased the size of Lake Pedder, drowning its beautiful beaches and the surrounding buttongrass plains. While conservationists were still smarting from this, plans were being formulated to dam the Gordon River farther down, as well as its tributary, the Franklin, one of the finest of Tasmania's mountain streams. Thanks to an unlikely coalition of the state Labor Party and conservationists, led by Bob Brown, director of the Tasmanian Wilderness Society, and following a barrage of letters from all over Australia, this proposal was voted down in July 1980.

In 1981 the Tasmanian Government called a referendum to break a deadlock between the two Houses of Parliament. The Labor Government favored a dam on the upper Gordon that would preserve the Franklin, while the Hydro-electric Commission and the Legislative Council favored a dam lower on the Gordon that would flood part of the Franklin. Tasmanians were made aware that because of the greater cost of the dam on the upper Gordon, every wage-earner would have to contribute $1,100. "And what does the average Tasmanian get for his $1,100?" asked *The Bulletin* (Sydney). "Little more than the assurance of knowing that the Franklin is still a wild river. Very few will ever see what they have saved. The Franklin is so wild and dangerous that only a handful of scientists and dedicated conservationists have visited it."

Nevertheless, when the chips were down, over a third of those voting in the referendum expressed a disdain for either dam by an informal write-in: No dams. The future of the Franklin remains in limbo. As conservationists often point out, when they win, it simply means they still have something to continue to fight for; when they lose, the battle is over, for there is nothing left.*

A new twist was added to this story in 1981 and 1982 with the discovery of several caves in the Franklin and Gordon river valleys that contain large deposits of human bones and stone artifacts. Radiocarbon dating has shown these deposits to date from 20,000 to 15,000 years ago. Archeologists from all over the world have written to the Prime Minister of Australia urging that damming of these rivers be prevented, since the caves represent the most southerly settlements of humans during the last glacial period, a critical period in human evolution. The national government has recommended that the valleys be placed on the World Heritage List, thus morally obligating the government of Tasmania to preserve the area. To what extent the state legislature will yield to these pressures remains to be seen.

One of the more encouraging developments in recent years has been the establishment of Kakadu National Park [colorplate 24], which includes much of the Alligator River systems and adjacent Arnhem Land escarpment, east of Darwin in the Northern Territory. This is a vast area of mangrove swamps, tidal flats, a forest of paperbarks, eucalypts, and cycads, and a great plateau of ancient sandstone being dissected by tributaries of the Alligator River. Much of the plateau is aboriginal reserve, and as we have said before, many of the rock shelters on the escarpment, as well as some of the outlying ones, contain paintings recording aboriginal life-style and Dreamtime. The swamps and woodlands teem with wildlife, but the country has hardly been settled at all by whites, and the crocodile and buffalo hunters that once roamed the country are now mostly gone.

Kakadu was the name of one of the native tribes of the area, and hence became the name of the national park established here in 1978. Ulti-

*According to a sympathetic article in the *National Geographic* magazine, May 1983, members of the Tasmanian Wilderness Society demonstrated against the dams in the summer of 1982–83, resulting in nearly 900 arrests and the jailing of more than 400. The premier of Tasmania, who has called the Franklin a "brown, leech-ridden ditch," remains pitted against conservationists. In the meantime, the Labor Party has won the national elections, riding to power on a platform that included opposition to the dams.

mately it is planned to include 4,826 square miles in the park—more than a thousand square miles larger than Yellowstone. So poorly known to science was the area that several expeditions were sponsored by the government in an effort to learn more about the flora and fauna.

Establishment of the park was complicated by the fact that in the early 1970s some of the richest uranium deposits in the world were discovered along the escarpment. This led to endless negotiations between those who wished to mine the uranium and those who sought to protect the area. The result was a compromise in which it was agreed to exclude the uranium deposits from the park and to permit construction of a paved road and a village to accommodate the miners. The village was called Jabiru, after the red-legged stork of the coastal swamps. The aboriginal reserve has been left intact adjacent to the mines and to the park, and it is hoped that some of the natives will be trained as park rangers and interpreters of the wildlife and artifacts.

Some parts of the park are relatively unexplored. This is not a place one visits to fill an idle weekend, but a park that challenges one's stamina and one's ability to submerge oneself in a world where the white man is an ill-adapted stranger, a world owned by the eagles and the crocodiles.

Australia has another very large, potential park or wilderness area, and that is Cape York, the finger that points toward New Guinea. This is also tropical and thinly settled, but very different from Kakadu. Its 67,000 square miles (larger than Switzerland) provide a varied setting of beaches, rain forests, bushlands, and plains. Being close to New Guinea, the area contains many creatures occurring nowhere else on the continent—tree kangaroos, cuscuses, cassowaries, and a variety of orchids, forest trees, and other plants not occurring farther south.

Here there are also many aboriginal rock paintings, some of them known to be more than 13,000 years old. At one site there are nearly 400 separate figures on a rock-facing 100 feet long—perhaps the largest single mural of prehistoric art in the world. Discovery of this and many other sites resulted from the efforts of Percy Trezise, whom we have quoted in connection with the Great Barrier Reef. Trezise was a former bush pilot who became a painter, writer, and friend of the aborigines. As he explains in his first book, *Quinkan Country* (Quinkans are spirit figures of the Cape York aborigines):

> My occupation as an airline and aerial ambulance pilot involved almost daily flights over this region, and I took advantage of these flights to make an aerial survey whenever I crossed the sandstone country.
>
> During outbound flights to pick up patients in the aerial ambulance, I flew as low as conditions permitted, often dropping down into a gorge to follow its twisting course and to look for shelters at the base of the towering red cliffs. . . .
>
> I found that it was possible to locate likely shelters in this manner, and occasionally even to see the ochre paintings in the brief glimpse afforded. . . .

Trezise's second book was discouragingly titled *Last Days of a Wilderness* (1973), but thanks to him and other dedicated people, interest in Cape York has been kindled on a national scale. In 1976 the Wildlife Preservation Society of Queensland held a workshop on the subject, with financial assistance from the National Heritage Commission. In 1980 the Second World Wilderness Congress was held in Cairns, at the base of Cape York, and hopes were high that a major commitment would be made toward preservation of the Cape—and of the Great Barrier Reef, too. But the world's largest bauxite mine is at Weipa on the Cape, and there are many other opportunities for development both on the Cape and on the Reef. The mining interests, Cape York landowners, and others unsympathetic to conservation made their presence known at the congress. Perhaps the best that can be hoped for is preservation of selected areas of the Cape.

Of course, the problems we have been discussing are not peculiarly Australian; they differ only in details from efforts to preserve Africa's dwindling herds, the Amazonian rain forests, or the last of the great whales. But in Australia conservation is a matter of special concern to everyone, for here is a continent where, through long geographic isolation, there has developed a collection of living things that are especially precious. Many of them are ancient forms of life that have survived through unusual adaptations to environments that were sometimes physically harsh, but largely free of competition and predation by "higher" forms of life that developed on the major landmasses. Mankind is enriched by having the hairy-nosed wombat still digging on the Nullarbor Plain, the lyrebird still ringing in the dawn in ravines of the Dividing Range.

There are still large areas in Australia that are thinly settled, and there is hope that some of these may remain so. Australia is rated as one of the most underpopulated countries in the world, but the fact is that it will not conveniently hold many more people. The major cities are spread over so much of the countryside that transportation has become a serious problem. In the Outback, scarcity of water and dependable forage requires that viable sheep and cattle stations be of enormous size, and the human population correspondingly scattered.

There are places on the continent that undoubtedly would accommodate more people, we think, notably the villages and smaller cities back from the east and southwest coasts, where there are fertile soils and adequate rainfall. But it is not probable that Australia will become the last refuge of persons now living in countries already overcrowded (which is most of them). The real danger is that Australia will become the world's supermarket for food, fuel, and metals to the extent that it will become a withered remnant of its former self. It can, of course, share its resources cautiously and remain a home for its remarkable plants and animals—and a mecca for biologists and for everyone who takes pleasure in living things. There are hopeful signs.

We have seen Australia change a good deal over the ten-year span of our three trips there. Some changes are for the worse: more urban sprawl, more clamor for material goods, a greater presence of foreign and multinational corporations. And some changes are encouraging: a growing ecological conscience and ecological activism (especially among young people), a flood of new books on Australian natural history, and an effort to define and preserve the essence of Australia.

Australia is a country where Americans are liked and welcomed (for the most part), where they feel at home, and where all the conveniences of life are readily available. It is fine cities, surfing beaches, race tracks, and cricket fields (but one need not travel that far for those!). It is also gum trees, kangaroos, koalas, and other oddities pointed out in the travel brochures. It is still a great deal more than that: plains of red sand and spinifex, with wedge-tailed eagles overhead; forests hung with lianas, resounding with strange bird calls; coral reefs spangled with multicolored fish. But we have said all that before. Go and see for yourself.

Bibliography

1 Impressions

Bechervaise, J. M. 1967. *Australia: World of Difference: The Australian Transition.* Adelaide: Rigby.
Breeden, Stanley, and Kay Breeden. 1970. *Tropical Queensland.* A Natural History of Australia: 1. Sydney: Collins; New York: Taplinger.
Breeden, Stanley, and Kay Breeden. 1972. *Australia's South East.* A Natural History of Australia: 2. New York: Taplinger.
Gunther, John. 1972. *Inside Australia.* Completed and edited by W. H. Forbis. New York: Harper and Row.
Huxley, Elspeth. 1967. *Their Shining Eldorado: A Journey through Australia.* New York: Wm. Morrow.
Keast, Allen. 1966. *Australia and the Pacific Islands: A Natural History.* New York: Random House.
Reader's Digest. 1976. *Scenic Wonders of Australia.* Sydney: Reader's Digest.

2 Geography

Heathcote, R. L. 1976. *Australia.* (In a series, *The World's Landscapes,* edited by J. M. Houston.) New York: Longman.
Jeans, D. N., ed. 1978. *Australia: A Geography.* New York: St. Martin.
Keast, A., R. L. Crocker, and C. S. Christian, eds. 1959. *Biogeography and Ecology in Australia.* The Hague: W. Junk.
Keast, A., ed. 1981. *Ecological Biogeography of Australia.* 3 vols. The Hague: W. Junk. (An extensive revision and expansion of the preceding.)

3 Flora

Blombery, A. M. 1977. *Australian Native Plants.* Sydney: Angus and Robertson.
Holliday, Ivan, and Ron Hill. 1974. *A Field Guide to Australian Trees.* Rev. ed. Adelaide: Rigby.
Holliday, Ivan, and Geoffrey Watton. 1978. *A Field Guide to Native Shrubs.* Adelaide: Rigby.
Kelly, Stan. 1969 & 1978. *Eucalypts.* Text by G. M. Chippendale and R. D. Johnston. 2 vols. Melbourne: Nelson.
Richards, P. W. 1952. *The Tropical Rain Forest: An Ecological Study.* New York: Cambridge Univ. Press.

4 Mammals

Breeden, Stanley, and Kay Breeden. 1974. *Wildlife of Eastern Australia.* New York: Taplinger.
Frith, H. J., and J. H. Calaby. 1969. *Kangaroos.* New York: Humanities.
Morcombe, Michael. 1974. *An Illustrated Encyclopaedia of Australian Wildlife.* New York: Doubleday.
Ride, W. D. L. 1970. *A Guide to the Native Mammals of Australia.* Melbourne: Oxford.
Rolls, Eric C. 1969. *They All Ran Wild: The Story of Pests on the Land in Australia.* Sydney: Angus and Robertson.

5 Birds

Macdonald, J. D. 1973. *Birds of Australia.* Sydney: Reed.
Pizzey, G. 1980. *A Field Guide to the Birds of Australia.* Princeton, N.J.: Princeton Univ. Press.
Reader's Digest. 1977. *Reader's Digest Complete Book of Australian Birds.* Sydney: Reader's Digest.
Rowley, Ian. 1975. *Bird Life.* Australian Naturalist Library. New York: Taplinger.
Slater, Peter. 1974. *A Field Guide to Australian Birds.* 2 vols. Adelaide: Rigby.

6 Reptiles and Amphibians

Cogger, H. G. 1979. *Reptiles and Amphibians of Australia.* Rev. ed. Sydney: Reed.
Gow, G. F. 1976. *Snakes of Australia.* Sydney: Angus and Robertson.
Heatwole, H. 1977. *Reptile Ecology.* (Australian Ecology Ser.) Brisbane: Univ. Queensland.
Swanson, S. 1976. *Lizards of Australia.* Sydney: Angus and Robertson.
Tyler, J. J. 1976. *Frogs.* Australian Naturalist Library. New York: Taplinger.

7 Insects and Their Relatives

Common, I. F. B., and D. F. Waterhouse. 1972. *Butterflies of Australia.* Sydney: Angus and Robertson.
Commonwealth Scientific and Industrial Research Organization. 1970. *The Insects of Australia.* 1974, 1st Supplement. Melbourne: Melbourne Univ.

Goode, John. 1980. *Insects of Australia.* [With colored plates from R. J. Tillyard's *Insects of Australia and New Zealand*]. Sydney: Angus and Robertson.
Hughes, R. D. 1975. *Living Insects.* Australian Naturalist Library. New York: Taplinger.
Main, B. Y. 1976. *Spiders.* Australian Naturalist Library. Sydney: Collins.

8 The Great Barrier Reef

Bennett, Isobel. 1971. *The Great Barrier Reef.* Melbourne: Lansdowne.
McGregor, Craig, et al. 1973. *The Great Barrier Reef.* In Time-Life Series: *The World's Wild Places.* New York: Time-Life.
Wright, Judith. 1977. *The Coral Battleground.* Melbourne: Nelson.

9 Aborigines

Berndt, R. M., and C. H. Berndt. 1977. *The World of the First Australians.* 2d. ed. Sydney: Ure Smith.
Blainey, Geoffrey. 1976. *Triumph of the Nomads: A History of Aboriginal Australia.* Woodstock, N.Y.: Overlook.
Gibbs, R. M. 1974. *The Aborigines.* Hawthorn, Vic.: Longman.
Leach, Barbara, ed. 1971. *The Aborigine Today.* Sydney: Hamlyn.
Maddock, Kenneth. 1972. *The Australian Aborigines: A Portrait of Their Society.* London: Penguin.
Smith, Patsy A. 1971. *No Tribesman.* Adelaide: Rigby.

10 Exploration and Settlement

Blainey, Geoffrey. 1977. *The Tyranny of Distance: How Distance Shaped Australia's History.* Melbourne: Sun Books.
Carter, Jeff. 1969. *In the Steps of the Explorers.* Sydney: Angus and Robertson.
Clark, C. M. 1963. *A Short History of Australia.* New York: NAL.
Dutton, Geoffrey. 1970. *Australia's Last Explorer: Ernest Giles.* (In a series, Great Travellers.) London: Faber and Faber.
Feeken, E. H. J., G. E. E. Feeken, and O. H. K. Spate. 1970. *The Discovery and Exploration of Australia.* Melbourne: Nelson.
Langley, Michael. 1969. *Sturt of the Murray: Father of Australian Exploration.* London: Hale.
Mack, J. D. 1966. *Matthew Flinders: 1774–1814.* Melbourne: Nelson.
Rienits, Rex, and Thea Rienits, 1969. *A Pictorial History of Australia.* Sydney: Hamlyn.
Sigmond, J. P., and L. H. Zuiderbaan. 1976. *Dutch Discoveries of Australia: Shipwrecks, Treasures and Early Voyages Off the West Coast.* Adelaide: Rigby.
Smith, Bernard. 1960. *European Vision and the South Pacific, 1768–1850: A Study in the History of Art and Ideas.* London: Oxford.
Ward, Russel. 1969. *Australia.* Sydney: Walkabout Pocketbook.
Younger, R. M. 1970. *Australia and the Australians: A New Concise History.* New York: Humanities.

11 Final Impressions

Frith, H. J. 1973. *Wildlife Conservation.* Sydney: Angus and Robertson.
Marshall, A. J., ed. 1966. *The Great Extermination: A Guide to Anglo-Australian Cupidity, Wickedness and Waste.* Melbourne: Heinemann.
Serventy, Vincent. 1966. *Australia: A Continent in Danger.* London: Deutsch.
Webb, L. J., D. Whitelock, and J. Brereton. 1969. *The Last of Lands.* Milton, Qld.: Jacaranda.
Wright, Judith. 1971. *Collected Poems: 1942–1970.* Sydney: Angus and Robertson.
Wright, Judith. 1975. *Because I Was Invited.* Melbourne: Oxford.

INDEX

W

Y